Dorothee Niebuhr

Making Global Value Chains

Geographies of Market-Oriented Development in Ghana and Peru

Springer Gabler

Dorothee Niebuhr
Frankfurt (Main), Germany

D30

ISBN 978-3-658-13286-6 ISBN 978-3-658-13287-3 (eBook)
DOI 10.1007/978-3-658-13287-3

Library of Congress Control Number: 2016934951

Springer Gabler

Printed on acid-free paper

This Springer Gabler imprint is published by Springer Nature
The registered company is Springer Fachmedien Wiesbaden GmbH

Making Global Value Chains

ACKNOWLEDGEMENTS

This book is the result of my own research and work over the course of three years. I have received support and encouragement from several colleagues and friends who have been a source of motivation, inspiration and helpful feedback.

My supervisor Marc Boeckler, Goethe University Frankfurt, has guided me closely on this thoughtful, enriching and rewarding journey. He gave me the freedom to develop my own thoughts, which has been a genuine learning experience. I would also like to thank my second supervisor Christian Berndt, University of Zurich, for his support. Stefan Ouma has raised critical questions and has broadly inspired my research. I would also like to thank Katharina Abdo, without whom I would not have started the research project itself.

A great thanks goes to the Konrad-Adenauer foundation. Without the financial support, this research project would not have been possible. Beyond the financial support, the innumerable discussions with scholarship holders and members of the graduate school "Social Market Economy" have been a valuable source of inspiration and feedback.

I would also like to explicitly mention those who took part in this research project for generously sharing their time and ideas with me during the times of field research. Thanks in particular to Luis, José, Manuel, Carla, Ivo and Michel in Peru. In Ghana, I would like to mention especially Rita, Ernest and Ernest, Soule and Nii. They contributed a lot to this research project by providing access to the settings in which the value chain approach gains momentum. Their help and efforts are highly appreciated and go beyond the scope of this research project.

Carmen and Pia inspired me throughout the duration of the research project with their helpful comments. We grew closer at every stage of the research project. Ana and Julius contributed through their helpful comments and critical reviews. Finally, I would like to extend my gratitude to my family who has accompanied and encouraged me throughout all stages of this project. Without their support, their interest and their advice this work would look very different than it does today.

Dorothee Niebuhr
Frankfurt, January 2016

TABLE OF CONTENTS

List of Figures, Tables, Contexts and Abbreviations

List of Figures

List of Tables

List of Contexts

List of Abbreviations

AFD	French Agency for Development
AFDB	African Development Bank
AGRA	Alliance for a Green Revolution in Africa
ANT	Actor-Network Theory
APISI	Association of Industrial Producers for the Commercialization of Sacha Inchi-derived Products (Peru)
BMZ	German Federal Ministry for Economic Cooperation and Development
CAADP	Comprehensive Africa Agriculture Development Program
CIAT	International Center for Tropical Agriculture
CIDA	Canadian International Development Agency (dissolved into the Department of Foreign Affairs, Trade and Development)
CIP	International Potato Center (Peru)
CTA	Technical Centre for Agricultural and Rural Cooperation
DANIDA	Danish Ministry of Foreign Affairs
DFID	British Department for International Development (since 2012: UKAID)
DGCA	Directorate of Agricultural Competitiveness (Dirección General de Competitividad Agraria, Peru)
EU	European Union
EUR	Common currency of 19 European Union member countries
FAO	Food and Agriculture Organization of the United Nations
FASDEP	Food and Agriculture Sector Development Policy
GAP	Good Agricultural Practices (see also: Global GAP)
GCC	Global Commodity Chain
GDP	Gross Domestic Product
GHC	New Ghana Cedi (May 30, 2015, 10 GHC = 2.50 EUR)
GIZ	German Development Agency (former GTZ, renamed and restructured in 2011)
GLOBAL GAP	Global private standard for Good Agricultural Practices

GMP	Good Manufacturing Practices
GORESAM	Regional Government of San Martín (Peru)
GVC	Global Value Chain
HACCP	Hazard Analysis and Critical Control Points
IADB (IDB)	Inter-American Development Bank
IFAD	International Fund for Agricultural Development
IFDC	International Fertilizer Development Center
IIAP	Peruvian Research Institute of the Amazon
IICA	Inter-American Institute for Cooperation on Agriculture
IMF	International Monetary Fund
INDECOPI	National Institute for the Defense of Competition and Protection of Intellectual Property (Peru)
INIA	National Agricultural Innovation Institute (Peru)
ISO	International Organization for Standardization
ITC	International Trade Centre
KfW	German Development Bank
M4P	Making markets work for the poor
MDG	Millennium Development Goal
MIDA	Millennium Development Authority (Ghana)
MINAG	Ministry of Agriculture and Irrigation (Peru)
MINAM	Ministry of Environment (Peru)
MINCETUR	Ministry of Foreign Trade and Tourism (Peru)
MOAP	Market Oriented Agricultural Program (Ghana)
MoFA	Ministry of Food and Agriculture (Ghana)
NBPP	Peru National BioTrade Promotion Programme
NEPAD	The New Partnership for Africa's Development (Technical body of the African Union)
NRGP	Northern Rural Growth Programme (Ghana)
OVCF	Outgrower and Value Chain Fund (Ghana)
PEN	Peruvian currency Nuevo Sol (30 May 2015: 10 PEN = 2.50 EUR)
PPP	Public Private Partnership

PSD	Private Sector Development
PTB	German National Metrology Institute
RCN	Raw Cashew Nuts
SDC	Swiss Agency for Development and Cooperation
SME	Small and Medium Enterprise
SNV	Netherlands Development Organisation
UN	United Nations
UNCTAD	United Nations Conference on Trade and Development
UNIDO	United Nations Industrial Development Organization
UNVCD	United Nations Value Chain Development working group
US	United States
USAID	United States Agency for International Development
USD	American currency United States Dollar
VC	Value Chain
WTO	World Trade Organization

Figure 1: Selected sites for the study of value chain development
Source: Own draft

1. Introduction

"Everybody is talking value chains" is the bold claim of a development practitioner and professor in Ghana (2011_4: 15). In his statement, he refers to the wide and rapid expansion of a model of global markets that has recently gained momentum in economic practice and development policies all over the Global South.[1] The rising uptake of market-oriented approaches in development cooperation represents the departure point of this study: It is about markets, development, and politics, and how they are linked together. Rather than taking (developmental) markets as given or market-oriented development as a coherent construct that conform to an overarching logic, this work aims to analyze and unveil the practices, policies, and procedures that constitute them.

Value chains represent the "infrastructure of international trade" (Bair 2009b: 9; Figure 1) in which, according to the Swiss development agency SDC, 80% of global trade in commodities is transacted (SDC 2013). At the beginning of the 21st century, multilateral organizations and policy makers started to promote more inclusive and sustainable markets: Smallholder farmers and processing firms, mostly in the Global South, were to gain access to global markets via the integration into global value chains (GVC). There would be close cooperation of all actors involved in the production and transformation of goods, while quality management infrastructures and the modification of agricultural practices from production- to market-orientation became the means to increase value addition in producing countries. Three snapshots from Ghana, Germany, and Peru provide an initial illustration of how the GVC framework is translated into development practice through workshops, newsletters, and traveling development consultants.

[1] The notion "Global South" is a relational notion rather than a spatially fixed term that separates the world into two clearly bordered hemispheres. See Ouma, Lindner (2010) and Solarz (2012).

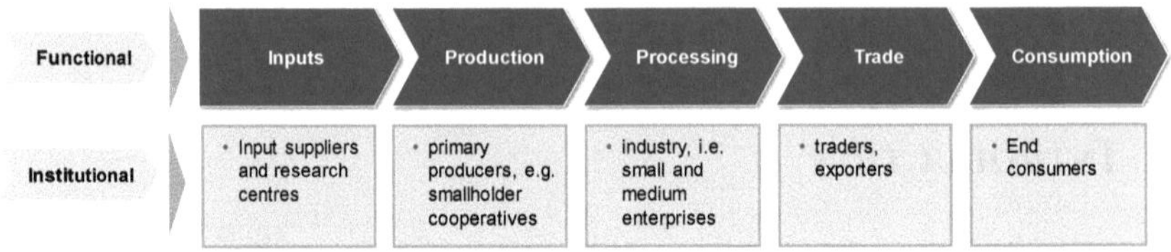

Figure 2: The functional and institutional organization of value chains
Source: Own draft

Snapshot 1: Transforming Ghanaian agriculture and agribusiness

In an interview with a so-called "value chain specialist", who has been working for a program that promotes rural development in the Ghanaian North, I learned about the challenges of translating a "global" model into the Ghanaian political and institutional setting:

> "So, value chain orientation is all about competitiveness, not about just comparativeness. It's all about the market. You must know who will buy your produce. Not just produce it and then go around begging for people to buy it. So you produce on demand (…) It was necessary because in 30 years, we realized that only some members of the value chain benefit. Others lose out. So the chains break (…). It was a jungle warfare. Agriculture was not a developed issue." (2013_7: 33-35)

Snapshot 2: Learning about value chain development in Peru

In one of the numerous workshops that are organized for value chain participants – i.e. farmers, processors, traders, public agencies, research institutions, and service providers – the participants are asked to build a value chain and illustrate how collaboration ideally looks like. The role play featured here shall demonstrate that every value chain is only as strong as its weakest component and builds on close cooperation.

Figure 3: Value chain development involves close cooperation
Source: Own photo (2013)

The recent introduction of policies that adopt a “value chain approach for development” in many countries of the Global South leads to a wholesale transformation of national economies, especially of the agro-export sector. This approach comes along with new practices, procedures and perceptions of the economy and introduces logics of competition, maximization of productivity, and enhanced coordination. Access to markets, it is maintained, is facilitated via the integration into GVCs.

The shifting contours of global markets

In the aftermath of the global economic crisis in 2008, international institutions such as the World Bank, UN agencies, the Organization for Economic Cooperation and Development (OECD), and various development organizations started to promote “appropriate institutions” to support defective market mechanisms (Sheppard, Leitner 2010) rather than adhere to laissez-faire policies. The end of the Washington Consensus, which represented a long era of enforced free trade policies by Washington-based institutions including the International Monetary Fund (IMF) and the World Bank, has been marked by profound transformations concerning the agendas of norm-setting agencies and the governance structures of global capitalism.[2]

Major international donor agencies have adopted value chain frameworks to tackle pro-poor development (e.g. DFID; SDC 2004; OECD 2011; UNCTAD 2013; UNIDO 2011). Participation in GVCs, it is assumed, spurs structural transformation and economic development in targeted countries once these countries adjust their trade policies around a nexus of foreign investment, trade, services, and intellectual property (Baldwin 2014, cited in UNCTAD 2014: 104). In order to make smallholder farmers and national economies benefit from value chain development, a plethora of interventions in the Global South accompanies this agenda. In Ghana, for instance, the shift towards a value chain-inspired agricultural development occurred when the

> "Ghana government took the decision that [it] will now use a value chain approach to promoting agriculture and rural development. Before that, (…) some people benefited disproportionately from that relationship from others, so in the long run it was not actually lifting everybody out of poverty. You know, some people ended up growing faster and getting a bigger gain of the project, and others were worse off. But now, if we turn to use the value chain approach and you get everybody integrated in a systematic manner, everybody will get a part of the cake that is proportionate to his or her input. The idea is not to share the cake equally, because the efforts are different, but the idea is that everybody gets remuneration proportion ate to his or her input in the chain. In that way, you will find that everybody benefits." (2010_3: 6)

The inscription of the market-oriented approach in Ghana materializes in market-friendly export policies, legal arrangements, academic courses, field schools, manuals, new agricultural practices and consulting services. The creation of practitioner forums, platforms, and associations underlines this trend as well. In

[2] Throughout the text, I use the term "global capitalism" to refer to the current international economic system which is based upon and governed by a (free) market-oriented rationale. The notion should not be understood in narrow ideological terms.

this realm, scholars have proclaimed 2013 the "year of the global value chain" (Werner et al. 2014: 1219) due to its rapid rise and uptake by international organizations and policy-makers. How have value chains become *the* prevalent model for organizing economies in the Global South?

Studying markets through global value chains

The study of global capitalism has long lacked a concept that links macro, meso and micro studies of markets across a variety of countries and sectors. Over the last three decades, economists, economic sociologists, economic geographers, political economists, and anthropologists have proposed concepts to unpack the functional complexities of global trade relations. Among the most prominent and widely picked up tools for the analysis of economic globalization is the analytical GVC concept. A value chain refers to all value-enhancing activities that are part of the conceptualization, production, and distribution of a good or service. The framework helps to analyze the "full range of activities that firms and workers perform to bring a specific product from its conception to its end use and beyond" (Gereffi 2014: 12). It also helps to grasp the terms and conditions for access to increasingly complex chains, the persistence of logistical bottlenecks, and potential for upgrading within chains. Within chains, the relations between producers, buyers, and suppliers can be categorized on a line that ranges from buyer- to producer-driven governance structures.

Historically, the framework is rooted in the critical Commodity Chain approach that has its intellectual lineage in dependency theory and world-systems theory of the late 1970s (Wallerstein, Hopkins 1986, 1977). The Commodity Chain approach applies a macro-perspective on spatial patterns of development and social reproduction with a focus on the sociospatially uneven development of the capitalist system. It conceives of such chains as networks of labor and production activities whose end result is a finished commodity. It seeks to unveil dynamics of accumulation, social change, and imbalances of power and knowledge between "core" and "periphery" countries – the latter being exploited by, and dependent on, trade with core countries. Subsequent approaches have withdrawn from the macro-perspective and dependency theory and focused on specific industries, sectors as well as managerial aspects of improving certain value chains instead: The idea of supply chain *management* has influenced later versions of the Commodity Chain approach. It introduces a business-oriented rationale into the originally analytical framework. Competitiveness enhancement replaces the former objective of unveiling accumulation patterns.

Value chain analysis guides a broad range of policy-relevant decisions related to industrial upgrading, economic development, and poverty reduction (Gereffi et al. 2005: 79). Improving the governance patterns and opportunities for upgrading constitute the core interest of pro-poor oriented development interventions. Hence, the GVC framework has become more than an analytic concept for the study of economic globalization. From an analytic approach that depicts, or criticizes, unequal conditions of production, it has evolved into a *tool* for economists, business leaders, and development experts to use to change the underlying governance structures. Value chains, in this sense, are both ontological and epistemological devices that shape global markets.

Matters of concern: Questioning the making of markets

Notwithstanding the valuable insights that value chain manuals, methodologies, and assessment reports provide about the structure of global markets, most of them lack a deeper and critical questioning of practical markets. The categories that are proposed – the market or pro poor development – have developed into stable and unquestioned assumptions that are taken as explanations instead of being investigated themselves. Such essentializations risk black-boxing the very matter at hand – the construction of (developmental) markets in the making. Studying the modalities and processes behind the circulation of market models and development policies in their own right, instead of raising hypothetical questions, enables a broader understanding of emerging market orders. The research questions can be subsumed under three categories:

Modelled markets

The overarching question of the project is related to how markets are constructed according to the premise of a circulating market model, the GVC framework. How has this model become prevalent and how are economies in the Global South constructed according to the model?

Associational politics

Development organizations mobilize resources to promote, implement, and inscribe the model into national policies and strategies. How does the model travel and by whom is it inscribed elsewhere? Which new meanings, attributes and rationales does the model take on when it passes through various ideological backgrounds and institutional settings?

Grounded market experiments

The translation and materialization of the GVC framework on the ground comes along with processes of framing, standardization, and valuation whereby global connections are created. Which activities and interventions contribute to stabilize market-oriented rationales? Which practical challenges and potential resistances arise in the process of making markets?

These questions around markets – in Latourian terms, they are "matters of concern" (Latour 2004b)[3] rather than matters of fact – cannot be approached without an assessment of the procedures through which markets are designed. Empirical insights into the study sites in Ghana and Peru and into global "policy pipelines", i.e. policies on the move (Cook, Ward 2012), are essential for understanding the conditions under which models of (developmental) markets become effective.

[3] "Matters of concern" must be distinguished from "matters of fact". While the first notion builds on the idea that one should not start from a priori statements, the second notion assumes a positivist attitude to the world: "matters of fact" allow scientific practices to pass as a simple description of a state of affairs (Latour 2008: 33).

Methodological reflections and research objectives

Studying and mapping the multi-sited fields, dynamics, and rationalities of global markets poses several challenges to the researcher. Where should one begin to study a market concept and its translation into a global policy? Whom, when and how to follow a concept, consultants, and objects in motion? And, finally, how to tackle the translation of economic models into practices and new guidelines for action on the ground?

In seeking to unveil how circuits of development expertise are maintained and assembled, I draw from geographical research about policy mobilities (Larner, Laurie 2010; McCann, Ward 2013; Peck, Theodore 2015; Peck 2011) and Ananya Roy's ethnographical approach to circuits of "development capitalism" (2012). When policies, models and ideas travel through distinct institutional, political, and ideational settings, they travel in bits and pieces. Not only do they mutate along the way, but they also remake the policy landscapes in which they gain traction. There are no perfect replications of a global model for value chain development. These approaches equally highlight the role of expertise that is embodied in development practitioners and technocrats who act within global policy circuits: It is important to take into account not only the models, but also the agents of change, i.e. the "travelling technocrats" (Larner, Laurie 2010) who assist and implement global policy regimes. In this vein, problematizing mobility means to engage with the modalities and purpose of flows, while staying attentive to how claims of mobility mask stubborn stickiness (Peck, Theodore 2015).

Such a perspective implies considering markets not as stable and abstract entities but rather as "practical accomplishments" (Garfinkel 1967: 3). They are shown to be dynamic arrangements – precisely, "sociotechnical agencements" (Callon 2007b: 319-320) – which are made of various components: market agents (value chain participants, development practitioners, policy-makers, and service providers), materialized models, embodied knowledges, techniques, and practices.

By tackling the conceptual trajectories, sociomaterial dimensions, and the effects of value chain development, I elucidate how market-making and development are entangled. What I subsume and understand by the "associational politics of markets" (Chapter 2) is hence deeply informed by the field of social studies of marketization (Çalışkan 2010; Callon 2007b; Callon, Çalışkan 2005). By fruitfully combining insights from these theoretical fields, I will explore and demonstrate the collective work that is part of making GVCs.

Accordingly, in this book I aim to de-naturalize the concept of "the market" and "value chains" by shedding light on the actors, processes, and effects that make market and development discourses mobile and effective in new contexts. Instead of simply challenging the accuracy of representations, I propose a critique of value chains in the Foucauldian sense of problematization (Deacon 2000; Bacchi 2012): From seeing them as given entities which generate new practices, tasks, and problems that must be resolved, I turn to seeing them as "a question" whose formation and obviousness must itself be subjected to analysis (Rabinow, Rose 2003: 13). Rather than emphasizing the ways in which economic models fail to capture the complexities of social relationship – that is, that economic models are "wrong" – attention is drawn towards the power of economic models to perform the reality they purport to describe. By following the conceptual and spatial trajectories of two value chains, I show how people and things – market agents and economic goods – are weaved together and reconfigured as they move from place to place and become central elements for organizational action (Müller 2015b). The network that emerges around value chains can then be situated within broader processes of marketization.[4] Accordingly, this research project aims to unveil the political, social, and cultural processes behind the making of market associations and the circulation of market rationales to two sites of the Global South.

[4] Marketization describes a series of definitional processes that define new systems of order and valuation (Ouma et al. 2013) and refers to the extension of the market rationale to all sectors and levels of society (Barber 1995: 406).

Following global value chains in the making

The selected approaches call upon researchers to follow various traces, devices, and people within market arrangements – i.e. GVCs – while accounting at the same time for the interconnections between their constitutive elements – variable times, spaces, rationales, and actors. Some nodes in the field of market-oriented agricultural development were selected as points of departure, after which a series of journeys were organized: from the centers of concept innovation and policy generation to places where intermediary adjustments were undertaken, to sites of negotiation and mediation such as practitioner forums and workshops for government ministries, and back again to the "centres of calculation" (Latour 1987; see also Jöns 2011) where knowledge is produced and fed back into global circuits. If not through such a mobile ethnographic approach, how else could I make claims about markets in the making and more generally about marketization processes in the Global South?

Consequently, I delved into the travel itineraries of policies and inscriptions of the GVC framework through documentary analyses, and subsequently contacted potential interviewees via online platforms. My investigation into the making and maintenance of global market relations draws on more than eight months of field work on three continents realized between 2013 and 2014. Alongside the study of academic articles and books, practitioner manuals, evaluation reports, policy papers and project proposals, I conducted semi-structured interviews, engaged in various informal conversations, wrote e-mails, conversed with development consultants and practitioners via telephone, and visited international fairs such as the Biofach in Germany to meet entrepreneurs and smallholders. I applied to become a member of a (rather exclusive) expert circle that promotes a pro-poor oriented value chain methodology and was indeed granted access to that association.

When I started the research project, I had no contact persons in either country. Neither the field nor scientific facts are simply "out there" and wait for the researcher who stumbles over them to be investigated (MacKenzie 2009: 8). Rather, access to "the field" and "gate keepers" are a "social product" of the researcher's ability to forge linkages and gain access to actors and institutions (Gupta, Ferguson 1997: 169; 83). Gaining access to potential interview partners is crucial but not quite plannable. Neither is it by any means predictable that the case studies prove to be as insightful or significant as anticipated. The research project evolved in the course of time through fortuitous encounters, informal conversations, and the persistent motivation to hang on when interview partners did not show up or when the field research suggested an unexpected turn in my research results. I was able to get in touch with key gate keepers – international and local[5] development consultants – with whom I worked for several months in two broad-scale development projects that promote economic development via the integration into GVCs in Ghana and Peru. In Peru, for instance, it all started with a Skype interview and a confirmation by e-mail of a program coordinator and my future team leader. This conversation was followed by an informal procedure: I was granted access and even material support with a shared office room, a proper working place, and a broad contact network. In Ghana, it was equally rather easy to access a development program in which I was provided with a working space, a computer, travel grants, and, most importantly, a broad network, and a supervisor who was charged with making my stay as insightful and valuable as possible. Through these extended cases of participant observation, I gained first-hand experience in terms of the practices and rationales of (mobile) development consultants, the processes of translating the market concept and development tool into national policies and educational systems, and the creation of linkages in the field.

[5] In this text, the term "local" is not to be contrasted with "global", nor are "macro" and "micro" categorizations understood in an antagonistic relationship. The "global" is realized through "the articulation of a complex interconnection of variously local relationships, not as something that is above or simply predatory of, the local" (Massey 1994: 154). Hence, as Massey (2005) claims, the global is always constituted locally.

Value chain development in Ghana and Peru

While conducting field research in programs for economic development, two value chains drew my attention as both were recently promoted on a larger scale and with the support of international development agencies. They promised to provide valuable insights into the making of markets from scratch. In both cases, no market existed for the respective products. Yet, based on methodologies and programs for value chain development, a connection was established between local smallholder farmers, entrepreneurs, and all kinds of intermediaries, which eventually created access to global markets.

In Northern Peru, I studied the making and dynamics of the Amazonian inka nut, known as *sacha inchi* in the regional language Quechua (Chapter 8). An international development organization had selected it as a commodity in a value chain development program, because it fitted the recent political interest in biotrade in Peru and was considered a promising product for rural economic development in the region. From the mid-2000s, the role of international development practitioners – with their methodologies and manuals, workshops and consulting services – in developing this value chain was remarkable. Previously, neither market demand nor political interest in promoting its commercialization existed. Within a few years, a regularly convening public-private exchange platform was initiated *by*, and created *for*, value chain participants, service providers, and public officials. Within less than ten years, sacha inchi had developed into a promising Peruvian specialty which made its way to global export markets and to the Biofach in Germany, the biggest international fair for organic foods.

For similar reasons, i.e. a particular interest in studying recently commoditized and commercialized products, I selected the cashew value chain in Ghana (Chapter 9). While working in a development program for the promotion of the Ghanaian Cashew industry, I learned how the market for cashews in West Africa and Ghana was constructed from zero. Native to northeastern Brazil, the cashew tree now grows in tropical regions from India to West Africa. The cultivation of cashew trees in Ghana started in the 1960s, but its use as a commodity has only recently gained pace. Falling prices for shea nuts in 2010-2011 animated local processors and global firms to shift to cashew, instead, and develop an industry around the promising, non-traditional export commodity. With the creation of the African Cashew Alliance (ACA) in 2005, the African cashew industry was united to capture market opportunities and improve its position in the GVC. In the meantime, institutions have been created that facilitate coordinated efforts to respond to global market dynamics and ensure that smallholders can access highly competitive markets.

The dynamics of strengthening each value chain must be seen in the global context of market-oriented development and the creation of trade infrastructures. Besides the adoption of market-friendly agricultural and export policies at the national level, technological infrastructures, and quality standards were in both cases adjusted so as to fulfill the requirements of international buyers and consumers. Both products were recently identified and qualified as commodities with the support of international development agencies and firms. In the process, they have been assigned qualities that aim at increasing local value addition. For instance, sacha inchi is promoted as an Amazonian superfood: vegan, organic and apt for cosmetic use. Global marketing strategies prominently stress its history of traditional cosmetic and nutritional application by ancient Pre-Inka populations. While the cashew nut counts on a global demand around which advanced technological infrastructures in Southeast Asia have emerged, sacha inchi is cultivated in small quantities in the Amazon and its production is technologically little developed.

Both products are barely accessible on national markets in Ghana and Peru: The investments made to comply with international standards and certificates have resulted in added value, which makes them unaffordable for local society. As a result, there seems to be no real alternative to their promotion on global markets. Both value chains exemplify how global market infrastructures emerge and stabilize over time and also how they are constantly adjusted in the wake of market failure, or rather, resistances.

Structure of this book

The book is divided into nine chapters. Some chapters have been written at an earlier stage than others and prove that the practice of conducting research is a dynamic process in which not only the mode of writing but also the perspective on the phenomenon changes. The chapters can be read separately from one another, but are complementary in that they provide different perspectives on the same phenomenon of marketization.

Theoretical foundations and methodological departures

Based on past and present conceptualizations of markets and global capitalism in the social sciences, alternative approaches can be elaborated that take into account the dynamic, disciplinary, sociomaterially distributed, mobile, and relational effects and dimensions that are part of marketization processes. In Chapter 2, I propose eight prisms for the study of markets in the making which I subsume under the notion of the "associational politics of markets". Moving beyond rational choice frameworks and positivist accounts of markets, the framework is attentive to the power of circulating discourses, legitimation strategies, knowledge embodied in traveling consultants, institutionalized routines, material devices, and the effects of traveling policies on particular sociopolitical and economic settings. It has developed in the course of field research and during analysis: It is a move from (studying) "the economy" to (studying) economization or marketization.

What follows in Chapter 3 is an outline of the methodological challenges that come along with such an investigation of marketization. While a text-based analysis and interrogation of mobile concepts is the starting point of this research project, such an armchair analysis must not be its end point. The investigation of markets and traveling market models must reach out to capture the particular "social situation" (Gluckman 2002) in which practices, discourses, policies, and market actors become linked to one another. Such an endeavor requires the researcher to be on the ground in order to follow models-turned-into-policies, practices and related documents such as evaluation reports and manuals to their multiple sites of enactment. Reflections on one's own positionality as a white female geographer from the Global North conducting research in the Global South are constitutive elements of a critical attitude towards the observations made in the field.

Policies in motion: The political realm of markets

For a study of the journeys of GVCs, a link must be made between the places of policy invention and the sites of translation and policy implementation. While the travels of policy regimes and their implementation sites are often downplayed in orthodox policy transfer research (Dolowitz, Marsh 1996), it is precisely at these moments and sites that programs, ideas, models, and policies take on a life of their own. This is why the modalities of mobilizing and inscribing models into particular sociopolitical, juridical, and cultural settings must themselves be topics of analysis.

Chapter 4 explores the rise of the value chain approach and its application in international development cooperation. While chain approaches were developed by sociologists in the 1970s to explain the global division of labor and uneven development, the GVC framework of the 2000s focuses on patterns of value creation and capture. It has been increasingly mobilized beyond academia to draw on business management literatures and converted into an operative management tool to enhance productivity and the efficiency of production processes. Moreover, its widespread adoption by international organizations in the last fifteen years reveals a noteworthy convergence around one paradigm, notwithstanding the differing rationales that are associated with it across development organizations. An investigation that pays attention to the agents of change who mobilize policies, to the tools (such as practitioner manuals) which enable ideas to circulate, and conferences and platforms in which best practices are shared and recirculated, shows how a comprehensive development apparatus has emerged and stabilized around the value chain framework in development cooperation.

Chapters 5 and 6 reconstruct the inscription of the GVC concept in Peru and Ghana. The traveling market-oriented paradigm, through its translation into institutional settings, policies, trade agendas, laws, and academic institutions, has reached enormous societal dimensions in both countries. It has become a powerful tool in the broader field of development policies, export strategies, and market-oriented agricultural development. Markets do not emerge from an "exogenous menu of market structures, from which one is chosen in a particular context" (Sheppard 2013: 402). Instead, they are shown to be shaped by political interests, institutional infrastructures, and geographical conditions. The insights of both, Peru and Ghana, demonstrate that circulating models of the market – market access via value chain integration – keep altering when they shift and travel between (academic) economics and (real) economy, profit-oriented interests of entrepreneurs and developmental concerns of donor organizations.

Experiments with markets: The framing of goods and market agents

The mobilization, interpretation, and implementation of the value chain concept cannot be grasped at the global or policy level alone. This is why Chapters 7 and 8 turn away from the politico-institutional context dealt with in the previous chapters to the concrete manifestations of value chain development. Processes of qualification, standardization, and ordering in markets are explored in detail and are identified as central moments in the construction and stabilization of value chains. They result in the "ontological reconfiguration" (Holm 2007) of products as economic goods and people as market agents. The different elements that are all tied together by one overarching market-oriented framework will be studied using two examples: the construction of the sacha inchi value chain in the Peruvian Amazon and the promotion of the cashew value chain in Ghana. Each chapter deals with one aspect and one perspective of value chain development as it is performed "on the ground".

Chapter 7 discusses the commercialization of sacha inchi in Peru, which is an endemic plant that has only recently been embedded in a GVC infrastructure. The process of enrolling institutions with partly diverging interests into the value chain involves investments and efforts of regional market actors, public and private ones alike. Unsurprisingly, international donor organizations oriented the emerging value chain towards export markets primarily, while nationally oriented value chains tend to be sidelined – if only at first, as the case of sacha inchi will demonstrate.

Chapter 8 deals with the cashew value chain in Ghana, which – similarly to the sacha inchi value chain in Peru – has more recently taken off and enabled cashew farmers to integrate global markets. In this chapter, attention is drawn to the processes and practices that enable the transformation of farmers into accountable, responsible, but also empowered market agents. Contracts, internet and communication technologies (ICT), and calculation tools such as weighing scales are part of this endeavor. They enable farmers to take part in trade relations and become full-fledged market participants.

The conclusion in Chapter 9 situates the insights of value chain development in Peru and Ghana within current trends towards market-oriented modes of global governance that shape policy agendas throughout the Global South. The insights gained in two localities go beyond the geographical boundaries of these countries: They stretch out into multilateral organizations, ministerial offices, consulting firms, mediated in and through workshops, manuals, and policy papers before being fed back, modified and purified, into global policy circles.

This research project investigates the immense labor involved in constructing (developing) markets, which is a marked contrast to pervasive images of the market as a given entity. First and foremost, it aims at denaturalizing markets through an empirical investigation of how global market connections are performed and stabilized at two selected conjunctures in the Global South. Thereby, it not only contributes to recent studies of marketization, but raises questions about the processes and politics around the construction of markets.

2. The associational politics of markets

> "To grasp the economy one has to look at that which is economic since all that is visible are the qualities of the object, its characteristics, and not the object itself. This shift from a noun to an adjective is the first step on the path to the study of economization." (Callon, Çalışkan 2005: 5)

Markets usually stand by themselves, unquestioned and considered as naturally existing phenomena: The analysis of markets supersedes the investigation of how they come into existence. While such a perspective on markets is prevalent in neoclassical economics, critical political economics, economic sociology, and most chain and network approaches, it is rejected by scholars working in the social studies of markets or marketization (Çalışkan, Callon 2010, 2009). In this growing scholarly field, both the "performativity" lens (Fligstein, Dauter 2007: 120; Fourcade 2007: 1026) and Deleuzian-inspired assemblage thinking (Deleuze, Guattari 1987) have gained strong momentum as explanatory building blocks for the study of market emergence. From a performative vantage point, markets are practical accomplishments rather than abstract and stable entities that govern the dynamics of supply and demand (Callon 2007b; Mirowski, Nik-Khah 2007). They require manifold investments to temporarily stabilize them and they are (re-)produced by discourses, tools and practices of economists, policymakers, and various kinds of practitioners. Yet, the elements that compose markets can disintegrate. This is what policy mobility scholars have demonstrated in relation to various cases ranging from urban studies, economic geography to business studies on the contingent arrangements, modes, and effects of traveling policies (e.g. Henriksen 2013; Peck 2011; Temenos, McCann 2013). The mobilization of various bodies of knowledge including economic models, embodied expertise, and techniques must be investigated in their own right.

Inspired by the above-mentioned literatures, I outline the epistemological and conceptual claims of what I call the "associational politics of markets". This approach aims at broadening our understanding of the construction of markets by ascribing not only an important role but also agency to material elements, traveling disources, and capacitations of (market) agents. Thereby, the approach can expand the theoretical repertoire for understanding how markets and market-models take shape. First, I contextualize this approach within the disciplinary developments of the social sciences, human geography, and geographies of marketization (Berndt, Boeckler 2011, 2009) more specifically. Consequently, I aim to provide answers to the following questions: Which features inhere in markets (in the making)? What is political about the circulation of value chain models and policies? The departure point of the research on the making of *markets*, and more precisely on the global circulation of market models and rationalities, starts with the claim that "the market" is all too often treated like a black box. Instead, I propose to examine how markets are constituted and *assembled* and how their components are (temporarily) held together. To do so, I discuss eight prisms for the study of markets. Thereby, the focus shifts from the study of a preconfigured and given economic reality – i.e. the assumption that economics and markets pre-exist the economy – to the study of economization and marketization, as the quote in the beginning of this chapter suggests. In this endeavor, I do not pursue a narrow political agenda, but understand *politics* as ontological politics, whereby the power of market models to create new identities and indeed new worlds comes to the fore.

Cultural turns and actor-networks

In the 1980s and early 1990s, which is also known as the era of postmodernist thought (Ley 1993), an unprecedented convergence of intellectual investments around a common project swept through the social sciences. A shift in theorizing, methodology and epistemology led to the collapse of metanarratives and a turn towards interpretative and constructivist approaches. What came to be known as the "cultural turn" in human geography (Barnes 2001; Cook 2000;

Crang 1998) and beyond started to "question the constitution of the discipline – what we know, how we know it and what difference this makes both to the type of research we do and who participates in it with us, as either colleagues or research subjects" (McDowell 1992: 399-400). Specifically, the new cultural geography attempts to de-stabilize structurally determinist accounts of economic change, in which "singular notions of 'economy' invariably trumped 'culture' in a predefined hierarchy of epistemic significance" (James et al. 2008: 3; Berndt, Pütz 2007). It accommodates concepts from Marxian political economy, regulation theory, and neoclassical economics which dominated the discipline since the early 1970s. Nuanced understandings of globalization and the construction of "the social" or "the economic" in specific places have come to substitute the conventional focus on space and place. Holding against accounts of globalization that argue for the erasure of geographic specificity, space is no longer considered as pre-given but rather produced through, and constitutive of, social relationships.

Certainly, the use of the term "culture" could erroneously lead to the assumption that the cultural turn is primarily about "culture". However, as indicated above, the turn implied a radical shift to an openness towards pluralist modes of theorizing and a shift from epistemological to hermeneutic theorizing. Thereby, the very idea of theory is turned around. Theory is no longer considered to hold an exclusive truth or possess only one particular format (Woodward et al. 2009). Instead, theorizing is a profoundly subjective activity inherent in practices (Barnes 2001: 547). Methodologically, the cultural turn has led to the adoption of qualitative and interpretative methods which followed the quantitative turn of the 1950s and 1960s in the social sciences. At the epistemological level, the cultural turn called for sensitivity to the social construction of social and economic phenomena. In other words, the "cultural turn" has inspired a new sensitivity towards the contingency of economic and social phenomena by questioning pre-fixed scientific categories and social constructions of knowledge and power forms.

Cultural turns should be considered in the plural. Indeed, several turns have swept through the cultural and social sciences since the 1990s: the relational turn, the performative turn, the linguistic turn, the postcolonial turn, the spatial turn, the pragmatic turn and the practice turn (Barnett 1998; Cook 2000). These turns aim to withdraw from a mode of thinking using prefixed claims and categories that featured in the modernist body of thought. Instead, they are open towards more eclectic, modest, and experimental ways of theorizing the social world. Two broader claims can be distinguished therein: one is the call for more flexible, pluralistic and hybrid conceptions of "the economic" and "the social" that acknowledge the mutual constitution with, and its inseparability from, "the cultural" (Berndt, Glückler 2007). The second claim implies a focus on the practices that constitute everyday social interaction (Jones, Murphy 2011; Schatzki et al. 2001). A source of inspiration for both claims is found in ANT. Rather than constituting a "theory" per se (Latour 1996b), as the name suggests, it is an ontological project that departs from a radical assumption. Bruno Latour has audaciously argued that "the social" – and "the economic" – do not explain, but must be explained (Latour 2005b). As a consequence, any scholar can do social theory without being a social scientist, one can discuss a generic "science" without becoming committed to a generic scientific method, and "follow scientists around" without ever becoming subject to the disciplinary norms and codes that discipline the scientists (Mirowski, Nik-Khah 2007: 194). The questions posed in social and political theory, all of which presuppose the social as a sort of substance that explains rather than something that must be explained, should be replaced by accounts that shed light on the situatedness of "the economic" in a broader fabric of social relations and networks of cultural institutions. This de-essentialist approach emerged out of the social studies of science and technology (STS) (Callon 1986; Latour 1999, 1987, 1983; Latour, Callon 1981; Latour, Woolgar 1986) or science studies more briefly. Instead of researching "ready-made science", scholars are interested in "science in the making" (Latour 1987: 1-17). The original interest was linked to understanding the construction of scientific knowledge as a social and collective product of manifold connections between scientific laboratories and the external environment, the rapid uptake of

ANT and STS approaches has led to a large body of research that traces how all kinds of things – whether of a scientific nature such as academic journals, academic presentations or skills embodied in a scientist or related to other fields of knowledge and practice – are brought together in different ways through a process of "heterogeneous engineering" (Law 1992).

The radicality of ANT lies in the fact that it does not differentiate between science (knowledge) and technology (artifact). It ascribes the capacity to act to any purposefully and effectively aligned entity: All kinds of documents, technologies, artifacts, symbols, and places become active players in the ordering process. It is what Latour calls an "actant", which is "anything provided it is granted to be the source of action" (Latour 1996b: 373). Although it is through the associations that nonhumans acquire the capacity to act, nonhumans do not have identical agency as humans. As Latour rightly mentions, nonhumans will never have inertia by themselves (Latour 1996a: 86), since an actor is never isolated (Latour 1988: 108-109). Simply put, nonhumans do not have agency by themselves, if only because they are never by themselves.

The radical critique of prefixed categorizations by ANT and STS altered the thinking of space among geographers as well. More generally speaking, ANT appeals to geographers because it addresses many concerns at the heart of geographical research, particularly the question and theorization of distance/proximity and scale, the role of technologies and the relationship between the natural and social world (Müller 2015a: 30). It is even much more than that, since ANT "redefine[s] geography" (Murdoch 1997). Instead of trying to categorize space and landscapes into micro-macro dimensions and relations, ANT scholars propose a geography of "topologies" (Mol, Law 1995) or a "science of nearness and rifts" (Serres, Latour 1995: 60). Such geographies require no less than a withdrawal from a mode of thinking in terms of macro- and micro-dimensions, and the use of a relational perspective that is not constrained or bound by space. Moreover, geographers have started to acknowledge that their research does not simply represent the world as it appears, but cultivates new ways of formatting it by "actively experimenting with the production of space as an integral part of one's own practice" (Paglen 2009: 31). A greater methodological reflexivity in the research process and the handling of data comes along with the awareness that researchers co-construct social and economic realities through their practices:

> "We are in the business of creating links, of making them, of bringing them more or less successfully into being. Which means in turn that we are no longer trying to find good ways of narrating and describing something that was already there. Instead, or in addition, we are in the business of ontology. We are in the business of making our objects of study. Of making realities, and the connections between those realities. Of making the realities that we describe. Of trying to find good ways of interacting with our objects, ways that are sustainable, ways that make it possible to link with them." (Law 1997: 65)

Researchers not only describe, but act upon the world through their research and the drawing of connections. The diversity of connections that constitute economic entities should be investigated and taken into account as much as the comments, vocabularies and theories used by researchers (Latour 2005b: 49; Roberts 2014). Researchers constantly enact reality, or rather realities in the plural, through (research) practices and their ways and means of analyzing and depicting the world (Mol 2002). Research, hence, is a thoroughly performative practice.

Eight prisms for the study of markets

Since its original and rather narrow interest in the construction of scientific knowledge, STS- and ANT-inspired assemblage thinking has transcended disciplinary fields (Bosco 2015) and reached out into research areas that were hitherto reserved for traditional social theory. Of particular interest for this research endeavor is the adoption of these insights in the field of market studies. In the late 1990s, Michel Callon carried out a "market test" of ANT (Callon 1999) by asking how and if ANT can be rendered useful for the study of economic markets. This is a valid question given the fact that ANT-inspired approaches postulate distributed agency and hence an agential inseparability between humans and non-humans. The market, on the contrary, is a sphere marked by a "strict formal separation between what circulates (goods which are inert, passive and classified as non-human) and human agents who are active and capable of making complicated decisions (producers, distributors, consumers)" (Callon 1999: 182-183). This is why the experiment of constructing and assembling markets is a particularly promising case.

1. Agency in markets is sociotechnically distributed

Let me start with a very basic clarification of what I understand by the essence of an economic actor or rather, economic agency. Understandings of the sources of economic agency vary in different disciplines and fields: Economic agency in neoclassical economics is exerted by a calculating rational individual, represented by the construct of homo oeconomicus and linked to utilitarian market behavior. In political economy and the new economic sociology of markets, this construct is widely rejected on grounds of ideological or analytical misrepresentation (Foss, Klein 2010; Fourcade 2007) and it is argued that calculative behavior "is marginal and at best an ex post rationalization for choices grounded in other logics" (Callon, Muniesa 2005: 1230; Beckert et al. 2007). These logics include cultural norms, laws, and institutions. Economic sociologists oppose homo oeconomicus and substitute it for another abstract figure: homo sociologicus. Granovetter has withdrawn from this simplistic dichotomy by proposing the notion of "network" in which all economic and social interaction takes place (Granovetter 1985). Yet, in doing so he dissolves everything into networks. His approach cannot explain the configuration of economic actors, because it takes the identity and existence of economic actors as pre-given. The configuration of networks, however, depends precisely on the identity and equipment of the economic actor.

Actors become calculating market agents if they are equipped with the necessary tools. In the understanding of Michel Callon, an (economic) actor is “made up of human bodies but also of prostheses, tools, equipment, technical devices, algorithms, etc. – in other words, is made up of an agencement” (Callon 2005: 4; Context 1). His analytical emphasis is on the ensemble of market devices (Dumez, Jeunemaitre 2010a), rather than an exclusive focus “on what one might call [one actor’s] glamorous agential peaks” (MacKenzie 2009: 22). The agents’ calculative equipment (knowing how to calculate or how to keep records of farming practices) is co-produced by devices (calculator, Excel tables or paper sheets). In fact, calculative capacity must not be understood exclusively in numerical and mathematical terms (Lave 1988), but rather in broader sociopolitical terms as the capacity to act upon “economics at large” (Callon 2007b: 335). What does this mean for market agents who aim to become part of GVCs? Through all kinds of tools and investments – manuals, contracts, record-keeping books, workshops, and field schools – farmers (it could be any other market agent) in the Global South become familiarized with the functioning of global markets and thus equipped and capacitated. For instance, they are enabled to live up to the standards, norms, and rules of global markets through the documentation of their farming activities. A comprehensive set of tools – from agricultural technologies and practices to inscription devices such as policies, documents, evaluation reports, economic models – emerges around value chains and generates socio-technically distributed economic, i.e. calculative, agency. Calculative tools are at the heart of the emergence of economic agency.

Context 1: Markets as agencements – an etymological reflection

The French term "agencement" is a word-play borrowed from Gilles Deleuze (Deleuze, Guattari 1987) and often associated with what has been widely translated into "assemblage" in English. Although the two notions are sometimes understood and used as a synonym, they are not direct translations (Law 2004; Phillips 2006). While the French term "agencement" stems from "agencer" (to arrange or fit together) and "agence" (agency) and connotes "arrangement", "configuration" or "fixing" in English (Callon, Çalışkan 2005; Phillips 2006: 108), its English counterpart – the notion "assemblage" implies "joining" and "gathering". In French, its referent has a technical connotation, and can refer to the components of a machine (Hardie, MacKenzie 2007: 58).

The word-play opens up new ways of thinking about distributed notions of agency and distributed cognition (Bennett 2005; McFarlane 2011; Giere, Moffatt 2003). "Agence" in French is translated with "agency" in English and connotes the capacity to act and give meaning to action. An agencement denotes socio-technical arrangements (Callon, Çalışkan 2005: 24-25) in which all parts – independent of their human or non-human status – possess the capacity to act. The term's usual English rendering as "assemblage" or "arrangement", however, has too passive a connotation (Hardie, MacKenzie 2007: 58). They do not – at least not in their original meaning – grant agency to non-humans, and thus imply a divide between human market agents (those who assemble and arrange) and things that have been arranged. To the contrary, "agencement" has the same root as agency: "agencements are arrangements which are endowed with the capacity to act in different ways" (Çalışkan, Callon 2010: 9). An agencement is built up by the connections between its components, but insists on the autonomy of each component. Deleuze's original definition highlights the role of each component that makes up arrangements: "It is a multiplicity which is made up of many heterogeneous terms and which establishes liaisons, relations between them across ages, sexes and reigns – different natures. Thus, the assemblage's [it should be translated as "agencement"] only unity is that of co-functioning: it is a symbiosis" (Deleuze, Parnet 1977: 69). Consequently, "all the elements of a non-homogeneous set converge, making them function together" (ibid.: 39), but it never goes so far as that the parts lose their autonomy. Deleuze (ibid.: 52) stresses that "it is never filiations which are important, but alliances, alloys; these are not successions, lines of descent, but contagions, epidemics, the wind" (Anderson et al. 2012). Hence, parts within agencements do not possess a prefixed ontology, but are constituted by the agencements of which they are (temporarily) part.

What is missing in the understanding of agencement or network as proposed by Latour and Callon, is an explicitation of the spatial dimension that allows global markets and forms to function (Ong, Collier 2005b: 12; Anderson et al. 2012). Ong and Collier's book "Global Assemblages" (2005a) elaborates on this idea. They extend the key claims of ANT – including an emergent temporality of assemblages, shifting forms, and composite concepts – to the spatially informed concept of "global assemblage": "Global" refers to a broadly encompassing, seamless, and mobile form, while "assemblage" implies heterogeneous, contingent, unstable, partial, and situated determinations that are not reducible to a single logic (ibid.). The notion indicates that there are inherent tensions, and reveals in this sense a strong commonality with Callon and Muniesa's (2005) understanding of markets as socio-technical agencements which organize the circulation of goods together with the price and property rights attached to them through the contradictory encounter of quantitative and qualitative valuations. After all, one risk remains: The rich conceptual repertoire might draw attention away from what is really at stake in an ANT-informed approach to the study of markets. Concepts help to make sense of the world, yet it is through practice that they gain significance and it is in practice that they are enacted.

2. The design of markets is a collective project

The construction of markets is realized by both economists and practitioners who collectively test market models outside of the economic laboratory. Yet this argument is far from uncontested. It is widely assumed that economic theories and models are developed in academic laboratories by "confined economists" (Callon 2007b) who draw and control the boundaries between the outside of real society and the inside of economics. What happens in the scientific laboratory usually remains a sealed space for the outer world. Inside the laboratory, society is made up of abstract individuals with given preferences and predictable behaviors who match mechanistic concepts of market orders. The study and perception of the "laboratory" has been extended and indeed revolutionized by STS (e.g. Latour, Woolgar 1986; Knorr-Cetina 1981b) as it has brought to the fore the complete spectrum of activities and actors involved in the production of knowledge (Knorr-Cetina 1992: 115). The cultural and social dimensions of scientific practice must be revealed, since science and technology are never apart from the realities that they describe or manipulate. Instead, they must be considered as participants in the project of "shaping, bringing forth – performing – new worlds" (Barnes 2008: 1434). And this claim should reach beyond the academic laboratory: While writings in the tradition of STS and the sociology of science have chosen scientists and scientific laboratories as privileged objects of research, ANT scholars have challenged the assumption that science is solely happening in laboratories (Callon 2007a; Latour 1999). They extend the idea of the academic laboratory to society more generally. Bruno Latour goes so far as to claim that "laboratory life [is extended] to all of our collective existence" (Latour 2004a: 112).

The making of markets "involves joining together with others, both within the academy and "in the wild" [as opposed to "confined economists"], in "hybrid research collectives" (Callon et al. 2002: 195). This reflexive intervention is performed through the coordinated action of practitioners and academic economists alike (Mitchell 2005): Callon and Rabeharisoa (2002) have demonstrated in a study about patient organizations that both professional investigators involved in clinical and biological research and lay persons collectively enact technical innovation..[6] In the case of value chain development in the Global South, ongoing investments to make markets work involve a broad array of academics, business experts, development consultants, policy makers, and entrepreneurs who draw up regulations and certification systems and enroll researchers, technological engineers, certification bodies, business gurus, professional economists, and international organizations. All have their share in market construction.

[6] Callon claims that the conception of "economics at large" and its political implications is where the main difference between his and Latour's approach lies: "Bruno [Latour] has clarified the operations constituting a politics of networks by showing how to reconsider relations between politics and nature. With my colleagues Yannick Barthe and Pierre Lascoumes (2009), I have explored the institutional configurations that make it possible to reconcile scientific adventure and political concerns" (Callon 2008: 27).

3. Markets are always in the making

The enrolment of market agents and the qualification of economic goods is temporary, because "links and nodes in the network do not last all by themselves, but instead need constant maintenance work, the support of other links and nodes" (Law 1997: 52). Markets are mechanisms of ordering, separation, and evaluation of economic worth and they are contingent: "There is no social order. Rather, there are endless attempts at ordering" (Law 1994: 101). The terms "econom-ization" – and more precisely "market-ization" – illustrate that they are always in the making. Accordingly, markets are "an achievement as much as an outcome, a starting point or a reality already there that could simply be revealed. The diversity of scientific or vernacular definitions of the economy or of behaviors and activities qualified as economic, and the controversies triggered by these definitions, are an indicator of a state of relative indeterminacy" (Callon, Çalışkan 2005: 370). The open-endedness and variability of economic configurations also reveals itself, for instance, in those moments when they do not align or stabilize as previously expected. Andrew Pickering's *The Mangle of Practice* (1995) provides a useful framework that helps to grasp the experimental endeavor of science which can be applied to market-making as well. He demonstrates that the production of scientific knowledge is always linked to the development of technological, conceptual, and social apparatuses that enable scientific concepts to become effective and realize themselves. Machines and social systems are interrelated and must be continuously brought in line ("tuned") with one another. Market agents such as farmers are not passive subjects governed by external "higher" forces – global policy regimes, norms and standards, technological devices or specific forms of expertise. They can resist new entanglements and associations when they do not engage in the modes and practices which are valued by powerful market agencies.

Hence, such temporary configurations may not only lead to stabilization but equally cause friction (Tsing 2005). Materialized flows of people, ideas, capital, and politics are subject to transformation as they enter the "sticky materiality of practical encounters" (ibid.: 1). The adjective "sticky" points to the impact of all kinds of infrastructure in the establishment of global relations which can enable but also hinder mobilities. Material and technological infrastructure facilitates the transfer of objects, ideas, and people, yet it may equally hamper their mobility. Global market connections rather turn out as "awkward, unequal, unstable, and creative qualities of interconnection across difference" (ibid.: 4). In other words, markets cannot be enduringly framed or formatted. Externalities may prevent previously aligned entities from staying in an agencement. Callon borrows the notion "overflowing" from the sociologist Erving Goffman (Goffman 1961) to claim that anything that is mobilized in a specific setting "guarantees, simply by virtue of its presence, that the outside world is also present" (Callon 1998a: 5). While in the world of economists, framing seems to be the rule and possible, the framing of value chain interventions, agents, and goods requires in practice many investments, it is expensive and always precarious.

4. Market-making is about translations

Translation, a term borrowed from Michel Serres (1974), is central to market-making and "is both about making equivalent, and about shifting. It is about moving terms around, about linking and changing them" (Law 2007: 5), and more pointedly, it is about aligning things that were previously different. Translation of goods and agents is indeed the defining feature of markets, as Callon has argued elsewhere (2008: 25, original emphases): "*[A]gencements* are operators of translation, and translation is the basic module on which *agencements* are built". To return to the quote at the very beginning of this chapter, "economization" refers to the translation process during which "behaviours, organizations, institutions, and, more generally, objects which, in a particular society, are tentatively and often controversially qualified by scholars and/or lay people as economic" (Callon, Çalışkan 2005: 2).

Marketization represents one specific mode of economization which has currently become prevalent. In the course of marketization processes, what counts as economic is qualified and calculated and thereby separated from what is not part of markets (Ouma et al. 2013). The type of translation that occurs in markets involves on the one hand the qualification and singularization of a product: This occurs when a product is alienated from its original context, is made calculable and when its properties are defined and associated with an economic, ecologic, or other value. The valuation of goods must not be understood exclusively in economic terms. Cochoy has proposed the term "qualculation" (Cochoy 2008) for the double movement of qualitative judgement and quantitative assessment that are both central to markets. Through various safety and quality standards such as GlobalGAP, environmental, social, ethical, or Fairtrade standards, goods are become certified and are ascribed a particular economic value (Chapter 7). A glance at the anthropology of valuation provides insights into the inner logic of these processes: "The forces that explain the circulation-transformation of things are the same forces that give things value. In short, things circulate because they are valued and it is because they are valued that they become goods" (Dewey 1915, cited in Çalışkan, Callon 2009: 390). On the other hand, marketization embraces the configuration and framing of individuals as calculative and accountable market agencies who are technically and cognitively equipped to evaluate products ("subjectification" in Çalışkan, Callon 2009: 389; Chapter 8): "Farming as a business" is a credo that has gained momentum in market-oriented development programs. Farmers are by no means passive subjects upon whom a certain reality is imposed. Indeed, farmers actively enact valuations and engage with technical, cognitive, procedural, and material devices (Higgins, Larner 2010; Miller, Rose 2008): Mobile market information systems, managerial benchmarking tools, contracts, and certifications format sociotechnical relations, whereby farmers in the Global South are framed as responsible business partners. Such entanglements bring about entrepreneurial selves who adhere to logics of market rationality, profitability, and productivity.

Markets, then, are defined by a double movement of entanglement and disentanglement of products and market agencies. The association *with* and dissociation *from* market agencements through processes of valuation and qualification determines the "in" and "out" of markets. Otherwise expressed, marketization involves the alienation of ideas, concepts, products, and people from their original context.

5. Market-making has disciplinary effects

The framing of economic entities and agents comes along with disciplining. A study of market-making – and the micro-practices of market agencies – must at some point engage with what Foucault has called the "microphysics of power". Foucault's analyses of disciplinary mechanisms and governmental rationalities shed light on the "calculated management of life" (Foucault 1981: 140, cited in Mennicken, Miller 2012: 6). In this vein, Foucault defines "governmentality" (governance + mentality) as a mode of analysis that reveals "the who and what one should study in the critical investigation of the relations of knowledge, authority and subjectivity in our present" (Miller, Rose 2008: 5). This refers to administrative practices of bookkeeping and recording that farmers in the Global South have to adopt and follow meticulously. As such, a disciplinary practice and mechanism of sanctioning is, for instance, the fact that farmers in Ghana cannot receive awards as "best national farmers" if they do not keep records of their activities (Chapter 8). More broadly, the increasingly sophisticated and all-encompassing standardization, certification, and metrology regimes that govern global markets are technologies for the governing of conduct (Busch 2011). They impose procedural and product-related norms and regulations upon market agents and determine whether the latter can or cannot participate in markets. Indeed, such standards are much more than indexes along which a pre-defined social reality is regulated. As ontological devices, they configure and transform realities by valuing and rendering visible things while concealing others.

6. Markets materialize in (traveling) policies

Markets materialize in policies that can travel and act at a distance. Reports, charts, tables, maps, or figures facilitate travel over time and space while retaining their form and shape. Accordingly, a concept becomes powerful (only) when it is materialized whereby it can "act at a distance" (Latour 1987): Action, according to Latour, emanates from centers of calculation in which representational devices such as maps are assembled and molded into "immutable mobiles" (ibid.: 227-229). Values and political goals can be achieved when statements – such as the value chain approach – are entangled with technical devices, embodied competencies, rules, and procedures. It travels – spatially and also ideationally – from the headquarters of development organizations or from the academic laboratories to policy makers, entrepreneurs, and public officials elsewhere. Although ideas usually do not have a clear-cut origin, they are often associated with a specific time and place symbolically. This gives them authenticity and ideological convincibility (Peck, Theodore 2010: 170). Inscribed in policy agendas and legal arrangements, the value chain concept exerts considerable influence in the places where it touches ground. Manuals, evaluation reports, PowerPoint presentations, policy papers, and embodied knowledges in mobile consultants enact a multi-source type of power as they develop into relations that link geographically discrete locations (Cook, Ward 2012: 16).

Policy transfer has sparked broad debates among scholars in the social sciences (e.g. Künkel 2015; McCann et al. 2013). It was for a long time considered a result of structural forces, conceived either in the form of coercion, lesson-drawing, emulation or diffusion (Stone 1999). From such a perspective, policy-makers assume a passive role and policies themselves are considered as stable and replicable (Benson, Jordan 2011; Peck, Theodore 2010). Resisting orthodox accounts which suggest a simple and mechanistic replication of policies across different sites (Dolowitz, Marsh 1996; Rose 1991), I understand the traveling of policies as a social process involving multiple agents, tools, and techniques which leads to the transformation and remaking of geographically near or distant politico-institutional landscapes, but also of the policies themselves.

Accordingly what I propose is to enrich the study of markets and marketization using a policy mobilities perspective: An orientation towards the contingent features and multi-directional mobilities of market models acknowledges that ideas of the market take shape in policies that travel along ideational and socio-institutional settings. It directs attention towards the spatial effects of embodied practices, knowledge, and agency across "translocal fields of power" (Ong 1999: 159). The means of inscribing the value chain approach into the agendas of development agencies and guidelines reveal much deeper insights into the power of market models to gradually construct the realities they attempt to describe: This is achieved through the inscription of the value chain approach into institutional arrangements and policy agendas.

7. Markets are relational constructs

Market devices, agents, and technologies are qualified and gain significance in relation to others. Along the way to Ghana and Peru, the value chain framework is modified once it enters new market agencements and policy agendas in which, for instance, the pro-poor rationality may be sidelined while the business orientation gains the upper hand (Chapter 6). The model becomes meaningful only through the web of relations that it is situated in. This relational claim has important implications for the reading of spatial connections.

There is a tendency in the social sciences and beyond to differentiate between macro and micro level, areas, institutions, and interactions (MacKenzie 2009: 33-34). Accordingly, a macro phenomenon would be globalization or global capitalism, while a micro phenomenon refers to a seemingly mundane technicality or an exchange between two persons. ANT, for instance, has often been blamed to explore in too minute detail the relational and productive features of small-scale actor-networks while being incapable of making wider "macro" political claims. This critique disregards that from an ANT perspective, "there is no overall social, natural or conceptual framework or scale within which events take place: as webs grow, they tend to grow their own metrics. But then, without a foundational macro and micro, the distinction between macro- and micro-sociologies (…) makes little sense except as a performative effect of those sociologies: class, nation state, patriarchy become effects rather than explanatory foundations" (Law 2000, cited in Law 2007: 8). Accordingly, any a priori, essentialist categories and dichotomies (society/nature, knowledge/technology, market/non-market) must be questioned, since the practice of categorizing enables black-boxing and draws attention away from the very matter of concern. Put differently, "a macro-actor is a micro-actor seated on black boxes" (Latour, Callon 1981: 299)..[7] Certainly, in this book I cannot do away with notions such as global, local, micro, macro, national, international, etc. Yet, I do not use these terms as determinist geographical constructs. Instead, I approach them as fields that are connected in space and shaped by their relations and connectivity to other entities in broader agencements (Law 1999: 4). This has implications for the conceptualization of the "global" – a broadly encompassing, seamless, and mobile form (Ong, Collier 2005b: 12) – and "globalization" – the extension of functionally integrated economic activities across national boundaries (Dicken 1998: 5). The use of such terms should always reflect the processes and outcomes that, for convenience, can be called "globalization" rather than being used as a catch-all phrase that embraces broader economic and political dynamics. As a consequence, what should be foregrounded are the relational effects in networks, since they can reveal insights into the power that a macro-actor has temporarily acquired within a socio-material agencement.

8. Hence, markets are performative effects

Let me come back to the figure of homo oeconomicus (Prism 1) to conclude what the previous precepts ultimately suggest. Although it has often been rejected for its high degree of abstraction, this construct provides space for discussion. Callon maintains that homo oeconomicus is not a fiction, but can be configured as a temporary effect of the established associations (Callon 1998b: 22, 30, 51). How does homo oeconomicus become a reality? Homo oeconomicus and calculative behavior are not simply there, but can be configured cognitively "with the aid of economic theory, of technology and of much else" (MacKenzie et al.

[7] If the argument is followed one step further, the notion of network as a pre-established category could be challenged as well. Latour however sticks with the notion because "it has no a priori order relation; it is not tied to the axiological myth of a top and of a bottom of society; it makes absolutely no assumption whether a specific locus is macro or micro and does not modify the tools to study the element 'a' or the element 'b'" (Latour1996: 373). It fits ANT and the performativity approach, which aim at de-naturalizing and de-absolutizing phenomena. Rather than a deconstruction of the latter, these approaches seek to provide solutions and methods to unveil the inner workings of institutions, procedures and concepts to reconnect them to the "social" at large.

2007: 141; Callon 2007b). The cases of the stock ticker in financial markets (Preda 2006) or of trading screens that are linked to electronic networks (Cetina, Bruegger 2002) are strong arguments indeed. Both studies reveal the role of physical equipment that brings into being – or even reshapes (MacKenzie 2009: 13) – markets and market behavior.

The "performative turn" has caused broad debate in the social sciences and human geography in particular (Glass, Rose-Redwood 2014). The term "performative" was coined in the 1960s by speech-act philosopher J. L. Austin, who distinguished utterances that do things – such as "I apologize", which if one says it, is an apology – from utterances that report on states of affairs separate from the utterance, such as "It is raining". The first category embraces "performative" utterances: They define acts in themselves that perform the action to which they refer (Austin et al. 1976). They do things. Austin focused his attention on utterances, but did not include social (inter-)action and performances in his studies. Jacques Derrida, known for his elaborations on deconstruction theory, has popularized the works of Austin on the performativity of language-in-use across the humanities and social sciences (Derrida 1982). The concept has been refined by Judith Butler who related the concept to gender and questions of identity (Butler 1990) by arguing that bodies, norms, identities, and even biological sex is produced through performative, iterative acts.

Economists' modelling activities are entangled in representation and intervention, which has been illustrated more recently in several studies, of which I want to mention a few in order to explain what it means to say that economics is performative (Callon 2007b). Michael Goldman's study of the World Bank's new commitment to complying with environmental principles demonstrates the powerful entanglement of knowledge and expertise (Goldman 2007). Through the adoption of a "green neoliberal" approach, conventional forms of state power and agency were replaced which led to a sociotechnical transformation of property systems, production practices, and state agencies. Another illustrative case of the performativity of economics and the power of "Northern" expertise is Timothy Mitchell's *Rule of Experts* in which he reconstructs the politics of 20th

century Egypt to demonstrate how the introduction of private property laws and measurement methods generated a new concept of the "national economy" (Mitchell 2002). Julia Elyachar's study about the making of micro-entrepreneurs according to the concept of homo oeconomicus in Cairo is a similarly brilliant analysis of performative materializations of the economy (Elyachar 2005). Moreover, Brett Christophers aptly elaborates on the performative world-making of economic models through urban political-economic transformation in the UK (Christophers 2014). Marie-France Garcia-Parpet's study about the construction of a strawberry auction market in France shows how a perfect setting for market interaction was set up and transformed buyers and sellers into formal market agents, and the site of encounter into a model-like platform of market exchange (Garcia-Parpet 2007 [1986]). A recent study by Florian Weisser about international negotiations on climate change stresses the role of policy papers for organizational action in international politics (Weisser 2014). Documents are shown to act as agents by themselves and play a thoroughly performative role (Cooren 2004). They set hierarchies, designate areas of responsibility, assign roles, and organize workflows. The above mentioned studies indicate that theories and models are projects that transform rather than describe the world as they are applied by economists, policy makers, and society at large.

To say that economics is performative does not mean that economic models become reality as self-fulfilling prophecies, as some business scholars argue (Ferraro et al. 2009, 2005). Indeed, the performativity concept goes beyond self-fulfilling prophecies or prescriptions which suggest that economic models become real because they reflect human beliefs that people subsequently act in accordance with. A performative perspective on markets acknowledges the role of beliefs, statements, practices, and material devices. As a consequence, it is not merely the aim of economics and its adherents to better understand the world, but to act upon it. The models of economics become effective tools in performing the economy rather than being mere passive "representations" of reality: The value chain approach not only depicts the infrastructure of global markets, but has come to constitute their very organization through material, technological, legal, or procedural elements as well as the belief in its effectiveness by policy-makers, development practitioners, and entrepreneurs. It is a gradual process in which value chains become performative effects of contingent socio-technical arrangements (Barnes 2008: 1436).

The politics of markets

ANT- and STS-inspired studies have often been criticized for negating the broader political and societal framework in which the relations between entities of a network as market agencements unfold (Ausch 2000; Star 1991), for lacking a critical commitment and position (Mallavarapu, Prasad 2006; Roberts 2012), and for focusing on "networks" instead of more broadly defined "scapes" (Latham 2002; Santos, Rodrigues 2009; Whittle, Spicer 2008). The performativity approach of Callon has been the subject of critique for focusing exclusively on the technical sphere of markets while sidelining the political effects of marketization or for lacking an underlying theoretical framework (Barry, Slater 2002; Fine 2005, 2003; Holm 2007; Miller 2005, 2002; Mirowski, Nik-Khah 2007). We have to ask, and here I follow Stefan Ouma (2012: 66), whether we can study markets without studying capitalism? These critiques have inspired me to engage in a deeper reflection and clarification of what I understand by "politics at large" in the making of markets.

The scholarly discipline that is mostly concerned with the matter of concern, i.e. politics, "the political", and policy-making provides an initial pillar upon which subsequent reflections are based. The traditional field and understanding of politics by political scientists focuses on the sphere of institutions, political strategies, interests, or ideologies. While scholars in international relations have usually defined "the political" from a positivist and technical perspective which takes "the political" as a given, more recently there have been calls within the discipline to bring back ontological issues center stage (Wight 2006). Andrew Barry, for instance, defines and differentiates "the political" as "the ways in which artefacts, activities, or practices become objects of contestation" from "politics" in the sense of institutionalized politics of governments and parties as "a way of codifying particular institutional and technical practices" (2001: 201, 6). Politics has always tried to bridge the gap between competing visions of how the world is and how it should be. While ANT's original approach focused on describing the linkages between nature, technology, and society through the practices of scientists in academic laboratories, proponents of ANT have elaborated their own understandings of "the political" more recently. "The political" as understood by Callon et al. (Callon et al. 2009; Rabeharisoa, Callon 2002) highlights the "democratisation of democracy", i.e. the participation of laypersons and specialists alike in political decision-making. Latour (2005a) and others (e.g. Braun, Whatmore 2010) propose a material approach, a "Dingpolitik", that addresses things and issues of concern such as new infrastructures, mobile phones and genetically modified organisms rather than values and beliefs. Stengers proposes the study of cosmopolitics (Stengers 2011) and Mol has elaborated her version of an ontological politics (Mol 1999). Independent of the perspective one chooses, politics is, after all, ontology.

My interest lies in the political implications of investigating value chains by unveiling the associations that become powerful in the course of their emergence. While initially the research interest was oriented towards the (socio-)political outcomes and effects of traveling ideas of the market, it shifted to a concern about the mechanisms and means that allow the circulation of models, their mobilization and institutionalization in new settings and their adoption by organizations, public agencies, and academic institutions to take place in the first place. The question "what are markets?" becomes futile at the moment that the focus shifts to the tools that allow the social to be disconnected from the economic sphere, because "the question is not: what do we call economic behavior, or what is the economy, but how are behaviors, institutions, agencements, and rules of the game economized?" (Callon 2008: 22). Considered under this new angle, we must even go beyond and question not only how things, procedures, and agents are economized and reconfigured, but also how we as researchers contribute through our research to such "perceived" (and real) economization (Chapter 4).

The mobilization of market models in the Global South has political impacts in the traditional institutional sense, as the incorporation of the value chain framework in policy agendas and legal arrangements reveals (Chapters 5 and 6). Its inscription goes beyond technical shifts in wordings. "Market design", as Kera and Tuters argue (Kera, Tuters 2011: 5), "contributes to discussions over the issues of ecological, economic, and political crises by offering various scenarios of future interactions between actors". The circulation of the value chain framework moreover has political effects in another, less tangible, sense in that diverse forms of knowledge and expertise are co-created. Studying and writing up the making of markets "is not a simple description (assuming that such a thing were possible which it is not). It does not simply work in the world. It also works on it" (Law, Singleton 2013: 500; Gibson-Graham 2008). Then the process of designing and framing market transactions, market agencies, and thus market boundaries is political and transformative per se (Callon in Barry, Slater 2002: 286). Therefore, there is an ethical obligation for us to take account of the political implications and effects that our research has on particular sites, arrangements, and people.

The creation of "enabling environments" and the conditions within which market models develop is much more than a technical or purely scientific market framing. In fact, the creation or stabilization of what belongs to a market agencement and what does not is a politicized sphere of conflict over market boundaries. Of no less importance is the awareness that imagining other worlds as a researcher contributes itself to new ways of conceiving "the market". Understood in this vein, this research project about market-making in the Global South is a deeply political project. This comes little surprisingly, since "we always act politically" (Law, Hassard 1999: 7; Law, Singleton 2013). The question is: How do we do it?

Conclusions

> "Treating artifacts, organizations and expertise as black boxes is an inescapable aspect of daily life in high modernity: not to do so is to head for the hills of Montana with the survivalists. The point, however, of 'open the black box!' as a heuristic is that what may be inescapable as a practical matter is nevertheless unsatisfactory intellectually. Not to examine the contents of black boxes is to miss a critical part of how societies are constructed." (MacKenzie 2005: 557)

In this chapter, I have presented the epistemological and ontological underpinnings upon which my research of market-making in Peru and Ghana builds. The proposed research program that I have labelled *associational politics of markets* aims to overcome and denaturalize essentialist approaches for the study of circulating market rationales. Investigating the processes of market-making demands a close and critical observation of societal transformation on various levels: Market-making is reflected in formal institutional arrangements as well as in every-day practices that are required to make markets work. It is constituted by investments of various actors who draw associations between things that were previously different and disconnected: Poverty reduction has not always been linked to market-orientation: The value chain approach, however, has established a connection between management literatures and development policy (Chapter 4).

The proposed research program is the product of a circular and reflexive research process including empirical field work, the analysis of documents and audio transcripts, and the writing stage. It was not established in advance of my field research or only "applied" to the matters of concern, but was developed in the course of an intense engagement with the circulation of the value chain concept in countries of the Global South. Following MacKenzie's call to "open the black box", *associational politics of markets* facilitate investigations into the emergence, materialities, practicalities, socialities, and effects of an all-encompassing global market order.

3. Following value chains

Scholars working in the field of marketization studies have never settled on a singular methodology. Neither have they set disciplinary boundaries or a commonly agreed set of techniques for the study of markets. While scholars working in the social studies of finance often engage in ethnographic micro-studies of finance markets, trading floors, and stock markets (MacKenzie 2006; Miller, O'Leary 2007; Preda 2009), GVC studies are mostly based on interviews, as is most common among economic geographers more generally (Dunn 2007). Mainstream economists draw upon document analyses while often refraining from a deeper engagement with the messiness, practicalities, and uncertainties in the field. Michel Callon's concept of the performativity of economics (Callon 2007b) remains fairly abstract when it addresses the "mundane" worlds of market-making and leaves aside Bruno Latour's claim to study and follow the "little things" (Latour 1987) and connections of global markets. Following policies and actors by thinking through a mobilities "lens" (Urry 2007: 18) will not generate or reveal incontestable truths of global markets. Rather, it offers a "better" understanding of the world (Cochrane, Ward 2012) that takes account of the increased global circularity and interconnectedness of objects and subjects, policy systems, and forms of knowledge. Relations between elements are not given, but are, instead, produced and reproduced; they are inevitably done differently in different places and by different actors (Mol 2002). As a result, no thought is reproducible and no written account of the world can be "objective". My research findings therefore differ substantially from those observations and experiences recorded by another person in my place as much as my perspective differs from another researcher's reflections and conceptual influences.

Ghana and Peru: Exemplary sites for the study of marketization

Readers of this book may wonder about the reasons for choosing two countries on two continents as case studies. As indicated in Chapter 1, there are several reasons why Ghana and Peru lend themselves for a study on the circulation of the value chain development concept. The critical point was a research project over four years: In 2011, I began a comprehensive analysis of roughly 300 value chain development programs that operate globally (Context 2). Based on the databank, I could prove that, first of all, the value chain framework is indeed on the rise and widely prominent. The final result is illustrated in Figure 4 and indicates the places where the framework has been institutionalized and inscribed effectively at the political, institutional, and broader societal levels.

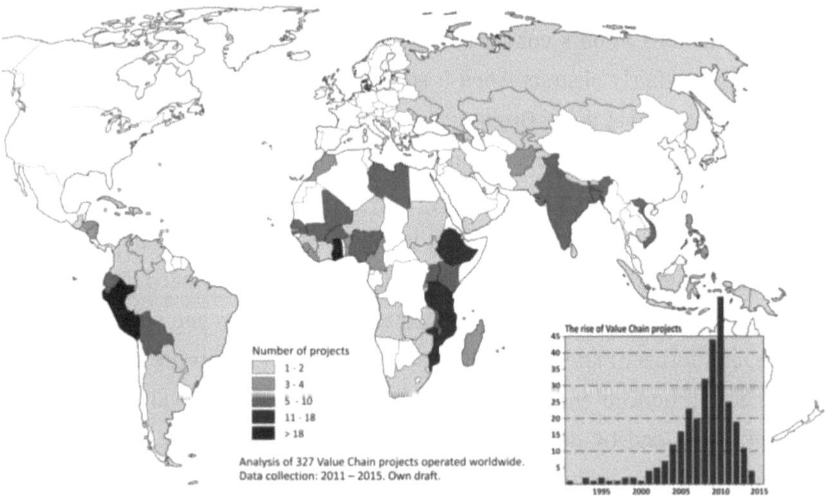

Figure 4: The global rise of value chain development programs
Source: Own data collection and own draft

Figure 4 shows that Ghana and Peru are the most outstanding cases due to the number of value chain initiatives which they host. The darker the contrast level, the higher the number of value chain interventions. Most programs are hence operated in countries of the Global South: Less than 20 out of 297 programs operate in the Global North. By studying more closely existing programs and policies that adopt value chain frameworks, I encountered more than 30 programs that have been or still are operated in Ghana and Peru respectively. National and regional policy agendas, academic curricula, and legal arrangements have been reframed according to the market-oriented rationale in each country (Chapters 5 and 6).

While the selected sites of value chain programs are not directly linked to one another, the incorporation of the value chain model into politics, academia, etc. creates a connection between multiple sites and people. It shows how varying interpretations and ideas are associated with a "global" model. In this sense, both case studies are heuristic sites which serve as a testing ground for global capitalism (Ouma 2012: 14). Many of the practices and relations I analyze are instances of broader processes of marketization that take place in (endless) other parts of the world as well. At the same time, these processes are, rather than generalizable, highly specific: The accounts do not pretend to be comprehensive overviews of the Ghanaian or Peruvian field of market-oriented development, nor are they comparable at the political or macroeconomic level.

The graph in the right corner of Figure 4 illustrates the timely dynamics of the analyzed programs – with a rapid rise to the climax of value chain interventions around 2010 and a decrease ever since. This dynamic suggests that the value chain paradigm has only been a short-termed buzzword, yet, a different factor explains this downward trend: An increasing number of value chain interventions are no longer labelled as such, although their rationale still adheres to the framework (Chapter 5).

Ghana and Peru as sites of policy implementation represent "centers of calculation" (Latour 1986b: 28-29), where models (of the market) are extracted from their original context, framed as "best practice" and transformed into global policies that travel and shape economic and political systems elsewhere. The selection of research sites was also conditioned by a socio-politically stable setting in which I could "calmly" conduct my field work as a young woman and foreigner. Language competencies equally played a role since I wanted to speak at least one official language in each country to an advanced degree to be able to conduct interviews, formal communication, and various types of conversations: Being fluent in both English and Spanish, no further concerns remained for the selection of case study sites.

Context 2: The intricacies of conducting social science research

While there has been considerable interest in value chain development by donors and policy-makers, no databank exists for the totality of value chain development initiatives, tools, and programs operated at the global scale. A consultant working provided a revealing insight in this respect in an e-mail exchange. Following my request in the very early stage of this research project for getting access to a global databank for value chain development activities – I had expected that there was some databank with an overview of approaches and types of projects – I received the following answer from him:

"We would also like to see such a listing! Even within one agency, it is challenging to get such a list – given that it is not always clear what the definition of a value chain project actually is. Also… most agencies are quite decentralized, and value chain projects may be spread across different departments (agriculture, PSD, trade, industry etc.)" (2011_1_E).

For the analysis, I thus faced the challenge of defining what counts as a value chain development initiative or guide and what not. Neither are programs presented in some common way by development agencies, nor do all of them carry the label "value chain" in the project description. I searched for buzzwords such as value chain manual, value chain handbook, value chain guideline, value chain tool, value chain initiative, value chain project/program, value chain promotion, and value chain development; I scanned through project descriptions and included also projects which carried the "supply chain" label but were SME-oriented development initiatives. Identifying the sponsoring organization, the implementing agency, and the length of projects was difficult because many websites provide only partial information. For instance, the American development agency USAID's projects are operated through partner organizations on the ground which they contract on the ground. The German development agency GIZ on the contrary provides funds and technical consultancy on the ground itself. There was no obvious line to draw as to which organizations to include or exclude from the research: Following Latour and his call to follow and unfold the "collective of action" (Latour 1987), the value chain development agencement no longer appeared as organic totalities but much rather as assembled from parts and temporarily stabilized (Latour 1986a). It has no natural borders. Due to time constraints, I finished the study after four years with a total of 327 collected and broadly analyzed programs worldwide..[8] By the end of the study, the analysis embraced the following multilateral organizations: AFDB, CFC (Common Fund for Commodities is an UNCTAD-related Fund), the UN Food and Agriculture Organization (FAO), the Inter-American Development Bank (IADB), the International Fund for Agricultural Development (IFAD), the International Labour Organization (ILO), UNCTAD, UNEP, UNIDO, WFP and the World Bank. Bilateral organizations include AFD, the former Canadian development agency CIDA, the Danish development agency DANIDA, GIZ, SDC, the Dutch development agency SNV, UKAID (former DFID) and USAID. Non-Governmental Organizations and implementing partners include ACDI/VOCA, Bill and Melinda Gates-Foundation, CARE, Chemonics, CIAT, CIP (International Potato Center), Cordaid, Helvetas, Hivos, IDRC (International Development Research Centre), Practical Action and Technoserve. The final outcome, illustrated in Figure 4, suggests a neatly ordered and finished research process, yet it is another example of never ending and pragmatic categorization struggles which reflect the challenge of doing empirical research. It is in these processes that "the social and natural worlds progressively take form" (Callon 1986: 224). This is why such fact-building endeavors must be problematized.

Ethnographies of associational politics

Local cultures cannot be understood from an armchair analysis of large scale political and economic processes alone. There is no global sphere "out there" that can be neatly separated from a local sphere. The latter is always already part of the global sphere and can only exist through variously connected sites, relations, and localities (Knorr-Cetina 1981a; Thomas 1991). Inspired by Marcus' multi-sited methodology (1995), I participated in patterns of movement of the value chain framework by researching the movements of either people (consultants), discourses (market-oriented development), or objects (manuals) as they circulate (Lins Ribeiro 2013; Peck, Theodore 2012; Weisser et al. 2014).

[8] At that point, I had to realize that a complete portrayal of value chain programs simply cannot be generated due to the nonexistence of a databank and of missing standardized terms of operation. The challenges which I faced in researching, reviewing, and documenting value chain-related initiatives are similar to those made by Nang'ole, Mithöfer and Franzel in their review of 32 manuals and instruments related to value chain development (Nang'ole et al. 2011).

The selected research methods were neither intended nor expected to result in systematic macro-economic comparisons between Ghana and Peru, but aimed at drawing attention to emergent processes, practices, ideas, and institutions. Only in this way was I able (or at least could attempt) to keep up with Latour's (1987) call to "follow the actors" and let the interviewees and other informants unfold their own frames of reference, perspectives and vocabularies while trying to back away from my own frames of reference as a researcher (Latour 2005b: 30). Nonetheless, the "search for order, rigor, and pattern" was not abandoned in the interviews and ethnographic field studies but "simply relocated one step further into abstraction so that actors are allowed to unfold their own differing cosmos" (ibid.: 23). And yet, as little as the direction and road map of research is clear and secure beforehand, as little can the research process be reconstructed in a detailed and verisimilar manner in the aftermath of research.

Entry points

The study of global market network with no pre-defined and visible boundaries poses a chicken-and-egg problem: Whom to start with and which associations to investigate and follow first? I chose an organizational perspective (Czarniawska 2012): From within a development agency in which the value chain approach is put into use, I was eager to find out how marketization around the Global South is being promoted and implemented. Hence, the research took off from the headquarters of a development organization and "ended" in two development programs in Ghana and Peru. Development consultants were chosen as key informants as they assume a central role in the mobilization of the value chain concept: They embody, translate, and promote knowledge about global concepts and development strategies elsewhere and among policy-makers and public servants (Chapter 4).

Another entry point for my research was the observation of the elaboration and circulation of a meanwhile broadly circulating practitioner manual that proposes a range of methods on how to promote, implement, and assess the value chain framework. A practitioner association with 100 members has emerged around the manual. This association is singular of its kind as it brings together experienced development practitioners from all over the world and thereby directs and steers the global circulation and deployment of the framework. I joined the practitioner association, participated in meetings to observe first-hand the negotiations around the creation of the second version of the manual, and conducted interviews with the members apart from meetings for a more detailed insight into their practices. From this center of calculation where the value chain approach is deployed and inscribed into manuals, modified and legitimized, I followed the approach to the implementation sites in the Global South by closely accompanying development consultants in their everyday routines.

Field access

For a study that is based on extended field work, gaining access to informants and insights into their practices, ordering processes, sites of encounter, and negotiations was an important issue to be resolved. In Ghana, there was already a network of practitioners that I could draw on. A previous research project on marketization processes in Ghana had been funded by the German Research Foundation (2010-2013). In contrast to that, I could not count on any contact or network in Peru at the beginning, but I was eager to establish it and succeeded in doing so.

Researching the practicalities of market-making meant collaborating and joining with others, both within the academy and "in the wild", in hybrid research collectives (Callon, Çalışkan 2005) instead of conducting an armchair's analysis. I engaged not in participatory, but in collaborative research. I understand collaboration here in the sense of considering informants as "epistemic partners" (Holmes, Marcus 2008: 81-101). This meant creating a trusting relationship of being partners instead of establishing hierarchical relations between a "research object" (practitioners) and the "expert" (researcher). This has deep implications: Scientists are no longer experts, but learn from and in the interaction with practitioners.

International consultants are difficult to access not only due to their highly mobile lives and tight schedules, but also for their broad exposure to international experts. Several interviewees were used to enquiries from foreigners, although most were not used to the kind of researcher enquiry that had precise questions, but also room for elaborate answers. However, once a personal meeting was arranged in which a personal relation could be established, for the most part I was able to quickly establish a trusting connection and was given broad access to information, personal viewpoints, and further contacts, and was helped out with answers in the aftermath via telephone and e-mail as well. Entrepreneurs were a different group of interviewees: They were interested in my evaluation and perspective about global market dynamics, yet not so much in my questions about the means and modalities of market-making. They probably accepted my interview enquiries because I was working from within the development organization which provided funds to their activities and to whom they felt obliged. Gaining access to informants was different in urban and rural areas. While in the capitals Lima and Accra interviewees often had tight schedules and therefore little time to answer questions from a researcher, it was much easier to fix interviews and meetings in rural areas. There were hardly any people from outside the regions and only a few sporadic researchers passed though in the course of the years on some specific research projects in those latter areas, more precisely in Northern Peru and Western Ghana, where I conducted in-depth field research and many of the interviews in the context of this project.

Intercultural communication

The research project aroused vivid interest among practitioners, although it seemed to be unusual for the interviewees that a German PhD student had selected both case studies about value chain development in Ghana and Peru and conducted research on the ground. My interest in the regions, their socioeconomic and political settings, and the personal experiences of the interviewees was always appreciated. There were situations which revealed particular power relations. One such situation occurred in a major Ghanaian university where I met one professor for an interview and asked him about his colleague who was known as a value chain specialist and who had an important node in the respective Ghanaian network. He led me to the professor's room, where his colleague was holding a lecture. My interview partner introduced me to his colleague as a "highly esteemed and special German guest and colleague" and made sure he sent out all the students right away for "the spontaneous visitor". The students were ordered to wait outside until I had asked all my questions. The situation not only revealed politeness, but demonstrated the somewhat uneasy relationship that one can be faced with when working in intercultural settings, where remnants of colonial structures and mindsets remain – I would have preferred to wait outside until the end of the seminar instead of having the students wait outside for me.

Other practical challenges awaited me during field research. The sporadic failure of power, internet, telephone, badly functioning public transport systems as well as misunderstandings due to "cultural differences" were a constant challenge to the effectiveness of the work and forced me to loosen my tight and rigorous research schedule. Punctuality was one such cultural factor: It was no rarity for me to wait for interviewees for one or two hours in both Ghana and Peru, and without subsequently being given a reason. External factors such as sudden tropical rains equally affected the punctuality of interviewees on the one hand and the accessibility of remote villages on the other. Another factor was the reliability of interviewees: Without at least one extra phone call for confirmation of the day of the encounter, meetings were not considered to be fixed appointments.

Some conversations, especially those with farmers, were shaped by linguistic barriers of varying degrees. While I encountered no problem in conducting interviews and all kinds of conversations in English or Spanish, several farmers in Ghana only spoke the local language Twi so that I had to rely completely on the translation of local entrepreneurs who accompanied me to meetings with farmers. Sometimes the challenge lay simply in choosing the right words that were simple enough to get answers to my questions. For instance, I quickly realized that I could not ask farmers in the field about the value chain framework or about their idea of what the market was. They were not able to make use of these rather abstract questions. As a consequence, I started to paraphrase my questions: Rather than asking what they understood by a value chain and the recent rise of market-oriented development approaches, I would start asking about their idea of a market, how field schools affected their practices, and what shifts they had perceived more recently in their relationship to buyers.

My roles

In the field, I often had to play multiple roles and assume partly contradictory identities: I was seen as

- a white-skinned "expert" coming from the Global North by the simple fact of having received a broad academic education and three Master degrees
- a "colleague" and visiting researcher in a team of development practitioners;
- a friend of the locals with whom I lived, worked, and spent many days and weeks in the field and in the bureau
- a PhD student trying to make sense of the observations and insights that I gathered during the field research
- a young woman often facing middle-aged or senior interviewees in two patriarchal societies.

The moment when professional interviewer-interviewee relationships turned into friendships was a double-edged situation. On the one hand, I gained deeper insights into the cultural context, personal understandings, and rationales for action. On the other hand, it was harder to get back to the professional level and relationship afterwards. I faced such a situation during a four-month research stay in Peru, where I lived in the house of a colleague and gained profound insights in the activities, practices, and rationales of local development consultants. At times, it was challenging not to "go native" (Flick et al. 1995) and identify too much with the research subjects. Indeed, proximity to the latter is both a responsibility and an advantage: There is a risk of insufficient theoretical reflection and the modification of research subjects' comments in presence of the researcher. Overall, I consider that chance as a great opportunity for enhanced access to the cultural background and perceptions of locals.

By always remaining in-between different worlds, roles, and spaces, I was not only torn between them but was confronted with sociocultural issues that went far beyond this PhD project and which are always part and parcel of doing research elsewhere. As both Ghana and Peru constitute patriarchal societies in which it is highly unusual for a young woman in her mid-twenties to conduct a PhD project, I found myself in interviews and contexts where senior men treated me rather as their daughter, a bachelor student, or as the "exotic" white-skinned woman with blue eyes. In the beginning, it therefore seemed difficult to build a relationship on the professional level with several interviewees. It seemed to me as if I did not fit any social or professional category due to my age and gender in combination with my status as a PhD fellow. This, however, was surprisingly different when I conducted the last part of my field work in Ghana. I worked in a development project where I had been formally presented and introduced by the executive director of the program to the colleagues as a PhD student right from the beginning in oral and written form. The colleagues did not question my status, but instead asked me for my theoretical perspective and how program adjustments could be linked to insights from academia.

I also had to switch roles and become a practitioner and consultant myself. Getting involved first-hand in practitioner settings and activities brought about conflicts that arose in the duality of being embedded within worlds of market policy formation and the worlds of academic analysis. At the end of my field research, I prepared a comprehensive assessment of the program, its strengths and weaknesses and challenges that I saw for the future of the development of the value chain. I was treated as an external consultant who could provide an "outsider's view" and critical feedback to the team. I was fascinated by, yet torn between, the worlds of academia and the practitioners' activities and programming. The attempt to follow the actors and enter into the practitioner world temporarily made me withdraw from my own (academic) frame of reference. Although I was close to the practitioners' view, practices and rationales for action can never be fully grasped by another person. Different frames of reference co-exist and different degrees of engagement may cause frictions (Delaney 2013). It must nevertheless remain the goal to "find a way to register the links between unstable and shifting frames of reference (...) by trying to keep one frame stable" (Latour 2005b: 24). At one point, I created a toolbox for a value chain practitioner manual. Becoming part of that latter world meant engaging with the objects of study, their perspectives, and practices and entering into an ambivalent relationship. It requires much tact and sensitivity as it possibly touches upon intercultural conflicts and (mis-)understandings and also entangles the researcher in new and constantly negotiated power relations (Gille, Riain 2002: 290). Indeed, these experiences were revealing in that they demonstrated that one cannot remain outside the phenomena one studies, as Burawoy (2000: 4) has argued in his outstanding book on "global ethnography". This is why methodological and epistemological reflexivity are not only useful, but absolutely vital.

The technical handling of material

Two stages can be distinguished in the process of analyzing the gathered data. On the one hand, an ongoing back-and-forth analysis and evaluation of the data was conducted in the course of the field research, including initial reflections and documenting of interviews, observed encounters and situations of all kinds. On the other hand, there was a final phase of data analysis and writing in the aftermath of the field research. The analyses that were conducted in the early research process were useful in guiding categorizing activities and concerns of interest, while the final phase of data evaluation was more structured, as all texts and selected materials had been gathered. They were reviewed, interpreted, and annotated with memos so that associations between the materials could be made. Memos are helpful in that they may lead to the discovery of emerging themes. The broad collection of codes and categories was enriched with theoretical ideas and quotes and therefore allowed one to make sense of the theoretical and empirical material.

Between February 2013 and December 2014, four in-depth research stays in each case-study country and more than 80 interviews and recorded informal conversations had been carried out in English, Spanish, German, and French. I am aware of the fact that this book is (necessarily) written in only one language – English – may impoverish or alter the meanings and vocabularies that were expressed by interviewees. They physically took place in Germany, Peru, Ghana, and Colombia[9] or over the phone. For conversations with Ghanaian farmer groups in the field, I was partly accompanied by an entrepreneur who translated back and forth from the local language Twi to English. In Peru, I conducted all interviews myself, since the interviewees understood and spoke Spanish. The interviewees were development practitioners and consultants working for (inter-)national development organizations, NGOs, various institutions, professors, experts working in research institutions, policy makers and employees in the Agriculture/Environment/Export/Tourism ministries, processing entrepreneurs, and farmers whom I talked to once or was able to meet again during the second research stay in both countries (Appendix).

Depending on the time constraints of the informants, interviews lasted from 20 to 190 minutes. They were based on a questionnaire that comprehends the broad array of questions and concerns outlined above. It served as a road map that was being designed to stimulate explanations rather than asking suggestive questions which narrowed the focus in advance. The concrete questions differed from one interviewee to another according to the interviewees' position in the value chain network, work experience, relations to value chain "masterminds", and academic and geographical background. Consequently, the conversations often took unexpected turns and broached broader sociocultural and political topics that served as contextual knowledge. At first, the interview questions were narrow which was reassuring in the unfamiliar research environments that I found myself in in Ghana and Peru. Gradually, I started to frame interviews more openly to give interviewees more room to express their justifications and perspectives. A sum-

---

[9] In Southern Colombia, I participated in a 10-day workshop on value chain development with regards to climate change mitigation, during which I could conduct a few interviews with participating development practitioners and researchers.

mary was produced directly after each interview and after the transcription at a later point in time. Due to various practical reasons such as time restrictions or surrounding noises, not all interviews could be recorded. Every interview was read several times and assigned codes and categories that structured the final analysis, which was done using MAXQDA, a software for qualitative data analysis, and drawing upon methods for the analysis of qualitative data. The quotes from interviews were corrected in cases of incomprehensibility. Fillers used by interviewees such as 'um', 'ehh', etc. have been excluded from the quotes. Word omissions on my side are marked by '(...)'. My additions to quotes for clarification are put in square brackets "[ ]".Quotes covering less than four lines are integrated into the normal text and indicated by "…". Each quote has a source assigned. Words written in italic style are pronounced emphatically by the interviewees. Quotes from Spanish or German interviews and sources were translated by me into English.

The interviews were complemented by participant observation on the ground. The insights gained through these observations and informal conversations were documented in a field diary. They provided information on "background" processes and helped to document ad-hoc impressions, observed behaviors, or encounters in the field. Such contextual information was useful for the later evaluation of data. The categorization and codification of interviews follows a simple logic: Every interview has been assigned a number and reveals the year in which it was conducted. A number after the interview code in the text relates to the line of the quote in the respective MAXQDA file. For instance, 2014_3: 15 refers to the interview with the code 2014_3, which was the third interview I conducted in 2014 and relates to line 15 of the MAXQDA transcript (Appendix).

Parallel to the coding process, in the course of which interpretations and analytic topics of the interviews were developed, field notes and additional material such as manuals, project evaluations, and project brochures, policy papers and contracts provided important contextual information and were partly marked with and linked to memos as well. These memos and codes were grouped together into thematic groups and then integrated into more abstract categories. In the course of the field work, a huge amount of material had been gathered which made it quasi impossible to follow a rigorous documentary method (Bohnsack 2008) or a detailed analysis according to the objective hermeneutics program (Wagner, Oevermann 2001). Therefore, a pragmatic compromise was made that would allow both for a reduction of the text material in order to get a better overview of the field and for the extraction of concerns that really seemed to matter to informants. The recursive categorizing and coding procedure was inspired by "grounded theory" (Corbin, Strauss 2014), a methodology that involves the construction of theory through the ongoing analysis of data. In the field, sensitizing concepts directed research concerns and emphases (Bowen 2006). They helped with following actors and action while not prescribing one single and narrow approach. Sensitizing concepts are "those background ideas that inform the overall research problem (...). [They] offer ways of seeing, organizing, understanding experience, they are embedded in our disciplinary emphases and perspectival proclivities" (Charmaz 2003: 259, cited in Bowen 2006: 3). Without broader guiding principles to provide a sense of direction, research of this scope risks not being successfully concluded.

Writing up ethnographies

> "Writing is a process, yet only the finished product is published. Nevertheless, the process and practice of our writing remains masked by its product, as the polished published work obscures the means of its production and even the production of our most frequent output (a scholarly publication) is, with few exceptions, seldom spoken of, let alone written about." (DeLyser, Hawkins 2013)

Ethnographic writing and research can go beyond the production of interesting and readable papers by improving one's understanding of people, cultural particularities, and lines of thought, and enhance one's ability to reflect on one's own culture and perspectives. Methodological reflexivity benefits the research process in that it allows for a circumspect handling of data and may lead to new forms of representation by experimenting with style, voice, structure, and purpose. It enables the reader to learn about the knowledge struggles and intricacies that underpin social research and qualitative research more generally (Boeckler 2005). For me, one such struggle was related to the fact that I never received a grounding in ethnographic research and writing, but learned along the way about the challenges and technicalities of doing ethnography.

The ongoing interplay between theorizing, collecting data, and writing up thoughts is central to my research. Through ongoing reflections on my own research practice and observations, I aim to show that my perspective has no superior claim to validity than others. Herein, I follow Andrew Pickering who argues that we should consider "science-as-practice" rather than "science-as-knowledge" (Pickering 1992), as this implies reflecting on one's conducting of research by making the processes of interpreting experiments and building statements transparent to the reader. As Gibson-Graham and Roelvink put it (2010: 342), "[w]e are less required to function as critics who excavate and assess what has already occurred, and more and more pushed to adopt the stance of experimental researchers, opening to what can be learned from what is happening on the ground", because

> "it is always part of an artificial experiment to replicate and emphasize the traces generated by trials in which actors become mediators or mediators are turned into faithful intermediaries. There is nothing less natural than to go into field work and remain a fly on the wall, pass out questionnaires, draw maps, dig up archives, record interviews, play the role of a participant-observer, compile statistics, and 'Google' one's way around the Internet. De-scribing, inscribing, narrating, and writing final reports are as unnatural, complex, and painstaking as dissecting fruit flies or sending a telescope into space." (Latour 2005b: 136)

The mundane and seemingly simple act of documenting ideas and visualizing information on paper already marks a transformation that requires the utilization of creativity, artifice, and skills by the researcher. As a consequence, all (social) research is (at least to some degree) political, whether or not it purports to be.

For instance, in the view of the people with whom I have worked in the Peruvian Amazon, it must have meant something that a German researcher came to them to study value chains. The meticulous and ongoing enquiries, the repeated return to the case study sites and the continuing interest I expressed through phone calls and e-mails contributed, as some informants told me, to putting the value chain model center stage in their perception.

The anonymization and fictionalization of informants and interview partners is a recognized practice and forms part of every social research project that builds on a deeper engagement of the researcher with a group of people. It guarantees not only the privacy of those people who are at the heart of the debate, but requires the researcher to deeply engage with his/her objects of study and the arguments he/she wants to make. The people studied are defined using abstract features such as the professional position, gender, ethnical background, or the relations in which they engage rather than their names. Individuals, development programs, and organizations have been anonymized or otherwise made general to ensure confidentiality. In some cases, sources such as reports or webpages which could identify my case studies have been withheld and the wording of the information derived from these sources has been slightly changed to ensure anonymity. These are marked with an "*". After all, "anthropological writings are (...) fictions (...) in the sense that they are 'something made', 'something fashioned'" (Geertz 1973: 15, cited in Alexander et al. 2011: 59), because they are themselves interpretations of a reality. Rather than considering such writings as unfactual, they are what Ouma calls "fictitious artifacts of scholarly practice" (Ouma 2012: 92) in that any written document is always an artifact of one's research. It is only "after the fact" (Mol 2002) and through one's writing that observations, documents, and all kinds of information take shape and a life of their own.

Conclusions

Researchers are not merely passive onlookers onto a social reality. They have an impact on the researched objects, not just on how reality is perceived but on reality itself. Reality, in other words, is not simply there to be observed, or for science to reveal it. Reality is constantly being enacted and performed through (in this case: research) practice. Therefore, the reflections, research practices, and methodologies that were developed in the course of the research process were problematized and brought to the fore.

I have outlined a range of methodological, epistemological, and ethical concerns that are deeply intertwined with this research project on global marketization. The production of knowledge and ethnographies is a deeply relational, practical accomplishment which is mediated through power relations, processes of (intercultural and material) translation, and social positions related to ethnic background, academic formation, gender, or age. The hardships of doing research "out there" is made visible to the reader, from the challenge to find and follow the actors to finding one's own role and making sense of the research findings out of the abundance of material that is both technical and entangled in one's own sensitivities, feelings, and affective decisions (Katz 1994: 498, cited in Herbert 2000: 563). By engaging in multi-sited ethnography, the intention was not to contrast the perspectives from each side, but instead to create a collage that lends broader insights into the connections and arrangements of circulating value chain models. This research project aims at a "refinement of debate" (Geertz 1973: 29) on marketization via value chain integration, which combines theoretical reflections on markets and creates new grounds for discussion.

4. Mobilizing market models

It would not be an exaggeration to claim that the value chain approach has recently turned into a prescriptive policy field for the design of industrial and economic policies. Within little more than a decade, the value chain approach has been hailed by development organizations all over the world. Since it is a rather slippery framework built on diverging interpretations, ideals, and ideologies, it allows donor agencies a broad space of action.

When market concepts such as the value chain approach are mobilized – and meant to endure in foreign settings – they require the support of adherents. Their success and outreach depends upon the construction of a vast network of instruments and the expertise and work of market agents ranging from chain participants – global retail firms, processors, intermediaries, and aggregators to smallholders – to government agencies, NGOs, and all kinds of service providers such as consultancies. And yet, the practical work that goes into their making is often neglected. Seriously engaging with the making of global markets requires an investigation of how global market linkages come into being and are stabilized, who designs and mobilizes market models, how market experiments are conducted, and how impacts are evaluated (Callon 2009: 21). This chapter engages with the conceptual, ideological, and material mobilities of the value chain model.

Conceptual trajectories of global value chains

Over the last decade and a half, the GVC approach has emerged as one of the most stimulating instruments for the analysis of spatial and economic dynamics of globalization and the circulation of market-oriented policies. Chain or network frameworks were developed to conceptualize and analyze economic globalization, global production linkages, and their spatial effects on the development of firms, regions, and countries (Coe et al. 2007). Following Staritz (2012: 7), two main strands of chain approaches can be distinguished: The first stems from within development studies and links the process of value creation along chains to broader issues such as global capitalism and debates of income distribution and entry barriers (Altenburg 2007). The second has its roots in management literature and is related to Michael Porter's Value Chain (VC) concept (Porter 1985). The analytical focus is the firm, its role in governing supply chain and opportunities and constraints to increase firm-level competitiveness.

The first type of chain concepts is rooted in critical development studies and world-system theory of the late 1970s. The American sociologists Wallerstein and Hopkins invented the term "Commodity Chain" (CC) and provided a tool for the study of (hierarchical) links between producers of raw material, processing and trading firms, and their activities involved in producing goods and services at the global level (Wallerstein, Hopkins 1977, 1986). They analyzed patterns of development and historical change in a system based on capitalist trade relations. They proposed to follow the production process of commodities as a way to trace the incorporation of new areas into an emergent worldwide division of labor during the 16th century (Wallerstein, Hopkins 1986). The authors illustrate their macro-level approach on international trade relations as follows:

> "Let us conceive of something we shall call, for want of a better conventional term, 'commodity chains'. What we mean by such chains is the following: take an ultimate consumable item and trace back the set of inputs that culminated in this item-the prior transformations, the raw materials, the transportation mechanisms, the labor input into each of the material processes, the food inputs into the labor. This linked set of processes we call a commodity chain." (Wallerstein, Hopkins 1977: 128)

In the same article, they argue that uneven production conditions are strengthened through trade between industrialized "core" countries and less-developed "periphery" countries. World system theorists reject modernization theory as a "developmentalist illusion" and highlight the role global power relations and exploitive structures that are embedded in commodity chains. The CC framework provides the first analytical account in a set of three loosely related chain approaches. More recent literatures on global production chains and networks differ from the former CC approach in two aspects: They attend to firms and producers, strategic decisions of single actors, different forms of governance within a chain and discuss types of market relations, such as networks, as compared to other modes of exchange. Consequently, their focus shifts from the macro-level of global capitalism to the meso-level of industries and firms. Second, the point of recent chain approaches is not to describe chains but to *change* them (Bair 2009a: 193).

The Global Commodity Chain concept (GCC), developed by Gary Gereffi and Miguel Korzeniewicz (1994), aims at understanding "where, how and by whom is value created and distributed along a commodity chain" (Appelbaum, Gereffi 1994, cited in Bair 2005: 157). It builds on the idea that chains can be regulated in a way to shift the sites of value appropriation and power asymmetries between lead firms and other actors in chains. At that time, concepts in comparative sociology were poorly equipped to make sense of emerging patterns of social and economic organization. In contrast to free spot-market relationships, the study of commodity chains enabled sense to be made of the emergence of close market relations in functionally integrated structures. As Gereffi et al. put it the appeal of the GCC construct is its ability to move across different levels of analysis:

> "Our GCC framework allows us to pose questions about contemporary development issues that are not easily handled by previous paradigms, and permits us to more adequately forge the macro-micro links between processes that are generally assumed to be discretly contained within global, national, and local units of analysis." (Gereffi et al. 1994: 2)

Several approaches were developed by scholars with differing emphases on the spatial dynamics, the role of institutional arrangements, the logistics behind production processes, or power relations in transnational trade systems. Notions such as commodity, production, and value on the one hand, to chains, networks, systems, and circuits on the other, were proposed to address the dynamics and structure of international trade. Examples include the Transnational Production Networks (Borrus et al. 2000), Global Production Systems (Milberg 2004), Commodity Systems (Friedland 1984), Global Production Networks (Henderson et al. 2002), and the French filière approach (Raikes et al. 2000). Although the discussion about the "right" terminology has been extensive, the application of the approaches in practice has resulted in studies that are "converging with more conventional approaches to competitiveness and losing touch with its more critical origins" (Levy 2008, cited in Coe et al. 2008: 275).

A profound conceptual shift came along with the terminological transition from "commodity" to "value" (Table 1): In 2000, leading academics and development practitioners gathered in Bellagio, Italy, to morph various concepts into the GVC approach (Bair 2009b; Gibbon et al. 2008; Sturgeon 2009). More than a simple terminological adjustment, this shift implied the departure from an analytical approach to a policy-oriented framework which increasingly appealed to development organizations. Contrary to the CC approach, which was perceived to be ideologically rooted in "fatalistic" structuralist development economics (Cramer 1999), the new terminology could be easily linked to previous works of Michael Porter (Ponte, Gibbon 2005). The shift towards the GVC framework was inspired by management literatures and Michael Porter's VC concept (Porter 1985). It is also known by the notion "supply chain" (SC) and embraces the technical concept of "management" (Bair 2009b: 6) to include the coordination and governance of logistical activities from production, supply, purchase, to the delivery and disposal of goods. These managerial frameworks did not take account of either the institutional settings or of the social dimensions of governance, coordination, and upgrading as previous politico-economic chain approaches did (Appelbaum, Lichtenstein 2006; Tsing 2009). The emphasis on technical questions of value allocation, generation, and enhancement transformed the framework into a market device through which systems of production are oriented towards economic efficiency, productivity, and enhanced profitability. Influenced by this economistic lens, the GVC framework lost its critical component.

Table 1: Theoretical approaches for the study of global chains

	Commodity Chains	Global Commodity Chains	Value Chains and Supply Chain Management	Global Value Chains
Year	1970s	1990s	1980s / 1990s	2000s
Key Question	How is global inequality (re-) produced?	How are global firms organized?	How can chains be organized to maximize efficiency and profits?	How can firms and actors improve their position in global chains?
Key Focus	Production of inequality	Governance & upgrading	Governance & transaction costs	Governance & upgrading for development; Policy orientation
Perspective	Historical & macroeconomic perspective on global capitalist system	Inter-firm networks and sector perspective on global industries	Meso and micro level	Meso level Institutional perspective
Key pioneers	Wallerstein, Hopkins (1977, 1986)	Gereffi, Korzeniewicz (1994); Gereffi (1999)	Porter (1990)	Gereffi et al. (2001); Gereffi, Humphrey, Sturgeon (2005); IDS Bulletin 2001, 29(1)
Theoretical background	World-systems theory	Organisational sociology and world-systems theory	Business management	Organisational sociology; Development studies
Influences	Dependency theory	International political economics literature; Comparative development literature	Trade economics	Global Production Networks (GPN); Trade economics

Source: Own draft (inspired by Bair 2005: 160)

Value chains for development

The GVC approach sparked broad debate among academics and policy-makers alike. Unlike the majority of social science concepts and paradigms, which remain limited in their outreach to practitioners and policy-makers, international organizations, development agencies, and NGOs have adopted the value chain approach to tackle pro-poor development. A change in the governance structures of GVCs should empower producers and small and medium enterprises (SMEs) in the Global South to improve their position within GVCs. Only through the access to global markets, it is argued, can smallholder producers have a share in economic development. As proclaimed by the Swiss development agency, "better integration and positioning within local, regional and global value chains can help producers in developing and transition countries to participate more in markets and increase their benefit from the added value created in the chain" (SDC 2007). The objective is to increase value capture at the level of the firm and local economy (Dolan, Humphrey 2000; Gereffi 1999; Gibbon, Ponte 2005). The attention has shifted to ethical questions, environmental concerns, and issues such as gender dynamics, labor, and sustainable livelihoods (Gereffi 2014).

The framework reconciles a focus on institutions and governance with agendas of economic growth and market liberalization (Weinberger, Lumpkin 2007; Werner et al. 2014; Context 3). The practicality of so-called "value chains for development" or "value chain development" approaches lies in their emphasis on meso-level analyses of the global economy which enable multi-scalar analyses of local and global dynamics.

Context 3: Value chain development and the international development agenda

Not only, but in particular since the daunting global financial crisis in the late 2000s, there have been widespread calls to reform the rules of the international economic system. Influential economists such as Joseph Stiglitz, former chief economist of the World Bank, have called upon policy makers and leading international institutions to introduce structural reforms of the leading principles underlying the current global economic system which have led to growing inequality within countries and, moreover, persistent global imbalances (Stiglitz 2014). A general consensus seems to prevail among international organizations and policy makers that markets are "not self-correcting" (ibid.), therefore necessitating corrective interventions in order to be more accessible to smallholders in the Global South. Acknowledgement of the ambivalent impact of radical trade liberalization has not always dominated.

In the 1980s, a broad consensus seemed to prevail over the role of trade, in particular export expansion, for overall development. Structural adjustment programs of the IMF and World Bank were promoted in countries all over the Global South, proclaiming and enforcing laissez-faire policies through standardized reform packages that incited these countries to liberalize their markets. The outward trend was reinforced in the 1990s when UN agencies such as UNCTAD proclaimed that "fast and full integration with the world economy was the key to seizing the opportunities of globalization and minimizing the chances of being left behind. (...) Global integration began to replace national development as major policy objective of governments" (UNCTAD 2006: 293). This overly optimistic perspective held sway in liberal Washington-based institutions and maintained that states should refrain from interfering with trade. The Monterrey Consensus Agreement of 2002, in which the international community convened to help low-income countries in achieving the MDGs, built on the assumption that trade (alone) is the engine for development and the way towards achieving the Millennium Development Goals (MDG).

While in the Washington Consensus era economic growth was the main goal of development, the Post-Washington Consensus era turned away from radical market liberalism. The lines of the debate around trade and development policy have shifted in favor of "sustainable, egalitarian and democratic development" (WHO 2015). Through a prioritization of pro-poor policies and measures that bring the state back in to support market systems, neoinstitutional approaches gain momentum (Brenner, Theodore 2002; Carroll 2012). Structural constraints to open markets persist in many countries of the Global South due to hierarchical and bureaucratic structures, as well as primary resource-based economies. They are conceived alongside further political, economic, and legal aspects as relevant indicators that shape the conditions for sustainable economic development. The 2014 UNCTAD Trade Report marks an important shift in development policies as Polanyian thoughts are taken up in it: "Markets are rarely – 'free' – and never operate in isolation; they require a framework of rules, restraints and norms to operate effectively. As such, the market economy is always embedded in a wider legal, social and cultural setting, and is sustained by a panoply of political forces" (UNCTAD 2014: 44). World market integration, it is argued herein, cannot rely on market forces alone. Effective industrial policies, strong public-private sector cooperation, and investments to upgrade into higher value-added sectors and strengthen national technological capabilities are considered determining factors (Springer-Heinze 2007).

Hence, the design of development policies in the most recent phase of "deep marketization of development" (Carroll 2012: 14) continues and expands the patterns of accumulation (Cammack 2012) while attempting to "fuse the public and the private into a liberal market reality like never before, variously working on, through and around the state" and attempting to create "enabling environments" (Carroll 2012: 26-27). A defining feature that comes along with this recent shift is the trend towards more contextualized policy propositions. The World Bank proclaims a new development approach which is called "new structural economics" (Lin 2012). It is meant to be carefully tailored to specific characteristics and needs of countries. From that angle, the discussion about GVCs assumes a key role in developing an appropriate design for policies that draw upon targeted, sector-oriented measures for broad-based pro-poor development.

Given the fact that GVC analysis is originally rooted in critical sociology, it comes as a surprise that the major proponents of the Washington Consensus have converged their policies around that single paradigm. First and foremost, the concepts have shifted from questioning whether producers can be integrated into GVCs to how it can be done (Altenburg 2007: 04). Critical scholars claim the framework's success is due to "the persistent ability of dominant actors and organizations to co-opt social theory and perpetuate prior commitments to a neoliberal development project" (Neilson 2014: 2). Value chain development strategies as mobilized by practitioner and policy circles today, remain closely tied to neoliberal agendas, while recent writings about "new heterodox models of development thinking" (Gereffi 2014: 23) suggest a departure from it. One of the pioneers in highlighting the link between the critical origin of the model and the shift towards its mere application as a business tool was the author of the GIZ manual *Shaping value chains for development* (Stamm 2004). Academics have also acknowledged the link between the CC and GVC approaches (Bair 2009a; Hamilton, Gereffi 2009; Kaplinsky 2005; Lee 2010; Neilson et al. 2014; Sturgeon 2009). Such works reveal the interest in bringing back the critical tradition of the GVC literature into the development debate. The disembedding of the academic GVC approach, i.e. the intended isolation of its critical component and history, demonstrates that policy transfer is ideologically exclusive and politically channeled much rather than an open process (Peck 2011: 6). This case is a far cry from keeping the critical "sedimentations" (Brenner et al. 2010: 190) of the approach upright. Instead, its rapid rise and uptake by multilateral and bilateral institutions demonstrates that the GVC approach has been hollowed out of its critical intellectual lineage.

The GIZ ValueLinks manual is one of the few manuals that explicitly distinguishes between supply chain management as a "business management tool" (Springer-Heinze 2007: Glossary 5) and the value chain approach as a "development tool" (ibid.: Module 0: 11). The former being a "private management instrument (...) [that is] much more limited in scope" (ibid.: Module 0:2), is delimited from the pro-poor oriented value chain development approach. The conceptual origins of the approach are rooted in two traditions and disciplines. While the latter refers to a group of academics who have used the GVC approach to explain industrial global networks in a systemic research tradition (Gereffi, Korzeniewicz 1994), the first tradition is linked to management economists and consultants who draw upon Michael Porter's business concept which extends beyond firms and can be applied to direct supply chains and distribution networks.

Early adaptations of the value chain approach by development organizations are closely linked to Porter's business-oriented value chain concept, as it is continuously made explicit by the practitioner community: "first comes the theory (...) the father of competitiveness is Mr. Porter, Michael Porter. He starts to speak about the competitiveness of countries from a theoretical perspective" (2014_26: 17). A senior planning officer in Germany relates how it was

> "not only Gereffi, that's for sure. And it was not always and only a question of global value chains. Yet, as such, it was introduced into the development field. There is also the French debate. (...) The filières are quite important in this respect. They [the French] have practiced it over years and also in their former colonies. In the practical application, there existed also an[other] approach. It was USAID's Gemini approach. The subsector approach, it was called, not value chain. It stems from the 1980s and they published a practitioner manual in 1991. This was the departure point. (...) But now it's promoted under the notion value chain development and not subsector approach. But there were several sources, also the French in Montpellier who used the CADIAC approach." (2014_4: 21)

According to the senior planning officer, the analysis of production processes via chain concepts in development cooperation goes back to two development approaches: the American Gemini approach and the French and Central-American CADIAC approach.[10] The Gemini approach was path-breaking in that it provided a conceptual toolbox through which the subsequently related steps of the production could be illustrated. Figure 5, which is taken from a practitioner manual, shows a early version of chain thinking before it was popularized and developed into today's widespread tool. The Gemini practitioner manual defines a subsector very closely to later versions of value chain methodologies as a "network of firms that supply raw materials, transform them, and distribute finished goods to a particular consumer market" (ibid.: 1). Mapping subsectors, industries, and value chains in order to analyze strengths, weaknesses and bottlenecks is a central part of value chain analysis until today, and has meanwhile been simplified and adapted to fit the chain illustration.

[10] In Spanish, CADIAC is the abbreviation for "enfoque de análisis de CAdena y DIálogo para la ACción", that is, value chain analysis and dialogue for action.

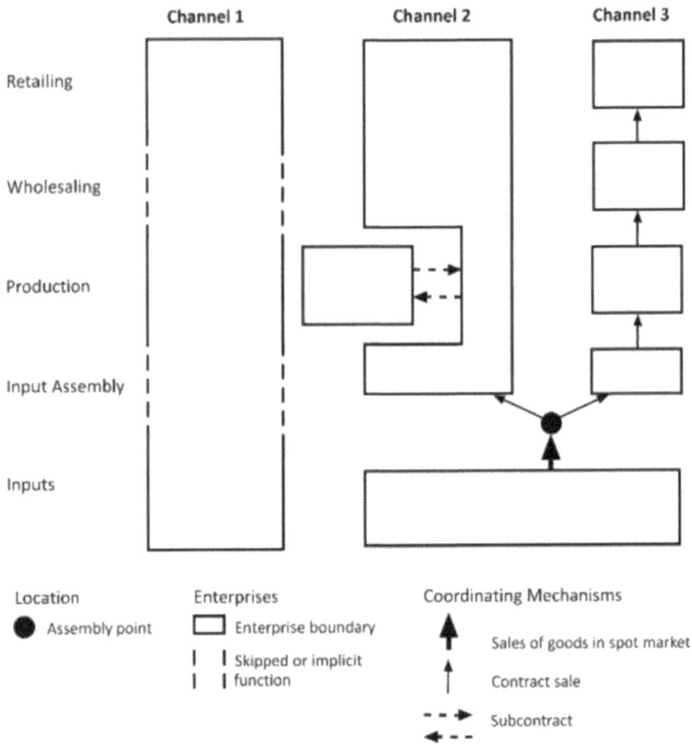

Figure 5: Subsector mapping: A precursor of the value chain approach
Source: Haggblade, Gamser (1991: 68)

The second approach has a different conceptual and geographical origin. The CADIAC approach was elaborated by the Inter-American Institute for Cooperation on Agriculture (IICA) based in San José, Costa Rica, and the French Agricultural Research for Development (CIRAD) based in Montpellier, France in the 1980s and 1990s. In the manual, references to the leading scholars in chain research from Wallerstein to Gereffi are not made. However, some references are made to French academic works, as well as to business school literatures on agribusiness and competitiveness. It focuses on participatory and actor-based development and (IICA 2000) builds on two components, namely, commodity chain analysis and action-oriented dialogue. Moving beyond a technical analysis of the bottlenecks of production processes, it conceives the competitiveness of agrifood-systems as a consensus-building process among the various actors of a commodity system. It is "an attempt to ensure, as much as possible, that expected benefits are shared among the actors concerned on a win-win basis" (ibid.: 6), which can be reached through preliminary consultations with public and private entities.

A consultant working for the IICA in Peru stressed that the emergence of value chain development approaches and different conceptual focuses must be related to the time in which they gained momentum: "CADIAC is born at a time when trade relations and the market were very important. It responds primarily to this context, to the fundamentally economic part of the chain: prices, productivity, information, trade circuits" (2014_26: 18). Here he stresses that different organizations have different emphases which can be complementary: "In GIZ, they developed from the beginning on an approach that addressed the territorial focus and sustainable development in general, the environment. These are strong points that the original CADIAC does not address" (ibid.: 19). And while the systemic research tradition is present in the practitioner's thinking, the link to the business-driven Porterian value chain approach is drawn more explicitly. But what is the difference between "supply chain" and "value chain", and how are the boundaries set between these circulating concepts in the eyes of development practitioners?

> "The concepts of Porter, they are rather from the perspective of firms. They say, you need to organize your supply chains. They are primarily interested in transforming raw material in the quality, volume and time that is needed to make use of the full capacity. (...) The notion 'value chain' rather takes the idea that surplus value is produced along the chain. We call it value chain because we want to explicitly want to address the issue where value is created. And who has what share in this process. Even in firms, there is a shift in thinking, especially in the agricultural sector. As the access to raw material is turning into a bottleneck, they open themselves to the "Creating Shared Value" concept of Porter and Kramer which they devel-

> oped in 2011. This concept proposes the idea that we have to share the created value among all partners along the chain in a fair way so that everybody is motivated to supply the quality and live up to his/her trade agreements that he has entered. The notion 'supply chain' is nevertheless so deeply anchored in the business sector that they [the entrepreneurs] say "you say value chain, you development people! For us, it remains a supply chain." (2013_12: 131)

The statement by the consultant reveals a long-standing controversy around the value chain paradigm. There is a persistent tension between those who apply value chain analysis and promotion primarily for developmental purposes, and those whom I tentatively call "supply chain proponents" with profit-oriented interests, who use the concept to optimize the structure and overall composition of a chain.

In the literature as well as among practitioners, however, the analysis and enhancement of supply chains on the one hand, and value chains on the other, are persistently used as a synonym (UNCTAD 2013). A senior consultant in Peru mentions that the terminological vagueness is prevalent, resulting in "infinite discussions what value chains and supply chains are. At the end of the day, we worked around the same object and tried to give definitions to both concepts, but actually what we were looking for was the same" (2013_16: 211). Similarly, a senior consultant in Ghana argues that the difference is close to none: "What is the difference? After all, in practice, they are very similar" (2013_2: 113). Both notions share common grounds, as confirmed by the statements of the interviewees. The smallest common denominator of the interviewees' comments is the chain metaphor, yet the conceptual origin and the objectives for promoting chain development strongly diverge. Should a clear distinction be drawn at all, as suggested by some? What remains certain in the end is the fact that a market-friendly thinking holds sway in the development practitioner community. A consultant in Germany summarizes the shift by maintaining that development practitioners have started to "think only in business cases" (2013_1: 43).

The statements of interviewees and their attempts to define and distinguish ideas that have been influential on the value chain framework indicate that a network of more or less closely related chain approaches has influenced one another. There is no single source, business concept, methodology, or organization that is unanimously recognized as the origin of the value chain framework by development practitioners. Scholars working with a policy mobilities lens stress that the outcome of policy translation is a social process that remains unpredictable and full of mutations (McCann, Ward 2013). Consequently, there may not be a need to link the origin of the value chain framework to one single influence or model. Such an attempt risks reifying one model instead of making the social processes of translation the object of debate. Development policies and paradigms evolve in environments where various ideas, approaches, and claims coexist and complement one another.

Value chains, the market, and the state

The GVC approach has gained a strong presence in the supranational agenda. It provides new analytical inputs for an array of technical assistance programs, financial projects, institutional advisers, conferences, and workshops that a few years ago were outstandingly and solely committed to self-regulative market theory (Fernandez 2014: 4)..[11] International organizations have come to perceive value chains as part of a new generation of PSD policies that are subsumed under systemic market development or the related approach "Making markets work for the poor" (M4P) (Werner et al. 2014: 1234). M4P is both an objective and a market systems approach developed by the British UKAID and the Swiss SDC (DFID, SDC 2008, 2004), which supports development practitioners in cooperating with business institutions to transform markets to make them work better for poor people. Value chain development is considered as a third way between

[11] The GVC approach is promoted by international institutions and donor agencies which are associated with "heterodox" economic policies and development approaches, but equally with those associated with Washington consensus principles. The first group of institutions includes, for instance, ECLAC, ILO, UNCTAD and UNIDO while the second group refers to institutions such as IDB, World Bank, IMF and OECD.

radical market liberalism and state-directed interventions due to the institutional bias that it applies. The market is seen as a force which should be capped by political regulation, as a senior project coordinator in Peru elaborates:

> "When the model was brought here, it was – how can I say it? – a useless model given the role that the public sector plays here, in particular in the agricultural sector. Certainly, the public sector has a huge impact here when it comes to govern and conduct politics and how to organize consultation. (…) I remember when Martin proposed his first draft: it was a retailer and market model. And so we said: 'Where is public policy in here?' He said: 'No, public policy mustn't enter. We are talking about a market economy.' And then a long discussion started about the role of the public sector. (…) I remember that in 2006 we had a large debate about market failures and how the market can resolve these failures by itself. The point at the time was that private actors tried to resolve them, and cheaper moreover, with lower transaction costs. There started the topic of asymmetry. It was a discussion that ended with him accepting the role that the state has in topics of value chain promotion in the broader context of development politics." (2013_16: 366-367)

Proponents of market-oriented development approaches see market-liberalization policies as a necessary, yet insufficient, condition for sustainable growth. Markets do not evolve in an abstract sphere, but are closely connected to political systems and agendas. The role of the state in market-making lies in providing a regulatory framework that facilitates the participation of marginalized groups in markets. Value chain development approaches acknowledge both the politico-institutional settings in which market agents act, and promote the creation of infrastructures and exchange platforms where market agents can determine the norms and regulations for the participation in markets. The authors of the ILO value chain development guide consider value chain development as a tool that can further sustainable socioeconomic development, although they remain vague as to the concrete configuration:

> "[This guide] reinforces the inclusive market development approach, which recognizes that conventional policies for market restructuring and reform, such as liberalization and privatization, cannot simply be assumed to reduce poverty. On the contrary, an inclusive market development approach accepts that explicit methods must be considered in order to encourage and promote participation by the poor." (Herr, Muzira 2009: 10)

Value chain approaches in the context of development draw on new institutional economics and theories of systemic competitiveness. Consequently, they acknowledge that markets, the state, and value chains are interrelated and interdependent spheres.

Crafting tools for value chain development

To claim that value chain development is happening everywhere is only one part of the story. To study and show how it is working is another one. Development organizations supporting agricultural development have produced a range of tools to help practitioners analyze and evaluate value chains. Methodologies of value chain development are illustrated and diffused through manuals, evaluation reports, fact sheets, and policy papers. These diagnostic tools constitute the necessary input for the design of interventions and play a central role for policy formulation, as they become their "scientific" point of reference. The proliferation of guides has taken place in an environment where key conceptual and methodological elements of value chain analysis and development are still evolving. That means that value chain analysis is being interpreted differently by development agencies with repercussions for the design of interventions and their impact (Altenburg 2007; Nang'ole et al. 2011; Chapter 4). Several development organizations have developed their own guides and tools, while others have adopted existing methodologies.

Table 2: The proliferation of tools for value chain development

Institution	Formal qualification	Training for practitioners	Manual / tools	Concept innovations
Agridea		Moderation and facilitation training formats Training on extension methods	Extension approaches and tools	Extension approach and adult learning
CATIE	Master courses	Technical backstopping/ learning in and on projects		Process innovation (marketing) PPP experience Value chain-specific technologies Product innovation
CIAT	Diploma program on enterprise development (Spanish, English)		Training manual for small producers in six languages	Value chain-specific technologies PPP experience
Global facility for underutilized crops			Guidelines on value chain development (underutilized crops)	
GTZ Competence Centre Social & Eco-Standards, Germany		Training formats Advisory services backstopping		Experience on social and environmental standards, codes of conduct

Source: BMZ (2007: 33-34)

Table 2 shows an extract from a list of qualifications and consultancy services that are offered in the development practitioner community. Various types of e-learning courses and academic studies leading to university diplomas in value chain development have been established and are important elements in the rise of chain approaches among practitioners (Chapter 5 and 6). A senior consultant for value chain development trainings indicates the authors of value chain manuals and guides basically “developed a toolbox of participatory instruments that you can apply in different phases of the implementation and mobilization” (2013_35: 171). The emergence of a vast assemblage of usages, modes of operation, and effects associated with the concept, which has meanwhile become a global policy regime, recalls Escobar’s account (2012) of how the concepts of development and modernity are applied, interpreted, and reproduced in various sites and regions.

Manuals may be the most comprehensive tools and attract particular attention in the institutionalization of value chain development. They explicate developmental objectives such as economic growth, poverty reduction, or decent work; they address target groups ranging from government agencies to NGOs and the private sector, and concretize action steps. Some manuals cover only value chain analysis, others address sector-specific, business-management or local economic development strategies, green finance, labor concerns, regional best practices, or policy implications and propositions. Some of the guides inform about the implications of globalization on countries of the Global South, while others are collections of case studies related to value chain development in particular regions. Ethnographers have provided stunning accounts of professional trading operations by linking the selection of trading techniques to aspects such as the corporate culture, training methods and technology (Abolafia 1998; Zaloom 2006, 2003). However, they stop short of an examination of the links between market beliefs and practices, or whether professional orientations reflect the experiences and practices of non-professional traders. Exploring how and why particular methods and technologies are utilized in the case of value chain development and how a market-oriented thinking is finding its way into the development policy community addresses precisely this issue.

A senior consultant, holding an MBA in development studies, recalls the process of translating the value chain approach into a manual for practitioners, and the mangling between "hard" science in the form of economic analysis and "soft" systems thinking which takes into account broader socioeconomic factors:

> "USAID asked me to stay, get involved again in the research and connect between research and applied research which is essential for how the project works, for me at least. (...) [W]e are trying to connect research to applied research. So there is some change in the handbook, with the aim of being less prescriptive about activities and trying to provide more guidelines and how you think about the problems, how you set up the kind of systems or processes in your project to manage information better. So you are using a lot more evidence-based decision-making about how to apply your research. That's the direction we are going, on top of the traditional standardized, you do your economic analysis of that. We are at the most cost, least efficient, most waste for parts of the chain. And we link it to the more systems-thinking that evolved here. And then you start "this is our starting point" of understanding [of] how the systems interact. You create a management system, so that if you start intervening you start getting more information about what works and why it works and what is the unknown role variety, this behavior." (2010_7: 59)

The processes behind the translation of the approach into a practitioner manual reveal valuable insights as to the practical transformation of scientific models into "conveniently portable 'best practice' " (Peck, Theodore 2015: 176). As argued above, there is a strong link between market beliefs, practices and material technologies. The making of a manual represents such a moment in which a market belief – that the market is constituted by transnational chains and that access to these chains contributes to pro-poor development among the most vulnerable market agents – is translated into a toolbox. This material market device thereby generates new practices among all kinds of market agents as it circulates to the Global South and further sites where it is applied. I had the chance to participate in a meeting of a development practitioner circle, in which a draft for an updated edition of a prominent value chain manual was discussed. The following observations shed light on those processes that occur behind closed doors and in the course of which manuals, and hence models, are rendered powerful instruments that subsequently circulate and "act at a distance" (Latour 1987) as global models. As member of a practitioner association, I could observe the little steps towards rendering the concept performative and realized that this global association is a central node herein.

> I am sitting in a seminar room of a development organizations' headquarter and am surrounded by 20 experienced development practitioners who have gathered for the annual meeting of their value chain development practitioner association. The members include staff of the development organization, freelance consultants from international and varying professional backgrounds, from senior to middle-aged and a few young development practitioners. To become a member of the association, one has to apply and, in case of acceptance from the board, pay an annual member fee. I am new to this association and am therefore asked to present myself and my professional background. It turns out, not surprisingly, that I am the only researcher and all of a sudden my hands-on experience with value chain development in the field in Ghana and Peru wanes to a minimum compared to the longstanding field experience of the present members. I am assigned the role of an expert with a valuable outsider's perspective and theoretical knowledge on value chain development. For more than three years, I had been trying to meet with Martin, the "mastermind" in value chain development, as everyone calls him – in Peru, Germany and Ghana alike. Martin welcomes me and even recalls my name. The associations' member appreciate his passionate engagement with the edition of the manual and the time he sets aside besides his senior planning officer position in the development agency. After everyone's personal introduction, he presents himself as president of the association and leads through the meeting based on a previously set program agenda.
>
> While the first hours are dedicated to compile regional experiences and best practices, the second part of the meeting focuses on his

draft of the manual, edition 2.0, which is about to be published. The second and bigger part of the meeting involves a broad discussion of the content, structure and topics to be addressed by the manual 2.0. In this quite informal and intimate setting, we talk about the modified modular structure, about the target groups, the role and link of the government and the private sector, and the development of policies that accompany the sustainable promotion and improvement of competitiveness via value chain development. A considerable part of the meeting is devoted to technical debates about wordings. For instance, a member wonders if "depending on the actors' perspective, do we classify value chain development activities as programs, projects, policies or initiatives in the manual?" Since 2004, consultants no longer speak of conducting projects, but programs: Interventions shall no longer be kept at the level of projects, but they shall be built into institutions. Policies are seen to be the outcome of programs. Initiatives are kept too broad and vague. At another point, appropriate terms and definitions shall be found for a chapter about standards covering product and process, voluntary and mandatory, norms and rules for the integration into global markets. Moreover, the manual will include rich illustrations, so that parts of the textual data can be illustrated through boxes and tables. We are asked to think about ways how to "put the theory into visualized models". The handbook should be easy to apply, handy and convenient for implementation, and address the practitioners' needs in the field. All members present are asked to send in success stories of the implementation of the value chain development methodology after the meeting. This can even lead to the value chain award (already mentioned in the snapshot at the very beginning of this thesis).

As I sit in the workshop surrounded by the development practitioners, my attention shifts towards the repeatedly expressed interest of the practitioners in framing projects, tables and models as success models. The association links experts who share technical expertise with one another and who share a belief in the positive contribution that the methodology offers – in practice and on paper. A responsible resource management is stressed in every program, since each

> must be legitimized to public entities and the media. Therefore, a senior consultant readily confesses, "small progresses [have] to be represented as [a] big success". The discussion continues with two more controversial issues. One consultant raises the question "Should private actors have a more prominent role in the promotion of value chains?" The practitioners seem to be rather uncomfortable with answering the question. Martin stresses that in the new manual there is an extra module for the crafting of business plans. Criticism and doubts, however, are expressed by another member who mentions that there are multiple tensions to bridge between the integration of local experiences and a universal approach, and the simultaneous orientation towards the global development community, national policy-makers and private chain actors such as firms. "How", the consultant asks, "can the approach be effectively put into a readable and practitioner-oriented format and from there into a methodology that could be taught within five-day workshops"? In order to enable the approach to become a "universal" model, the members agree that several issues have to be left out, while references of specific guidebooks and handbooks are added for further information. References to guidebooks of UN agencies are prioritized as they provide "more legitimacy" to the interventions in national economies, according to one of the present members. (Field note, 2013)

The making of a new edition of the practitioner manual manifests a key moment in the mobilization of the value chain development approach. Experiences collected from all over the world are put into technical terms, visualized by boxes, photographs and diagrams, and are then inscribed in the manual. Hereby, knowledge can circulate across time and space. The objectives have shifted over time, as an analytical comparison of the first edition of the manual and the draft of the new manual shows. While the first edition of the manual of 2007 focuses on pro-poor growth, the second edition of 2015 addresses more narrowly the promotion of a "green" economy.

The new version of the manual responds to the increasing concern for sustainability, that is, the social, economic, and ecological impact of economic growth. It distinguishes between procedures for the promotion of selected value chains and strategic approaches for changing the structures, politics as well as practices within value chains. For example, a key instrument proposed in the context of environmental considerations is the "hot spot analysis" through which major environmental problems of a value chain are identified. The application of tools of environmental assessment, such as the calculation of "footprints", life cycle analysis, and climate proofing is introduced and refined. These instruments are meant to calculate effects that were formerly disregarded or, at least, not measured through analytical tools. Hence, the effects of climate change and resource scarcity affecting the sustainability of a value chain as well as its negative impacts on ecosystems can be represented through numbers and tables. It is all about the shift towards "evidence-based decision making", as the senior consultant quoted above in this chapter has indicated.

Concern for sustainable development

Serving the idea of a "green (and inclusive) economy"
The guiding idea ("Leitbild") is a contribution to the "green economy" including economic, environmental and social dimensions

Economic growth and competitiveness
building on market opportunities and competitive advantage, seeking viable business solutions, calculating value addition and profitability

Economic inclusion of the poor, *gender equality, nutrition*
achieving positive impact on employment, income and other social issues
- to the extent possible
criteria for avoiding negative impact on all social issues ("do no harm")

Ecological sustainability
achieving positive impact on resource efficiency, adaptation to climate change
avoiding negative external effects of value chains development

Figure 6: The inscription of a sustainable growth agenda into manuals
Source: Practitioner association newsletter* (2013)

The slide (Figure 6) is part of a presentation from the practitioner association's meeting and provides insights into processes of including experiences, best practices and policy shifts into manuals which then evolve into facts in the updated version of the manual. Once the manual is published, the process of gathering and selecting information and formatting it into "scientific facts and figures" is rendered invisible. Yet there is much explanatory material that gets lost along the way. Simply looking at the final versions of the published manual would mean ignoring its sociology and "the arguments, interests and divergent points of view, that [it] encode[s]" (Mosse 2005: 15). In this context, Latour has introduced the notion of "circulating reference" precisely to describe how scientists meticulously insert and transfer "real world phenomena" into a chain of reflective arguments that stabilizes, and results in the creation of, scientific theories and figures (Latour 1999).

Documents and policies similarly contain "effects of practice" and "effects in practice" (Weisser 2014). On the one hand, policies, manuals, reports etc. are deeply entangled in corporate cultures and institutional frameworks and hence provide manifold insights about how these are assembled. On the other hand, documents and graphs are not passive artifacts but play a performative role: They contribute to bringing about the realities and statements that they describe. Inscribed in manuals, they can travel to other settings and become powerful sources of action. Gradually, sociotechnical networks become tightly enduring assemblages between peoples, objects, and technologies which can shift scientific findings across multiple and dispersed spaces and times. In the words of Latour, an idea, scientific theory, or a set of findings may turn into an "immutable mobile" over time where relative distance is a function of the relations between the heterogeneous components which constitute that actor-network (Latour 1987a: 215-257; Law, Hassard 1999). These immutable mobiles are ideas or concepts, which are mobile, yet immutable and stable as they are textual, cartographic, or visual representations that remain stable over time and throughout their travels. Things, therefore, "have to be able to withstand the return trip without withering away" (Latour 1986b). In other words, mobilities involve "hybrid geographies" of humans-and-materials that enable people and materials to move and yet hold their shape as they move across various networks (Whatmore 2002). Only then can models, ideas, objects become effective.

Translating the concept back and forth between powerful global centers of development, for instance, Washington-based institutions such as USAID, and the target countries is linked to strategic decision-making but also craftmanship. A study of the techno-politics of value chain development provides insights into the contingent outcomes of mobilities and the intentional efforts to create systems that are based upon global ideas and concepts of the state, the economy and governance. The term "techno-politics" (Mitchell 2002) stresses on the one hand the role of material and technical devices in the construction and functioning of markets. On the other hand it highlights the performative effect of economic theories in explaining how science and economics, hence, economics and the economy, interrelate and thus have political impact. In his book about the creation of the modern Egyptian state through the introduction of private property and the creation of a national economy through methods of calculation, measurement and exchange, the political theorist Timothy Mitchell stresses that "it is a particular form of manufacturing, a certain way of organizing the amalgam of human and nonhuman, things and ideas, so that the human, the intellectual, the realm of intentions and ideas seems to come first and to control and organize the nonhuman" (ibid.: 42-43). The formation of transnational value chain development networks and expert circles cannot be analyzed detached from the manuals and tools which they produce. When mobile consultants design, describe and rework models, norms and processes that constitute value chains, they engage in a process of "heterogeneous engineering" (Law 1987): Consultants as market designers mangle in workshops, field schools, conferences and institutionalized settings with policy actors, researchers and value chain participants. Indeed, the intentional efforts invested into crafting market environments leads to the paradoxical situation, as a senior consultant in Ghana argues, that "you're in much more engineering than free determinism" (2010_7: 77).

Who mobilizes models of the market?

International cooperation projects take place in environments of increased mobility and exchange of supra-local knowledge in which practitioners from different parts of the world gather and bring in their respective expert knowledge. The value chain development apparatus, or agencement, comprehends not only a whole set of practices, discourses, material tools, techniques and institutionalized policies, but also generates a specific type of specialist who mobilizes the approach in different contexts. An identification of those people who embody value chain development helps to "anchor globalization" (Rankin 2003: 709) and reveal the workings of circuits of embodied knowledge and traveling policies.

Current literatures on mobilities stress the role of consultants in mobilizing global ideas. The contingent processes through which new political and economic configurations emerge have attracted enhanced attention in recent academic debates, with a particular focus on entrepreneurs of ideas who mobilize ideas and concepts elsewhere (Czarniawska, Mazza 2013; Goldschmidt et al. 2014; Larner, Laurie 2010; McCann, Ward 2011). [12] What Larner calls the "new specialist elite" (Larner 2002: 663, cited in McCann 2011: 114) shapes the new contours of contemporary global development regimes. In the case of value chain development and based on various conversations and observations conducted during my in-depth field research in Germany, Ghana and Peru, I have come to identify three central elements that interact with one another and render the value chain development approach a powerful regime in contemporary development debates: local policy actors, globally mobile development consultants, and informational and material infrastructures. Such a typology and categorization entails the danger of narrowing down the variety of "real" actors in simplified typologies that hinder rather than facilitate an analysis of social pro-

[12] Several studies draw attention to the (political) effects of movements and translations of various forms of expertize through scientists, academics, activists, NGOs, recruitment agencies, management consultants, indigenous knowledges and to what extent they are involved in constituting neoliberal objects and subjects. See Barry (2006), Hall (2008), and Mosse (2011).

cesses. However, identifying the key policy transfer agents, various processes and means of mobilities helps to better conceptualize and tackle the driving agents behind policy mobilities.

As indicated above, policy mobilities are facilitated by a range of informational and socio-material infrastructures. Individuals, institutions, documents, and technologies frame, package, and represent information about best (policy) practices, successful interventions and cutting-edge ideas and circulate these through exchange platforms, digital libraries, newsletters, and directories of "resource people". These infrastructures are the glue that holds the different actors and elements of the value chain network together.

Local policy actors refer to policy professionals who are working for public agencies such as the Ministry for Agriculture or free-lance consultants being hired on project basis by the state or international development agencies and are residents in the project country with broad locally embedded knowledge. They ensure that national agendas harmonize with market-oriented value chain development and take care of its national and regional institutionalization in public agencies, expert committees and Public-Private Partnerships (PPPs).

Globally mobile development consultants usually work for a development agency or on a project basis and spend a lot of time working in projects abroad. These development and management consultants, conference organizers and workshop facilitators have an affinity for traveling and sharing experiences elsewhere and acquire supra-local project experience in the course of their careers. They work at the interface between governments, public institutions, research bodies and private entities, while some of them work from within ministries or hold an "academic-cum-consultant" position (Czarniawska, Mazza 2013). What further characterizes this group of consultants is their academic background in agronomics, economics, management studies, or development economics (see next section):

> "It's not just rhetoric. We are able to influence policy. We are able to influence business and government, and the sub-region. You

> know that's part of the process. When it began, it was comprehensive agriculture whatever. It was a nice word. But there were no tools. And it was immediately hijacked by the academia and the consultants" (2009_1: 66).

Far from including only policymakers, technical or academic experts traveling the globe while spreading policy recipes, these globally mobile development consultants perform and format market models in the Global South according to different – sometimes contradictory – logics and knowledge that they have acquired on their travels through different geographical, ideological, and institutional settings. They act in an environment that is certainly not devoid of academic reasoning, yet academic concepts play a minor role and gain traction only when they are translated into practical tools, as a senior consultant in Ghana recounts,

> "I see value chain development as following very much systems thinking, so I (…) wouldn't even say that we tried to take the theory of value chains and translate it. We didn't even make the caution of [an] effort to do so. We took some of the principles: Let's say in a value chain – what are the core principles in working on value chains? – we try to work along that side [rather] than [applying a] complete development project approach and not at all [did we focus] on [any] research approach. Or not at all on an academic approach. So you don't even spend time to look at the model. What it looks like, what's the framework like theoretically and how would you translate that framework into practice. We didn't make a conscious effort to do that. It would have been nice to do that, if we had a little bit [more] of [that] thinking and about research and maybe writing papers later on or something." (2010_6: 67)

Practitioners, as "middling technocrats" (Roy 2012), are trapped in the contradictions of market rule. They must constantly respond and bridge the expectations and satisfy requirements from their organizations and those concerns expressed to them by local policy-makers and value chain participants. Hence, they elaborate and negotiate the means for "market-oriented" development as dictated by international organizations such as the World Bank or UNCTAD, but have to translate and manage between differing logics and practical challenges on the ground: “We have our own challenges. (…) USAID still likes to have their core traditional indicators, because they have to feed that into a bigger system in Washington…because everybody is feeding that thing” (2010_6: 41). Practitioners are caught in the highly ambiguous development apparatus which may bring about effects that are not compatible with those originally intended. It is a fine line between global concepts and their grounded translation and effects; between complicity with noble motives of poverty reduction and resistance to the tools that are intended to bring about the expected results; between technical requirements, financially and institutionally imposed constraints, and the creative interpretation of what needs to be done and how it can be (effectively) implemented locally.

“El papá de esto”

> “When the translation of ideas into actions is well advanced, the actors involved feel a need to mythologize by dramatizing origins. (...) It might well be that, in the reconstruction of the past, an event is chosen or invented because it is rhetorically convenient (…) Alternatively, the incidental and disruptive character of the initial events is stressed to demonstrate the incredible touch of luck in the idea's timely arrival. Both types of memories serve the same purpose: to tie, meaningfully, the arrival of an idea to present problems experienced by people in organizations or attributed to the organizations themselves.” (Czarniawska-Joerges, Sevón 1996: 26)

While the rise of value chain thinking cannot be linked to one particular event or landmark, the quote from Czarniawska-Joerges and Sevón is helpful in explaining the role of arrival stories that circulate and become powerful among development practitioners. They create the common grounds of action and the boundaries of the practitioner network, as will be explored in this subchapter. In the case of traveling value chain frameworks in the Global South, these arrival stories always refer to a person, a global pioneer in value chain thinking.

> "Similar things were done previously, it was just not under the label of the value chain concept. Already at the time of my university studies, they told us to look at the entire process from the production to the marketing of a product. (…) It was called the "Linking farmers to markets" approach, it was in 2000, well, no, already in the end of the 1990s. But to pour it all into one concept, that came into focus in 2000s. And there was Martin* [a senior consultant] who said: This could be interesting for development cooperation. And then they offered a first course on value chain development in 2004. At that time still without a proper, sophisticated methodology." (2013_12: 42)

The idea of a systems approach to market development already existed before the ascendancy of the value chain approach. Yet only at the moment when there was a person to embody, elaborate and present the approach as a new concept, i.e. the arrival of Martin, did the framework became powerful as a comprehensive methodology all over the Global South. From ministry officials in Accra and Lima to technical experts in the Peruvian Amazon and workshop facilitators in Germany, Martin is seen as a mastermind of value chain development and a conceptual thinker for the global practitioner community. In 2013, I was sitting in the regional office of a development agency in the Peruvian Amazon from where I worked in a value chain development program. Listening to a presentation by a local expert on value chain development, Martin's name was dropped as precursor for the "value chain turn" in Peru – even in such a geographically and technologically-wise remote location. A similar situation occurred twice in Ghana when I conversed with project managers who delved into past experiences and workshops they had participated in, where they met him and kept remembering him vividly as the person who brought the approach to Ghana. A senior consultant in Peru with long work experience in Latin America recognized that

> "Martin is certainly the mastermind of the whole [value chain] story, he is globally renowned as a conceptual thinker. It's true. (…) And he is travelling through world history, spreading the word of value chains everywhere…" (2013_35: 155).

Beyond the recognition of Martin as a powerful conceptual thinker, he is seen as the father of the traveling experts on value chain development, as a workshop facilitator in Peru mentioned (2013_31: 138). Boundaries are drawn between the inside of the value chain practitioner community and the outside being embodied by those who do not know him, refer to him or apply his methodology.

Several development practitioners strongly urged me to get in touch with Martin if I was doing "serious research" about the circulation of the value chain approach. The first meeting with him and subsequent conversations about the rise of the value chain framework among global development practitioners revealed insights into the practicalities and rationales behind the circulating policy regime and his role as a central node for value chain promotion. Martin is a senior planning officer at one of the largest international development agencies, where he has been working on rural economic development and value chain development for many years. He is also editor and main author of a comprehensive manual with a specific methodology on value chain promotion, around which he has established an association for international consultants and facilitators. Over the years, he has become acknowledged as *the* pioneer of value chain development within the development agency and even beyond through his participation in global conferences on related topics and the publication of reports on the topic. Apart from his affiliation with the development agency, he works as a short-term advisor and senior trainer for these topics all over the Global South in Latin America, South and South-East Asia and Sub-Saharan Africa. Thereby, he constantly travels between the conceptual agenda of the development agency and the challenges, achievements and best practices on the ground. His capacity to do so is widely recognized, as a colleague admits: "He's a good academic and practitioner as well. He knew how to translate the discussions into a manual, even if I consider the manual to be very sophisticated, and one day one could write something easier to understand. Anyway, he was flexible enough to set the approach in relation to other value chain methodologies and approaches" (2013_16: 144).

The myths and stories around his person seem to have traveled as much as the value chain concepts in the Global South. The credibility and authenticity of one's claims, it seems, are enhanced when a reference to Martin is made. Such network nodes and arrival stories serve various purposes: First, they facilitate group identification purposes, because a commonly known and used terminology may define the boundaries of a social network: whoever uses the same terminology and refers to the same persons is part of the network, others remain outside of that policy community. Second, the creation of a myth around a concept serves legitimizing ends, and the authenticity and ideological power to convince the audience or reader of an idea, person, organization, or claim (Peck, Theodore 2010: 170). A network is, hence, defined by its nodes and linkages.

Behind the scenes: The politics of introducing value chains

The inscription of a "thinking in terms of value chains" as a crosscutting issue within development agencies is a condition for its mobilization elsewhere. Linking up actors to the value chain and enrolling public and private institutions is a process that involves many negotiations and investments. In order to understand how the value chain approach became recognized and anchored in development agencies, light must be shed on what happens inside development organizations, behind closed doors (Müller 2012). It is no secret that development politics are linked to strategic interests from donor countries. Where and for what purpose resources are invested depends upon a countries' economic interest in the target region, on the depth of political diplomatic relations and the historical links between two or more countries. A shift in national development policies resonates with changes in the composition of government. A German consultant reported that with a liberal candidate heading the German Ministry of Economic Cooperation and Development between 2009 and 2013 the shift towards PSD policies from supply side to demand side interventions was reinforced, with an increasing interest in and promotion of PPPs (2013_1: 44-48). The broader trend towards closer cooperation with firms and chambers of commerce had already started around 2000 when the private sector was being "sensitized for development activities". At that time, development agencies started to promote Good Agricultural Practices (GAP) as a common standard for farm management practice. The GlobalGAP certification system brought conformity to various existing retailer standards and soon became the most widespread private standard in agricultural value chains..[13] It was promoted through workshops and field schools, in which the value chain approach was used to draw attention to those segments and areas where (even more) profit could be made.

At the same time, there was a shift within development organizations when it comes to the staffing of development experts. When the "production-oriented colleagues left age-related to draw their pensions" (2013_1: 63-64), a general shift in human resource management came into effect. It was oriented along the lines of the trends in development policies. While the former colleagues had been agricultural engineers and animal-rights activists, from the 1990s onwards only agricultural economists were staffed, while no veterinary surgeon remained in the development institution. In his fascinating study about World Bank policies, Michael Goldman studies a similar phenomenon: How a "green neoliberalism" approach has gained momentum and became dominant through transnational policy networks of the World Bank. By tracing the routes of a new policy approach for the capitalization of water, he highlights the role of trained elites and global water policy experts who were staffed "in every node along the development production line, from Wall Street investors to the professional class actors who collect and analyze data, design and implement projects, and regulate them as government civil servants" (Goldman 2007: 789). What consequences

[13] GLOBALGAP is a private food certification and a management standard that promotes sanitary, phytosanitary and environmental safety along the production process. It was called EurepGAP until 2007, when its name was changed so as to reflect its expanding international role in establishing GAP between retailers and their suppliers. Meanwhile, it has become the most widely implemented certification scheme worldwide with more than 200 certified products and over 140000 certified producers in more than 118 countries (GlobalGAP 2015).

did this new staffing pattern have for the rise of market-oriented thinking and the directions of activities by development organizations? “Today it is a unilateral focus, based on a unilateral thinking model. It is strongly biased. We are running after political credos. Right now, everybody is doing PSD. Soon, with a political change there will be a new credo” (ibid.). Along with that shift, a new image of the farmer was promoted in development policies: the entrepreneurial farmer. In training sessions, farmers were called upon to act and calculate as entrepreneurs. What did the staff think about this shift? What is surprising is that “there is no discussion about that shift. Everybody is interested in the growth of the firm [development agency]. The seminars [for staff and target groups] are oriented along the principles of entrepreneurial thinking, and this is not going to change soon” (ibid.). By entrepreneurial thinking the consultant refers to a bundle of practices that farmers are called upon to apply, based on principles of productivity and efficiency. One consultant in Ghana put it bluntly saying that “[w]e want to transform the farmer community into a literate farming community. If you are not alphabetically literate, you should at least have business literacy, i.e. you are able to keep an eye on your cost” (2013_7: 25).

Through the replacement of technical experts such as agricultural engineers by economists, market-oriented thinking is taking the lead within development agencies. It gains momentum at all program levels. This turn is informed by a broader societal shift towards market-friendly policies, mentalities and social structures, as the processes of inscribing the value chain approach in Ghana and Peru will demonstrate (Chapters 5 and 6).

Mainstreaming: How a model becomes an immutable mobile

Various versions of the GVC concept are circulating. The GVC concept has started off as a critical tool to unveil unequal production relations, and has subsequently evolved into circulating techniques and accounts of “best practice” in the development practitioner community. The model of global markets meanwhile travels as little more than an inspiration or even just a label, a symbol of a new market system.

The market of value chain approaches

> "It was also the question to what degree we as development practitioners find ourselves in a market. You could say that there are the value chain manual market and the value chain training market, and in all these we are competitors as we compete with one another through our tools and products. Basically (…) there are standards for that market, how big is it, which market differentiation and segmentation are there? If you consider it from the market perspective, you would have to say that M4P [Markets for the Poor Approach] has acted as a clever entrepreneur, they have also invested many resources. SDC has also pushed it. GIZ has not provided any resources that would allow them to perform as a relevant market actor." (2014_4: 22)

The idea of a market of approaches illustrates a central aspect of recent attempts to mainstream value chain development. What the senior planning officer labels as "market of value chain approaches" refers to the variety of approaches, methodologies, and toolboxes which have emerged around value chains that compete with one another. Development methodologies are in a competitive market themselves, in which development organizations strive after attention and resources. Yet, how are the conceptual and methodological emphases mainstreamed into an immutable mobile that circulates globally while maintaining its core features?

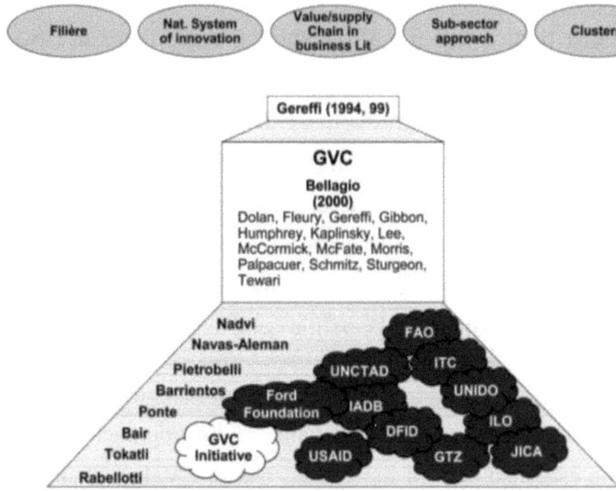

Figure 7: Conceptual lineage of the GVC approach
Source: Humphrey et al. (2008: 3)

A vast number of multi- and bilateral development organizations are active in value chain development. Many points of convergence exist between chain frameworks (Figure 7), as they pursue the overarching goal of strengthening the competitiveness of a subsector or an industry. A brief overview of a few approaches underlines the diverse purposes and focus areas addressed by value chain development initiatives. The International Trade Centre (ITC), a subsidiary organization of the World Trade Organization (WTO) and the United Nations Conference on Trade and Development (UNCTAD), provides trade-based technical assistance and stresses the role of market-driven development for marginalized communities. Accordingly, value chain promotion strategies should be derived from market opportunities, since it is markets that drive the performance of a value chain. ILO focuses on the role of labor standards in preventing a race to the bottom. Three issues are important in this regard: human resource development, local socioeconomic development, and comprehensive policymaking through a sector policy that enhances the competitiveness of specific sectors. IADB emphasizes the role of local value addition and entry points for gaining access to financial services, technology, and markets. One challenge lies in the design of contract farming strategies that do not invite free-riders and risk squeezing smaller participants out of the market. The American USAID emphasizes the importance of having a competitiveness strategy that is focused on the end-market and the increase in productivity through market access for the poor. However, that does not necessarily imply the need for a radical market liberalization, which would lead to the contrarian results, as the poor would be marginalized unless they can strategically position themselves in the market. The German GIZ focuses on the promotion of PPPs and the broad inscription of market-oriented guidelines and policies, rationalities and action plans into national institutions and agendas.

Initiatives to harmonize the market of value chain approaches are sparse, yet increasing. The establishment of the United Nations Value Chain Development (UNVCD) working group in 2010 is among the more prominent ones. This expert group includes academics and practitioners alike and gathers experts from ten UN agencies: FAO, IFAD, ILO, ITC, UNCDF, UNCTAD, UNECE, UNDP, UNIDO, and WFP. Its mission is to enhance effectiveness and recognition of the UN agencies in value chain development as well as coordination among these in formulating regional policy guidelines (Stamm, Drachenfels 2011). An evaluation report published by the working group underlines the fuzzy and inconsistent use of the value chain approach in UN agencies: the "interpretations range from a more or less technical description of the steps from the inception of a good to its consumption and the disposal of its residues, to the analysis of the complex interactions among the actors, based on concepts of political economy (ibid.: 3). This finding is consistent with observations made beyond UN agencies (Neilson 2014; Werner et al. 2014). The interest in merging and harmonizing approaches remains limited due to each organization's reluctance to give up their own approach and methodology.

Conclusions

> "Development projects and technology transfers to so-called developing countries present particularly intricate cases of idea materialization. Ideas are turned into things, then things into ideas again, transferred from their time and place of origin and materialized again elsewhere." (Joerges, 1976, cited in: Czarniawska-Joerges, Sevón 1996: 18)

While chain frameworks were once intended to describe global production processes, they are, meanwhile, used as business and development tools to change the modes of governance and the relations more generally between chain participants. The academic debates and conceptual trajectories around the GVC concept build the grounds upon which ongoing market-oriented programs and interventions in countries of the Global South are conducted. The key concern in this chapter was to reconstruct how the value chain framework became effective in the development practitioner community.

The circulation of the value chain approach in the development sector is facilitated through the creation of various market devices and techniques. As Czarniawska-Joerges put it in the quote at the head of this conclusion, ideas are materialized to then circulate and touch ground elsewhere. Manuals have been particularly important instruments that are used by development institutions. In an ANT-based reasoning, elements gain momentum and power in a network through their relations and interaction with other elements. I have selected development practitioners as a starting point for my research endeavor about the mobilization of economic models in the development sector due to their social, political and geographical outreach. The mobility of the "global consultocracy" (Saint-Martin 2000) and their tendency to gather information on best practices from various places to bolster their own recommendations makes them particularly powerful conduits of information among often widely dispersed development contexts. And yet, power and meaning unfold, are delegated through and formatted in sociotechnical networks (Callon 1999: 194). Consequently, I have suggested the need to study consultants not as stand-alone actors, but in close interaction and association with manuals and all kinds of devices that they apply and bring into circulation.

While mutating into a global fix, the original critical fervor of the framework has withered away with its expanding outreach and influence at the global scale. The process of mainstreaming, has been facilitated through the creation of platforms for exchange and coordination, (scholarly) attempts at stock-taking, and the creation of databases, as well as international conferences with academics and practitioners. They demonstrate the dynamics of the developmental apparatus that is currently emerging around debates of value chain promotion and economic development. The formation of transnational networks represents a remarkable shift in the mobilities of expertise, as the traditional one-way flow of expertise has been replaced through a multidirectional approach, in which academia and practitioner knowledge have started to step out of their respective worlds and seek stronger cooperation. Lessons and best practices from the Global South are taken into account, although most international development coordinators as well as the more prominent and well-known scholarly experts on value chain methodologies and analysis (still) come from the Global North, as the lists of participants and speakers of global conferences on the topic demonstrate. This also matches what anthropologists have more recently claimed: International development cooperation is no longer about an affluent Global North and its "others" (Mosse 2005: 1), but involves multidirectional flows of expertise. I have shown that despite the growing "market" of competing approaches, tools and methodologies, enhanced efforts are made to harmonize value chain approaches. The rising interconnectedness and exchange of people, materials and places have enabled better coordination. Yet, these efforts have also turned the framework into a simplified, somewhat "pasteurized" (Peck, Theodore 2015: 220) variant in the course of its circulation.

The mainstreaming efforts of development institutions and academics remain abstract when they are not linked to particular settings of mobilization and implementation. Thus, a study of concrete manifestations of the model in two settings, Ghana and Peru, allows a better understanding of the modalities of circulation, translation and implementation of this global policy regime.

5. Public policy and pro-poor development in Peru

> "Today, the value chain approach is pertinent in the development of the current global economy. (...) Agriculture and livestock farming are no longer elements that are detached from the rest of the economy. This approach allows us a systemic perspective of the agricultural activities that derive from the formation of clusters." (Ministerio de Agricultura del Perú 2012: 9)

In the last fifteen years, Peru has hosted a broad array of value chain development initiatives. The market-oriented rationale has gained momentum not only in agriculture, but also in various sectors that are linked to trade and production, as the quote taken from the Strategic Sector Plan of the Peruvian Ministry of Agriculture for the time period 2012-2016 highlights. To understand how the market-oriented rationale has become effective in Peru, one has to study the conditions under which it was introduced in regulatory frameworks, policy agendas and in society at large. In this vein, it is absolutely essential to look at the socio-spatial context in which the framework touches ground. Selected facts and figures provide necessary background information about the macroeconomic, geographical and sociopolitical setting in which the value chain framework gained momentum. Agriculture still plays an important role and contributes to 6% of the national GDP in 2013 while 25% of the labor force are employed in this sector (CIA World Factbook 2015b). Peru grows agricultural commodities such as asparagus, maize, potatoes, bananas, and coffee. Lately, Peru has become the world's primary source of high-quality organic coffee, the second largest exporter of organic cacao (USDA), and it provides half the global supply of quinoa.

Currently, Peru is in the transition stage from donor recipient to development partner (USAID-Peru 2012: 1). The economic recovery of the Peruvian economy in the last decade has prompted donor countries to reduce bilateral aid and shift their activities to other more "needy" regions.[14] GIZ, USAID, SNV and other international development partners are reducing bilateral assistance to Peru both due to political recovery after the terrorist outrages of the Shining Path guerillas in the 1980s and strong macro-economic growth in the last years. Socioeconomic inequality persists and is concentrated in the non-coastal, mountainous and rural areas, whereas the urban and coastal areas have benefited from recent economic growth.

Origins of the value chain approach in Latin America

Agricultural policies in Central and Southern America are coordinated by the IICA, a supranational institution with headquarters in San José, Costa Rica. Since its foundation in 1942, it has promoted agricultural development and strengthens the cooperation among currently 34 member countries. IICA develops agriculture-related policies and strategies that the member countries in Latin and Central America are encouraged to implement on a national level and as such, it has shaped the policy agenda in Peru. As indicated in an IICA manual on agribusiness, the interest in understanding, analyzing and enhancing the organization of production activities along chains is increasing:

> "Gradually, over the last years, the [value] chain approach has gained momentum and is utilized by technical experts, researchers, public officials, entrepreneurs, teaching staff and students in several countries of Latin America. As such, it has emerged as a topic of great interest and in different entities we hear about the importance of 'working in chains.'" (IICA 2006a: 20)

A new frame of reference for agriculture and rural life in Latin America emanated from the Summits of the Americas in 2001, 2004 and 2005 in which the ministerial delegates of agriculture endorsed the concept of agrifood chains. This marks the departure from a singular focus on production-oriented agriculture

[14] Recently, the US government has drastically cut its Official Development Assistance to Peru. Yet, USAID remains the largest absolute donor with 87603 million USD spent in 2010 (GIZ 2015b).

towards a systemic approach that considers rural territories and agricultural production chains in the national and international context. In the IICA Medium Term Plan 2006-2010 it is maintained that

> "[t]he concept adopted by the ministers of agriculture goes beyond measures intended to improve the productive and trade-related aspects of agriculture. It addresses rural territories where productive activities take place; the agricultural production-trade chains, which add value to primary production; and it extends to the national and international contexts that condition agricultural development. Further dimensions of sustainable development, such as the social, environmental and institutional aspects of those territories, chains and the national and international context are also considered." (IICA 2006b: 85)

Agriculture is envisioned as a network of agrifood systems which are related to other sectors of the economy, society and natural resources (IICA 2006: 14). The lines of action outlined in the IICA AGRO Plan 2003-2015 call for institutional mechanisms which strengthen the cooperation of micro and small-scale rural enterprises in regional clusters and connect these to agricultural production chains (ibid.: 36). Hence, in 2006, "production-trade chains" (ibid.: 85) as the IICA called them at that time, were seen as "the most appropriate spaces for the articulation of policies for rural prosperity" (ibid.: 14). In the Strategic Plan 2010-2020, market-oriented production is linked to the goal of improving "production, productivity, value-added processes and access to input and product markets, to financing and to agricultural insurance" (IICA 2011: 26). Value chains are the devices used to reach these objectives. A technical expert in agribusiness and capacity development working for IICA in Peru relates that the approach had always been oriented towards inclusive markets,

> "In our case, the value chain approach means to enhance the competitiveness of the economic actors. Understanding competitiveness herein as sustainable [market] access (...) and [generates] inclusive markets. I think that this is the departure point why there is rising interest in the value chain approach. (...) How it was introduced?

> Well… in the IICA we teach a methodology that we call CADIAC: CAdenas y DIálogo para la ACción [Chains and Dialogue for Action]. In the late 1980s we had the methodology and during the 1990s we started to intensively work on capacity development in ministries, at the level of ministries of agriculture. This CADIAC approach, what it does, is that it proposes an analytical tool with a value chain perspective." (2014_26: 11)

IICA introduced a chain-oriented approach already in the late 1980s and early 1990s – yet, under a different name and methodology. The CADIAC methodology is a participatory methodology promoted by IICA, which circulates in a modified version (Bourgeois, Herrera 1999). It is not the only origin of value chain thinking in Latin America. A senior project coordinator working with an international development agency in Peru does not question IICA's role in expanding the value chain approach, yet he argues that the approach was first introduced in Colombia in cooperation with the Colombian Ministries of Agriculture and Rural Development and of Production. Subsequently, it was transferred to countries in the Andes region:

> "[T]his approach is the one that comes later to Peru. We have brought it here (…). I came here after working in Colombia with the World Bank, where we worked on productive partnerships. We started to work on that and how we could adapt it here. By pure coincidence, the person working at the IICA here who was charged with value chains was Colombian as well – it was the former Minister of Agriculture and IICA director here in Peru. And there was another technical expert working for the IICA here in Peru. The three of us worked closely together for three years and developed the first edition of a value chain manual that was published by IICA in conjunction with GTZ." (2013_16: 265)

In Colombia, the value chain approach was and still is referred to mostly by the term "cadenas productivas" by IICA and national ministries. Indeed, all over Latin America, cadena productiva ("productive chain") is used to refer to both to the integration of smallholders into global markets and profit-oriented business management. A consultant in Lima was even afraid of being asked about the difference between the two concepts:

> "Honestly, I can only try to respond to this question, but I don't understand it [the difference]. According to what they explained to me, (...) a value chain means working on the relations between chain segments with the aim of generating added value. The value chain can only survive if everyone is on board. The cadena productiva is [a model in which every actor is] independent. This is what I understood, but it doesn't convince me either, because I don't think that it can work independently. Someone has to sell you their services and some has to buy from them. So that's the link." (2013_15: 115)

The historical emergence of the concept is linked to the modernization of the industrial sector in Colombia, which is constituted by large agro-industrial and manufacturing firms. The idea behind the approach is to maximize the profit of the overall chain. The Colombian model targets sectors and industries that shall become competitive at the global level. In the agribusiness sector, this includes globally traded agricultural commodities such as cocoa and coffee. In Peru, the Colombian approach is criticized for three reasons: "First, it did not involve small and medium producers; second, it was not a participatory model, and third, it was strongly academic" (2013_16: 53). The representational power of the Colombian approach has nevertheless contributed to inspire policy-makers in Peru. And it shows that across distant sites of invention, inspiration and implementation, globally circulating policy models can take on lives of their own and remain with little more than a symbolic linkage to their "supposed" places of origin (McCann, Ward 2010; Peck, Theodore 2010).

Rising concerns arose concerning the effects of the shift from the production-towards market-orientation for rural development and agriculture. Potentially also due to the focus of the Colombian "cadenas productivas" on market demand and powerful retailers at the end of the chain, the framework was associated with a "greedy" capitalist system that would hand over smallholder producers to the forces of the market. The market was seen as a destructive force that should not interfere with public policy.

> “The value chain approach raised a strong debate from the ideological political perspective. The left and extreme-left [party] said that this [shift] meant to “surrender” smallholders in the hands of the rapacious capitalist and private entrepreneur. They stood up for the former model that meant that the state bought all from them [smallholders], the state subsidized them, gave them grains or should give them anything. This paternalism was typical for the politics towards smallholders. Then they proposed a distinct solution, a solution – how do I say – based on a tripod institutional: market, state and the [smallholder] communities. And they search for the right balance between these three components to resolve a problem: beforehand the state gave all to them, which was like ‘State, resolve the problem of poverty of these smallholders!’” (2013_16: 41)

> “We have passed already tests of presidents who have been leftist: we hoped that they would work with the [value chain] model, and they ended up maintaining the model. Peru as a country opts for progress, for the market economy, but with a better distribution of wealth. With major equity, liberty and democracy.” (2013_21: 195)

The claims of both the senior consultant and the technical advisor in Peru reveal the importance of adjusting the framework to particular (national) political and ideological debates. Mindsets were in favor of the traditionally market averse production system, where producers received subsidies regardless of market demand. Agricultural production was dominated by regulation from the state. Markets were nearly left out of the equation. In Peru, the market-oriented rationale was perceived as a neoliberal policy that gradually took over the previously inward-oriented approach to agriculture. Indeed, at first the value chain framework was not perceived as an approach to solve problems and issues of economic and pro-poor development:

> "[I]t was not perceived as a methodological frame of reference oriented towards problems of development. It wasn't seen as a tool to incorporate in public policy. It was rather linked to the private interests of firms, this was the classical version of the value chain concept. What happens here in the scenario of countries such as Peru and Ecuador, is that there is a discussion in which this tool draws nearer to development policies." (2013_16: 208)

The "developmental approach" to value chain development targets a new relationship between market, state and producer communities while targeting the improvement of livelihoods of smallholder producers and the conditions for their participation in (global) markets. Hence, it becomes evident that during the transfer to other Latin American countries the original concept – or whatever version is taken to be the "original" – mutates into new policies, strategies, discourses and practices.

Value chains in politics, law and academia

As a tool for market integration of smallholder producers and rural economic development, the value chain concept was introduced by various agencies into the Peruvian economy: IICA, development organizations and NGOs in partnership with national ministries have all played their roles in the institutionalization process. It became pervasive in the last years in Peru because of the influence of multiple institutions and ideologies:

> "First, the influence of allied countries and multilateral organizations like the World Bank [and] the Inter-American Development Bank, to whom we pay our foreign debts. These institutions exert much influence on the government and propose reforms, like the National System of Public Funds. Then, the influence of the international cooperation linked to topics of development. It influences policy makers and local NGOs via technical cooperation. Through these channels, the [value chain] perspective entered and it positioned itself to reach up to our public policies." (2013_38: 12-13)

The influence of international institutions on national politics has been remarkable in sectors linked to economic development, trade and export policies, tourism, environment and climate change mitigation and further sectors. Among all ministries, the Ministry of Agriculture was mostly targeted by development partners in terms of adapting a value chain approach to development.

The Peruvian Ministry of Agriculture and its subordinated General Directorate of Agricultural Competitiveness (DGCA) were the first to introduce the value chain framework to policy outlines in 2001 in Peru. In its mission statement for 2001-2008, the Peruvian Ministry of Agriculture claimed to promote the formation of farmers into farmer groups: This would contribute to an easier integration into GVCs and lead to a more competitive agriculture system that is economically, socially and environmentally sustainable (Ministerio de Agricultura del Perú 2013). Economic development, it is said, can be reached through a better organization and positioning of producer groups in value chains (ibid.: 1, 3, 4). One of the first introductory workshops on value chain development for government officials took place in 2004 and was organized by the Peruvian Ministry of Agriculture, IICA and GIZ. At that time, diverse approaches and understandings of value chain development circulated in the different directions, offices and projects of the Peruvian Ministry of Agriculture. The workshop therefore aimed at the harmonization of concepts at the national context and led to the publication of a guide for the "promotion, support and implementation of agro-productive value chains in Peru" (Alvarez et al. 2005), which served as an orientation for the further incorporation of the perspective in different ministries and sectors. This guide inspired a directive that served to align agricultural policies and approaches.

The rising uptake of the framework is reflected in several policies and programs (see Table 3 below). The Strategic National Export Plan for the period 2003-2013 was a key element in institutionalizing the value chain concept and rendering it a powerful instrument of public policy in Peru. Alfredo Ferrero, former Minister of Foreign Trade and Tourism, stressed in the foreword the role of the value chain perspective especially for the agro-export sector in Peru:

> "The agro-export sector is doubtless one of the most promising sectors for development in Peru. The agro-ecological advantages of our country enable the production of a wide array of cultures, in many cases with a higher output per hectare than in competing countries and with clear seasonality advantages. Therefore, the agro-export sector was prioritized in the Strategic National Export Plan, defining a diagnostic and strategic guidelines using a value chain perspective." (Ministerio de Comercio Exterior y Turismo del Perú 2004: 5)

In the Strategic Sector Plan for the Promotion of Agriculture 2007-2011 and its annual operational plans, the value chain perspective remains the focus for agricultural development. For instance, the improvement of technical assistance for the development of productive systems and improved watershed management has been explicitly linked to the enhancement of associated value chains. The Operational Plans emphasize the role of identifying, selecting and prioritizing value chains, the organization of smallholders in groups and the enhancement of quality management within production networks. Beforehand, the lacking capacities and infrastructures did not permit to address other chain links apart from producers. From 2009 on, the Operational Plans include objectives and criteria for value chain development that address all chain links. In the Strategic Sector Plan of the Peruvian Ministry of Agriculture for the time period 2012-2016, value chains are presented as *the* central tool for development (see quote in the beginning of Chapter 5). The objectives for agricultural development for this time period are all framed through the value chain framework, and the agrarian policies reflect the incorporation of this perspective as well (Ministerio de Agricultura del Perú 2012).

Table 3: Policy landscape around value chain development in Peru

Time-line	International Policy Frame-work	National Policy Framework	National Agricul-tural Sector Policy	Important land-marks beyond
2000				First courses on value chain devel-opment (IICA)
2001			Supreme decree as a first move to-wards value chain approach	
2002				
2003	IICA Plan AGRO 2003 - 2015 (in-cluding a pillar on value chain devel-opment)	Strategic National Export Plan, Ministry of Tour-ism, 2003-2013		
2004				First workshop on value chain ap-proach, Ministry of Agriculture, IICA, GIZ Publication of the first value chain manual (SNV) Creation of practi-tioner circle "Ali-anza del Aprendi-zaje"
2005				
2006		Law on value chain develop-ment for enhanc-ing production chains & clusters		

Time-line	International Policy Frame-work	National Policy Framework	National Agricul-tural Sector Policy	Important land-marks beyond
2007			Strategic Sector Plan for the Pro-motion of Agri-culture, 2007-2011	Creation of su-praregional "Competence Team on Value Chains & PPPs"
2008			Agriculture Pro-motion Plan, 2008 – 2015	
2009			Agricultural Competitiveness Programs I-III, 2009-2013 Starting in 2009: Operational plans	Guide on value chain develop-ment facilitation for Latin America (GIZ)
2010	IICA Strategic Plan for technical cooperation in Peru, 2010-2020 IICA Medium-Term Plan Peru, 2010-2014			
2011		Bicentennial Plan 2012-2024		
2012			Strategic Sector Plan for the Pro-motion of Agri-culture, 2012-2016	
2013				
2014	IICA Country Strategy Peru and Plan for the Amer-icas, 2014-2018			

Source: Own data collection and own draft

The Peruvian Ministry of Agriculture introduced the value chain approach as a crosscutting frame of reference, linking it to concerns about sustainable development, the conservation of the environment and biodiversity and the adaptation of the agricultural sector to climate change. Whereas it may have mostly impacted the policies of the Ministry of Agriculture, it was also adapted by the Ministry of Environment, the Ministry of Export Promotion, the Ministry of Production, the Ministry of Culture and the Ministry of Foreign Trade and Tourism. These public entities developed their own tools and approaches to value chain development in order to support national competitiveness with each ministry.[15] The Ministry of Production deals with chain segments involved in the (industrial) transformation of a product, while the Ministry of Agriculture deals with the first chain node, represented by producer groups and raw agricultural commodities. In other sectors covered and addressed by the Peruvian Ministry of Production or the Peruvian Ministry of Tourism, they similarly "work with a chain perspective, looking at the services provided by different segments" (2013_19: 29) without persistently calling it "value chain". Some entities have continuously called it "cadena productiva", and also applied a different logic, as a coordinator of an ongoing value chain development program recounts:

> "In the Ministry of Culture, they have talked about value chains for ten years now. Since 2002, the Ministry of Culture has promoted value chains but in the beginning they called it "cadenas productivas". The perspective at the time was not necessarily a meso-level concept. (...) They promoted basically productive chains, not vertical articulations." (2013_19: 17)

The value chain approach caused malcontents in some ministries for being a crosscutting framework, for instance, for both touching the topics of the Ministries of Agriculture and of Environment. At times, as a senior project coordinator related, the coordination between both has not been easy: "They have to resolve rather sooner than later this disarticulation of politics between the agricultural

[15] The Ministry of Production has its own website on value chain development: http://www.cadenasproductivas.org.pe.

and the environmental, between biodiversity and agriculture, but for now there is no short-term solution" (2013_16: 444). Although such disarticulation of politics is not related to capital or labor circuits, the consultant's quote reminds Jennifer Bair and Marion Werner's call for a deeper engagement with the processes that engender the forging and breaking of links of production, people and places within commodity chains (Bair, Werner 2011). Politics of disinvestment and disconnections are indeed deeply entrenched in the constitution of such chains. Institutions like the National Council for Competitiveness have started to promote national value chains, such as the timber value chain and the textile value chain. These were early pilot projects to learn how an articulation of the actors at the national level could be reached. Without success though, as a project coordinator in Lima mentions, "these initiatives did not function" (2013_19: 40). While the cocoa value chain is highly institutionalized, having become an exemplary export-oriented value chain with a national platform in which public and private actors cooperate, other earlier examples of supported value chains – textile and timber – are rarely successfully institutionalized value chains at the national level.

Challenges related to the decentralization have arisen in the course of implementing the value chain perspective in Peru. During a workshop on value chain promotion in September 2013 with public officials of the Ministries of Agriculture, Environment, and Foreign Trade and Tourism, a participant mentioned that government agencies in Lima operate autonomously while neglecting regional bodies and realities. According to him, the national government did not consider policy actors and policy agendas beyond the outskirts of Lima, nor invest in strengthening the links between the capital and the regions. This resulted, inter alia, in differently prioritized value chains in Lima on the one hand and the regions on the other hand. While some products have been promoted by national and regional bodies alike such as cocoa, coffee or quinoa, many products and sectors lack a coherent value chain policy and support at the national and regional level. The articulation of regional policies and national strategies intensified in the wake of decentralization efforts, yet the coordination between agencies at the national and regional level still lacks common ground, as a project coordinator argued:

> "Every Ministry has its own prioritization. And its own perspective. The Ministry of Production has prioritized chains and the Ministry of Agriculture as well. Here, there are 6 [prioritized chains], over there, there are 20, and after these 20 there are 4 [more being] prioritized. But they are not the same ones, they are not linked. Then it gets to regions and in the regions they have their proper prioritization as well. It's not that the prioritization here marks a politics of the State to promote chains. In other countries maybe that is the case, but here it's not like that." (2013_19: 44)

Public officials and development practitioners in Peru perceive a gap between national policies, their interpretation by different public entities and their implementation in various regions of Peru. The practical challenges associated with the incorporation of the value chain framework into policy agendas and guidelines as presented above confirm a feature that is common to all global policy regimes: The frameworks that they are based upon are slippery in application. Apart from a core set of principles, such models are elastic and can be interpreted in various ways (Peck, Theodore 2010: 170), as a senior project coordinator indicated:

> "[T]here was a moment when the Value Chain concept was misinterpreted, you understand, it was dispersed, without any [conceptual] unity, people had different ideas about chains: at the Ministry of Agriculture, at the national level and then the emerging regional governments, at the level of other provincial ancillaries of the Ministry of Agriculture, at the Ministry of Production, at the Agrarian Bank, at some NGOs... in all those they had different concepts." (2013_17: 85-87)

As much as their flexibility can be advantageous, introduced frameworks must nevertheless be rather narrowly defined so as to create a common ground upon which policy propositions and solutions can be effectively elaborated. Besides the analytical part of identifying the bottlenecks and dynamics of a certain industry and sector, the enhancement of value chains requires long-term technological, financial and human investments. This refers to the creation of coordination mechanisms for all chain segments and supportive political and legal environments. A project description of a value chain development program that was funded by GIZ, reveals the comprehensive efforts in transforming the agricultural sector in Peru quite pointedly:

> "The construction of a competitive environment is, in sum, a long-term process that depends on the interaction of efforts and roles of the State (at the national and regional level), entrepreneurs and the academic sector. This network of actors touches on issues such as the generation of aggregated value, entrepreneurial development, innovation, quality, productivity, access to technology, infrastructure, the simplification of transactions, and, predominantly, the guarantee of economic, environmental and social sustainability along value chains." (PDRS 2013: 1)

The choice of words in the quote stresses that markets are "constructed": Markets are indeed politically *made* and the creation of market-friendly environments requires the support and intervention of the state. A complex amalgam of public and private actors at the regional, national and international level are at work in the endeavor of building market-friendly environments that enable the value chain approach to create the very setting that it purports to describe and explain.

Market devices for value chain development: Mesas técnicas

Instead of applying a ready-made set of policies for export enhancement, policy actors in the region have developed their own understandings, tools and models for economic development. An extract from a long conversation with a consultant in Northern Peru illustrates the efforts and dynamics impacting the inscription of the value chain framework into regional policy agendas and institutions.

"In the Regional Directorate of Agriculture as much as in all public establishments at the regional and local level, there was no clarity of how to start the work in practical terms. (...) GIZ proposes its methodology on local economic development to the Ministry of Foreign Trade and Tourism with a recommendation to increase exports and proposes the elaboration of a Regional Export Plan. At the same time, the department of economic development of the regional government [of San Martín] proposes the creation of regional export committees. The intent was to have a regional Export Plan linked to a national Export Plan, and those who were in charge of executing and following those would be the Regional Export Committee. I was there as a guest... what happened? All the year 2006 goes by and the Regional Export Committee never functioned. I think, the Regional Export Plan was established, but it was never implemented. There were changes in government: Presidential changes, regional changes and Cesar Villanueva comes in, and becomes President of the San Martín Region in 2007. The difference was that Cesar Villanueva had worked with international cooperation, the world of the NGOs. And somehow, this world arrived also at his government. The Ministry of Foreign Trade and Tourism coordinates the work with the regional branch of the Ministry of Foreign Trade and Tourism. (...) And they retake what the former government did - a move that rarely occurs. So they try to rescue the export committees. They had already done an assessment of this tool, which demonstrated that it would be valuable for the work that needed to be done. Part of the promise was to look if the region was ready to export. They do all that work, and start to analyze the territory and they realize that, I tell you, at the national level there is a profound knowledge about the regional dynamics. The national level comes in and says 'they need to make a regional Export Plan'. In the region, we had strong problems with the production segment in all our chains. We had nothing to offer, or if we had anything to offer, it just did not comply with international standards that were required to export. (...) These regional committees served as a basis for the formation of mesas técnicas for each product: mesas técnicas for cocoa, mesas técnicas for coffee ... The idea to create export committees evolved and they

> developed into dialogue platforms in which specific products and problems in value chains were discussed. This is why I tell you all that. It's the origin of the mesas técnicas. Until the year 2006-2007, they re-establish the mesas técnicas because at that time the regional government puts together its development strategy, which is – this step seems important to me – to prioritize chains. This element did not exist beforehand, the fact of prioritizing chains and they chose seven [value chains]. We have few resources in our proposition, so in matter of economic development we will prioritize flagship products. Those products which have a huge potential and towards these we will direct all our efforts." (2013_21: 33)

This extract unveils several features of policy mobilization processes. While analytical attention has often been drawn to small groups of policy mobilizers (Larner, Laurie 2010), which comes close to the role of the GIZ in this extract, policy making processes should be studied in their surrounding political, ideological and institutional contexts. A first Regional Export Plan was elaborated and adopted, but remained on paper due to missing coordination with national strategies for export promotion (Figure 8). The political interest withered away and the efforts had been shattered. With a new regional government in power, which proved to be more open towards export promotion strategies like the ones that had been proposed by development organizations, a new attempt was made not only to analyze but also to put into practice a Regional Export Plan. Based on an analysis of all value chain segments, the new strategy took into account the entrepreneurs' and producers' level of production.

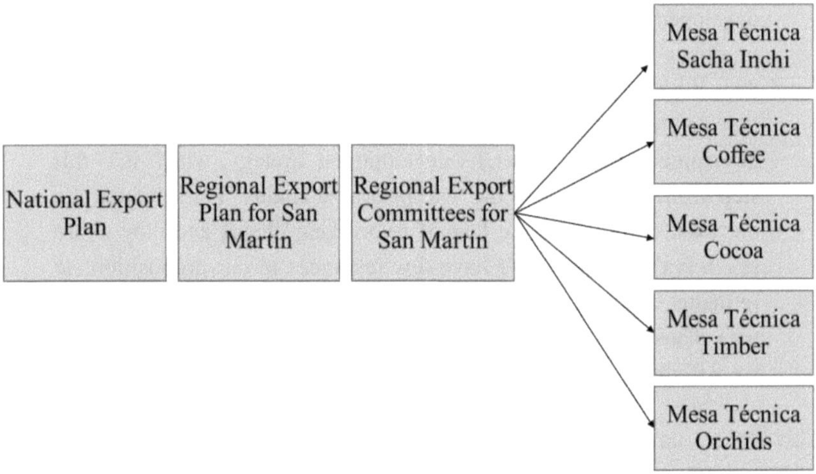

Figure 8: Operationalization of the Regional Export Plan
Source: Own draft (based on Guzmán 2013: 7)

In accordance with the National Export Plan, a market-oriented approach was (re-)inscribed into the regional policy framework by the regional government. Selected commodities from the region were prioritized. The Regional Export Plan became effective because of the mutual efforts of policy making actors, including public officials working for the regional government; and consultants of international development organizations. These efforts were canalized by an institution that was created to strengthen the linkages between value chain participants: the so-called mesas técnicas or technical roundtables, which are regional exchange forums of value chain participants, service providers and representatives of the regional government. As Figure 8 illustrates, the mesas técnicas implement the National and Regional Export Plans. For every commodity, a specific mesa técnica has been established. These exchange platforms have become key drivers for the stabilization of value chain development in Peru, as Chapter 7 will show with regard to the mesa técnica for sacha inchi(k).

The inscription of the value chain approach into regional and national policy frameworks involved the alignment of various levels of policymaking, and the support of manifold advocates. This process demonstrates the politics of market-making which involve various spaces, times and actors. The existence of an institutional frame in which economic activities take place determines the shape that the models are going to take on as a consequence. The same holds true for the broader spatial setting in which a model is inscribed. As Kevin Ward (2006: 70) put it: "The 'making-up' of policy is (…) a profoundly geographical process, in and through which different places are constructed (…) It is not only policy that is 'made-up' through the involvement of a network of actors: the identities, rationalities and subjectivities of those that are doing the making are subject to change through the process of 'inter-local policy transfer.'" Hence, institutional, geographical and ideological contexts are as important as the policies themselves: They impact one another. One market device that enabled the value chain approach to become performative is the mesas técnicas: These public-private platforms implement market-oriented export policy agendas, and bring together chain participants to exchange ideas and coordinate a common strategy for the value chain. Hence, they serve a more general purpose: the performativity of the value chain approach.

The emergence of a legal framework

> "[The value chain approach] was raised to the level of a regulation, to the formal political level, and then to agreements that were all indicators of what the future of the chain should become in the medium and long term. It was a unique experience." (2013_16: 44)

In the last decade, several public policy instruments were created to produce an enabling environment for enhanced competitiveness via value chain integration. Besides policies, plans and strategies, laws are common instruments of public policy. In Peru, Congress has launched three laws that buttress agricultural development based on a value chain perspective: Law N.° 28062 of 2003 for developing and strengthening agrarian organizations, law N.° 28846 of 2006 for strengthening production chains and clusters, and law N.° 29064 of 2007 for the establishment of an Agricultural Bank. As a consequence, four steps were undertaken: First of all, national councils on value chain development were founded to foster dialogue and coordination of private and public agencies. Moreover, commercial agreements between producers and entrepreneurs were established. Third, farmers were organized into groups, and fourth, access to financial services was enhanced.

A closer look at law N.° 28846 of 2006 for strengthening production chains and clusters serves as a basis for a few remarks about its purpose and background. Through this law, the Peruvian government pleaded for a market-oriented approach to reach competitiveness and emphasized that henceforth this approach would serve as reference for agricultural development. It explicitly promotes the establishment of platforms for dialogue between chain actors and supporting entities. Public agencies are called to foment the cooperation and better organization of chain participants and provide funds for SMEs, smallholder groups and for institutions. The law addresses all stages and nodes of the value chain: from production to transformation and services around value chains. This was previously different: In the early 2000s, policies promoting a market-oriented perspective targeted only producers, while other chain participants and segments were blinded out. This changed following this law, which remains superficial, though, as a senior project coordinator argued: "There is a law that promotes the value chain perspective, right? You have read the law? It's very general. It's basically the type 'it's good to promote value chains'" (2013_19: 44). Ministry officials and development consultants equally consider the law on value chains as a rather unspectacular enforcement tool and see it just as another paper with the only difference that "by law, the [regional] government in San Martín must support the economic promotion of its value chains" (2013_32: 154), as one entrepreneur argued. Despite the broadly indifferent attitude towards the law, the introduction of legal norms and regulations for value chain development has enabled the approach to gain stronger legitimization among policy actors and development organizations.

Anchoring the value chain perspective in academia

The value chain concept reached out beyond policies and laws and into academia. One of the early efforts to inscribe the value chain concept in educational institutions was a course on agribusiness in rural associations and firms that was developed by IICA and FAO (IICA 2006a). In the meantime, the value chain approach has been incorporated into several bachelor and master degrees on agribusiness development, international economics and sustainable development at universities all over the country. A prominent example is the Master's Program "Biotrade and Sustainable Development" at the Pontifical Catholic University in Lima, in which development consultants have had lectureships to teach practical knowledge on value chain development. They are "academic-cum-consultants" (Czarniawska, Mazza 2013: 128) and hence occupy a central position which provides these experts influence in both spheres – development practice and academia. In the Master's program, the consultant's influence has been remarkable, since the analysis and governance of value chains has been linked to biotrade, which is one of the "hot" topics in political debates on competitiveness, export promotion and agribusiness development as well (cf. Chapter 8). A virtual course on value chain management has been developed by GIZ and the Ministry of Production at the University La Molina.[16] Several attempts by development agencies to institutionalize the value chain approach in university curricula of agribusiness departments at the national level have, however, not been a sure-fire success, as the experience of a senior project leader confirms:

> "Here in Lima, I have been teaching a seminar on value chains for three years in the context of the Master diploma on Biotrade and Sustainable Development, but before there were also attempts. (…) In 2006, we succeeded to establish a diploma with a university in Chiclayo in the North of Peru, at the University Santo Toribio, and we established a curricula for the diploma course. The idea was to provide a formation to public officials of the Ministry of Agriculture

[16] The "Management of value chains" is taught in a 5-months course at La Molina University (http://www.lamolina.edu.pe/agronegociosvirtual/dip_cadenasproductivas.htm). A diploma can be obtained as well (http://www.cadenasproductivas.org.pe/diplomado.htm accessed on 10.10.2013).

> and the Ministry of Production who work there, but the problem was at first place the lack of qualified people who could then do the implementation. For me, this is the central issue, the inexistence of a methodological line of research. This was what did not provide sustainability to the model and the diploma. Basically, the diploma was installed, a group of people was capacitated and that was it." (2013_16: 368-369)

Two workshops for academic staff took place in Northern Peru in 2013, which aimed at enrolling universities to integrate the value chain development methodology in curricula. However, due to a lack of capacity among teaching staff to develop new lines of research, initiatives to inscribe the framework consistently in universities outside of Lima failed. Beyond lacking human capacities, a key challenge were the diverging interests of partner institutions: Universities aimed at diversifying their academic offer; development organizations sought to develop capacities for the promotion of local development; and the Institute for Irrigation Management, another financial donor, hoped to position itself as an expert institution in the topic of value chains (Alianza de aprendizaje Perú n.y.: 9). After these experiences, efforts to inscribe the methodology in public institutions focused on ministry officials, as the outcome seemed to be more promising.

Value chain development in Peru

The activities of various institutions have fostered the creation of a supportive environment for value chain development in Peru. Multilateral institutions such as the IADB, IFAD, the International Center for Tropical Agriculture (CIAT) and the European Union (EU) have financially and technically contributed to foster market-oriented rural development in Peru. IICA continues to be a leading institution for agricultural development strategies at the national level. The prominent donor organizations and development banks which have pushed value chain development in Peru are listed in Figure 9. The overview allows to assess the role that international development organizations have assumed in value chain development since the late 1990s.

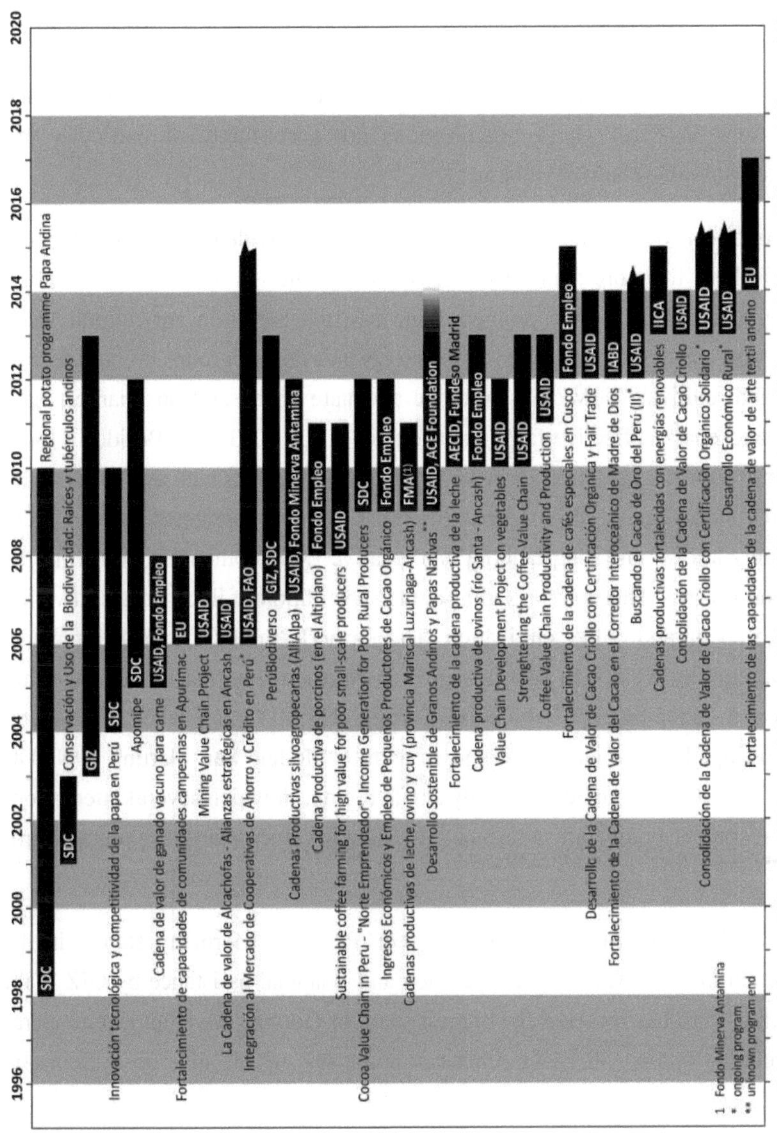

Figure 9: Value chain development programs in Peru
Source: Own data collection and own draft

Bilateral development cooperation

Bilateral cooperation is a precondition for value chain development. The selection of USAID, SNV and GIZ for a detailed record is based on interviewees' perceptions in Peru: These organizations are accordingly of particular importance for value chain development.

The American development agency USAID has provided development assistance in Peru for more than 50 years. Operating through the NGO Chemonics, among others, USAID has promoted and assisted SMEs in agricultural value chains and capacity building for cooperatives and farmer groups on how to prepare land, cultivate new crops, provide adequate shade and post-harvest handling, and realize effective farm management (CTA 2013: 42). Besides a focus on improved management and quality of public services as well as better natural resource management USAID-Peru 2012: ix), USAID operates programs under its widely known and longstanding "Alternative Development" approach in the Amazon Basin.[17] This approach aims at the substitution of illicit coca cultivation through cocoa and coffee cultivation. The formerly insecure, violence-plagued and structurally weak San Martín region in Northern Peru has made important progress in reducing coca cultivation. Through USAID's assistance, San Martín has developed into what is now known as the "Modelo San Martín" (UNODC 2011), a politically and economically stable region, in which several international development organizations are active through value chain development programs.

Bilateral development cooperation between Peru and Germany started in the 1960s and involves technical cooperation and financial assistance by GIZ, PTB and KfW. Peru has received the biggest share of German development cooperation funding among all Latin American countries, which adds up to 2 billion

[17] In Peru, this broad initiative is widely known under the term "Desarrollo Alternativo". Assistance is provided in five Peruvian regions which have been hubs for coca cultivation, drug trafficking, and illegal logging and mining: San Martín, Ucayali, Amazonas, Loreto, and Madre de Dios. For instance, areas of coca cultivation were reduced from 23000 to 1725 hectares in San Martin between 2000 and 2010 (CTA 2013: 42; USAID-Peru 2012: 4). In total, USAID invested 250 million USD in coca eradication in San Martín.

EUR since the beginning of financial and technical cooperation (GIZ 2015b). GIZ is most active in value chain development and has initiated several workshops on the topic for public officials and university professors all over the country. It has operated through a main office in Lima since 1975, but has ancillary offices in the regions as well as in the Peruvian Ministry of Agriculture and the Ministry of Environment. Programs address the strengthening of democratic structures and good governance, water management, rural development, mitigation of climate change and the management of natural resources (GIZ 2015a). In the priority area "sustainable rural development," German-Peruvian cooperation focuses on the sustainable use of natural resources and on the conservation of biodiversity (BMZ 2015). Programs such as the "Programa de Desarrollo Sostenible" (PDRS, 2003-2013) or "PerúBiodiverso" (PBD, 2007-2013) draw explicitly on the value chain development methodology and perspective.

The Dutch SNV also plays its part in the institutionalization of market-oriented rural development in Peru. As one of the first organizations it produced a Spanish manual for value chain analysis and the Promotion of Rural Development for Latin America (SNV 2004). Although it recently reduced its activities and interventions with Peru's improved status as upper middle income country by the World Bank (World Bank 2015b), SNV argues that it maintains "a current, robust portfolio in value chain development, inclusive business, and renewable energy" (SNV 2015a). It provides consulting services to firms interested in sustainable local development and operates projects in Latin America from its regional head quarter based in Quito, Ecuador.

The donor community in Peru comprises not only state-based development organizations. NGOs such as Practical Action, Technoserve, Chemonics, Helvetas and Oxfam have operated programs for market-oriented agricultural development as well and have published guides, evaluation studies and handbooks. Among other organizations that for the sake of space and focus are not mentioned here, they contributed equally in spreading the value chain perspective in Peru.

The role of practitioner circles

The development organizations and NGOs mentioned above are all members of the "Alianza del aprendizaje" (in English: Learning Alliance). This regional development practitioner network was founded in 2004 and convenes regularly in Lima to discuss value chain development measures. It differs from the mesas técnicas by bringing together program coordinators of different donor organizations. Its purpose lies in gathering sources of information about past and ongoing programs and institutions that are active in value chain development, and influencing policy-making (Alianza del aprendizaje Perú 2008). In 2006, it advised the Ministry of Agriculture in passing the law for value chain promotion. Members of the Alianza del aprendizaje have also worked together with the Ministry of Agriculture on a program for competitiveness enhancement in 2008, which aims at strengthening associativity and the use of appropriate technologies in small-scale farming. The alliance maintains strong ties with the CIAT in Central America, the CATIE network in Nicaragua and has equally ancillaries in Central America and the Andes. As of 2014, its members were international development organizations, NGOs and representatives of public agencies including AGRORural, CARE Perú, CIAT, CIP-ISSANDES, CTB, DGCA, GIZ, IICA, Helvetas, Lutheran World Relief, Ministry of Production, Practical Action, PRISMA, SDC, SNV and SwissContact. Distinct value chain promoters and approaches are discussed and coordinated that at times compete with one another.

Another supra-regional expert tackles value chain development and PPPs in Central and Latin America which is different from the Alianza del aprendizaje by being limited to practitioners within GIZ. Covering an area from Nicaragua to Brazil, the "Competence Team on Value Chains and Public-Private Partnerships" is a network of development practitioners from six countries in Latin America and the Caribbean.[18] It was founded in January 2007 and promotes the exchange of experiences made with value chain development in GIZ programs.

[18] It is called "Equipo Regional de Competencias: Cadenas de Valor y PPP". Member countries were Brazil, Ecuador, Guatemala, Nicaragua, El Salvador and Peru.

A former leader of the committee stressed the committee's impact on policy-makers and the institutionalization of the value chain approach in ministries of the respective project countries. Out of project funds from members, GIZ's value chain development methodology was translated from English into Spanish and Portuguese, which has enabled its global circulation. In Peru and Ecuador the methodology has been broadly circulated which is why "the [value chain] methodology develops most" (2013_16: 213) in those areas. The practitioner circle has impacted the shape and content of the globally circulating GIZ methodology, since it stressed the introduction of a module on territorial development that was not part of the first version of the manual. According to a senior project coordinator, the expert circle represents "a very interesting model for the collective construction of knowledge" (2013_16: 340). Knowledge was created through direct encounters with experts working with the same approach at different sites; the program outlines, emphazes and best practices were discussed and inscribed into newsletters and publications, and then disseminated to policy makers in Latin America. However, after 2012 there have been no reunions or formal exchanges among the practitioners.

Profile of the "Peruvian" approach

The value chain approach alternates and mutates in a dynamic field of connections in time and space. If there is something called a "Peruvian approach" to value chain development, it features four particularities:

First of all, and to tie in with claims made earlier in this chapter, value chain development projects do not solely deal with enhancing economic growth. When they travel, value chain models turn into policies that are adapted to surrounding politico-institutional contexts and associated with political interests and priority areas. The introduction of a market approach to development in Peruvian politics implied a profound change in understanding and approaching agricultural development. The crosscutting approach has been adopted and adapted in different ministries. It ties up with programmatic emphazes of international development actors. Beyond its market orientation, the value chain approach translates into an environmental bias in Latin America, as a senior planning officer argues:

> "[Value chain promotion comprises] not only the promotion of economic development. It can also be projects for environmental protection or resource conservation (…) In particular in Latin America and Brazil, the focus is on resource conservation and the protection of the tropical forest. This then becomes an important aspect of the project. They may not carry the label "global value chain" enhancement in their title, although they work with the methodology. If we do not take these regional examples into account, then hardly any projects would be convenient for evaluation. Most project outlines do combine different approaches and focuses. Indeed, there is practically no "pure" GVC approach that does not draw upon other approaches or policy lines, without watching out to the right and to the left." (2014_4: 59)

Rising concerns about climate change in the Global North put environment protection on top of the political agenda, with a particular interest in the protection of the Amazon and its rich biodiversity. Peru has indeed been heavily affected by natural disasters, floods and earthquakes in the last years. For value chain interventions, this agenda has translated into programs that combine both targets: environmental protection is linked to market-oriented development. The fact that programs in Latin America often do not carry the "value chain" label in their title, even if they operate according to a value chain logic, complicates the search *for* and analysis *of* respective programs. In African countries, however, programs mostly carry the label in their title (Chapter 6).

In this vein, the promotion of biotrade has become a priority issue on the Peruvian policy agenda. Apart from traditionally promoted cash crops such as coffee, cocoa, asparagus and palm oil, products drawn from Amazonian biodiversity are now targeted by national initiatives and development programs. In Northern Peru, for instance, native products including medicinal plants, sacha inchi, maca, kiwicha, chia and camu camu are prioritized. The development of respective value chains around these products is very promising – if not for global competitiveness, then for specialization in niche markets.

Second, value chain development has been increasingly linked to a focus on territorial linkages for rural development. Indeed, a focus on biotrade necessarily goes hand in hand with a concern for regional development (2013_20: 219), because there is no sound "environmental strategy without its economic foundation". Equally, "if you want to develop a territory, it is not enough to target solely the economy" (2013_21: 106). Systemic competitiveness through territorial development requires more than the development of market relations. A workshop facilitator and technical consultant in Lima mentioned that "it is very important to understand where the chain originates, this link to the territory" (2013_31: 47), while stressing that the spatial component has always played a prominent role for economic development in Latin America. Value chain promotion programs in Peru address rural development with a concern for the creation of jobs and sustainable growth rather than one particular product regardless of its spatial context.

Third, the state as partner and supporter of value chain promotion plays a key role in Peru. Certainly, the public sector assumes in most parts of the world a primordial role in fostering economic development. Yet its role in shaping agricultural development to compensate for the "failures of the market" is outstanding in Peru. When international consultants proposed market-driven development approaches, their counterparts in Peru made them become aware of the preponderant role that public policy support plays in Peru. Without public entities coming on board, they maintained, development of the agricultural sector could not be achieved. Others, mostly entrepreneurs, argue that international development organizations offset the lack of support from public entities: "International cooperation supported our project through shared funds of our firm and the development organization. There has been quasi no support by the government, so that, yes, international cooperation has given us very strong support" (2013_32: 114). Development cooperation fills a gap in the new pattern of transnational governmentality, which attributes states one role among other powerful institutions in governing national territories (Ferguson, Gupta 2002). Entrepreneurs have repeatedly pointed to the importance of supportive sectorial policies to develop value chains and expressed demands for a more active role of public policy in agricultural development. The role of the state is considered across all groups, from value chain participants to service providers, as key to fostering broad-based growth through value chain integration. Value chain development depends on the public making of private markets.

Fourth and last, manuals and publications that address the Latin American practitioner community for value chain interventions focus on participatory methods for market development. Respective value chain manuals were developed by practitioners in and for the region (Bernet et al. 2011; Escobar 2013; GIZ 2009; Springer-Heinze 2004). Enhanced institutional coordination between each segment of the chain is generated through mesas técnicas in which smallholders, entrepreneurs, distributors, service providers and representatives of public entities come together. There, they discuss quality management issues, the creation of technical norms or the professionalization of production:

> "We always tried to develop this participatory scheme, (…) it's like a demonstration that in order to achieve [development], we need a good mechanism, and then the results follow. There are the mesas técnicas… many of them! In cocoa and sacha inchi, we have them. In medicinal plants, we haven't succeeded in developing mesas técnicas because the strengths are rather not developed, but what we have is a rapprochement between public entities and native communities who are the target groups of PPP interventions. There is even an unexpected side-effect which is the formation of an entrepreneurial space, the 'cooperative.'" (2013_20: 243)

For farmers to make their voice heard and actively participate in capacity development and improved coordination, the creation of farmer-based organizations and buyer associations comes first. The creation of mesas técnicas allows them to speak up with one respective voice and encounter one another in a protected place for discussion. Does the Peruvian variant of the value chain approach represent a completely new approach to market development? "Not really", as a program coordinator with long working experience in Central and Latin America argues. "[W]hat they [the editors of the value chain manual in Latin America] did, is that they basically built a toolbox. They haven't re-designed or adapted the concept. It's a box full of (...) participatory instruments, which you can use in the specific phases of the implementation" (2013_35: 171). The implementation of the value chain framework leaves thus room for flexible interpretation and needs-based adaptation.

Conclusions

The mobilization and inscription of the value chain approach at various levels manifests itself as a process which requires the efforts of many institutions and actors. The analysis of the rise of the value chain perspective in Peru shows that it has meanwhile gained broad support (Figure 9). A senior project coordinator links its appeal to its flexibility, as it addresses various target groups and policy objectives: "[T]he value chain topic (...) is obviously multi-disciplinary. You have land management, rural development, economics, technical questions, statistical issues, politics, ingredients based on technical indicators" (2013_16: 175). Value chains have become immutable mobiles which act at a distance: Being widely inscribed into manuals, project outlines, evaluation reports and policies, the framework circulates in the form of material objects, workshops and techniques. Taken together, these create socio-material agencements that allow the projection of power across space. The performative effects of the framework are reflected in the creation of various tools and practitioner circles in Peru. In the next chapter, we will revisit another site in which the value chain approach has gained momentum, thereby modifying the economic and developmental policy landscape as well as mindsets and perceptions of the market.

6. Technocrats and technologies of trust in Ghana

> "Value chain development is critical to the growth of the economy of Ghana for a couple of reasons: First, Ghana is mainly an agricultural country and will gain from its agriculture produce if value is added. Second, when there is value addition, farmers become the gainers, and poverty is reduced. Third, the more actors are involved in the chain, from production to consumer, the wider the distribution of benefits. There is therefore a strong link between poverty reduction and market orientation." (2015_2: 20)

Value chain development has become a "buzz word" (2010_3: 24) in the practitioner community. The quote from the Ghanaian university professor shows not only the popularity that the value chain approach enjoys in Ghana, but also that an explicit link is made between market orientation and poverty reduction. In order to understand how the "thinking in terms of value chains" has traveled to Ghana, I will take a look at the ideational background, the macro-economic setting, as well as the regulatory and political conditions in which the concept gained momentum. This allows us to understand the functioning and effects of global policy regimes and how they play an increasingly dominant role in national public policy.

The Republic of Ghana is endowed with natural resources ranging from oil to minerals (e.g. gold, industrial diamonds, bauxite, and manganese), timber, cocoa, and horticultural products. Gold and cocoa production represent the major sources of foreign exchange. Due to persistent investment in the creation of a competitive business environment, sustained reductions in poverty levels, and economic diversification in the last two decades, Ghana was ranked as a lower middle-income country in 2010 (World Bank 2015a). Yet a glance at the country's economic part and present reveal remarkable dynamics: In 1983, Ghana turned to the IMF and the World Bank for assistance in the form of the controversial Structural Adjustment Program, which imposed Ghana to liberalize its markets. It was the beginning of an epoch of austerity programs and reforms in Ghana. Socioeconomic development based on political stability and rapid trade liberalization in the 1990s transformed Ghana into an attractive destination for international investors (Abdulai, Crawford 2010; Fosu 2013; Whitfield 2011). Indeed, as one of the continent's strongest and politically most stable economies, Ghana saw five years of more than 8% GDP growth between 2007 and 2012 – despite the global recession. In 2014, the promising economic trend in Ghana slowed down and even reversed. It resulted in a renewed request to the IMF for a bailout to stabilize the Ghanaian GHC and restore investor confidence. The GHC was devalued to 50% of its original value (UNCTAD 2014) and subjected to a depreciation of 40% against the USD in 2014 alone (Allison 2014). Turmoil was caused by a falling gold price, stagnant oil production, bloated civil services and bureaucracy, and general over-spending by the government. As Whitfield reports, "the results [of the World Bank's Structural Adjustment Programs] have led to growth without economic transformation. In particular, the country has witnessed recurrent macroeconomic instability, a haphazard process of privatization of state-owned enterprises, and no serious attempt to build up productive sectors outside of cocoa and gold" (Whitfield 2011: 6). A news agency headlined in 2014 accordingly that "[o]nce a model for Africa, Ghana's economy loses its shine" (Allison 2014). Ghana has one of the highest GDP per capita in Africa, yet it is dependent on international financial and technical assistance and remittances from the broad Ghanaian diaspora (OECD 2012: 16). It remains a "donor darling" (Lawson 2010: 2; Newiger-Addy 2008) of the international donor community. It is among the few in Africa expected to meet the Millennium Development Goal 1 (MDG) of halving the poverty rate by 2015. Indeed, one interviewee mentioned that donor organizations would not dare reduce funds and programs in Ghana, as Ghana is a reference model for West Africa, and no other country in the region could alternatively serve as such. Indexes, rankings, and the politics of numbers more broadly, serve a powerful cause: they posit

Ghana within Northern discourses and circuits of expertise and contribute to legitimizing development interventions.[19]

Since Ghana is an agricultural country, poverty reduction and smallholder upgrading are linked to the improvement of agricultural infrastructure and productivity. The agricultural sector accounts for roughly 25% of GDP and employs more than half of the workforce (CIA World Factbook 2015a), of which the majority are small landholders and subsistence farmers. Similar to the situation in Peru, the population who lives below the poverty line in Ghana remains high at a rate of 28% (ibid.) In the Northern regions, roughly 80% of the population live below the poverty level, of which most live in rural areas (Harsch 2008). A technical consultant stressed that "the value chain concept can be employed in virtually every sector, (but) for us it has mostly been agriculture, because it works, we found entry through agriculture" (2013_2: 109). It is reflected in the emphases of development programs and the agenda-setting of the Ghanaian government, as this chapter will demonstrate.

African agendas for market-oriented development

The member states of the African Union have aligned their efforts to increase assistance for agricultural development. Based on economic growth, competitiveness shall be increased and poverty and hunger reduced. Therefore, the New Partnership for Africa's Development (NEPAD) was adopted by the Assembly of Heads of State and Government in 2001. As an integral part of NEPAD, the Comprehensive Africa Agriculture Development Program (CAADP) constitutes the overall framework for agricultural transformation, wealth creation, food

[19] Certainly, rankings and indexes provide only a biased representation of the real economy and serve the interests of scientists and experts to shape and transform the economy by juggling with the politics of numbers. They enable the circulation of knowledge, policies, development and money to the Global South, and the making of the national economy more broadly, as Mitchell (2002) has argued: This is why one must examine how they are set up and by what social practices they are surrounded.

security and nutrition, and economic growth. This "African Owned Agenda" places the value chain approach at its heart by declaring that

> "[t]he renewed focus on agriculture and agribusiness, as priority sectors for spurring economic growth in Africa, calls for developing value chains that integrate producers and markets to make the agricultural sector more responsive to consumer demand. The value chain approach builds on conditions in the consumer market and emphasizes the interface, linkages, and segments that connect the final product demanded by consumers all the way to agricultural commodities produced at the farm level. This market-driven approach to formulating investment plans, public policies, and partnerships to integrate smallholder farmers can bring about significant changes being sought in Africa's agriculture and agribusiness sectors." (CAADP 2009: Area C)

The member states of the African Union committed themselves in the Maputo Declaration of 2003 to two targets: First, to allocate 10% of their national budgets for agricultural development and second, to achieve at least 6% growth in the agricultural sector (Brüntrup 2011). In West Africa, the Economic Community of West African States (ECOWAS) coordinates the implementation of CAADP under its regional agricultural policy ECOWAP since 2005 (Republic of Ghana 2009) by elaborating joint action plans for the development of the agricultural sector. Yet it is at the national level that CAADP ultimately reveals its impact. Ghana, for instance, has been a good performer as it surpassed the 10 % target every single year since 2003 (ReSAKSS 2013).

Some argue that the value chain approach was not a new framework to agricultural development in Ghana. Before the instauration of CAADP, as a ministry official in Ghana claims, "[the NGO] Technoserve where I used to work (…) was using the value chain approach for about a decade, but that time we were just calling it the 'Technoserve approach' to poverty alleviation" (2010_3: 32). Hence, value chain thinking prevailed before in Ghana, but was not labeled as such. Smallholders and processors were simply not aware, as a technical officer in Ghana argues, that

> "[t]hey were already working along the value chain… just that they didn't know. (…) Mr. Harley [a buyer in the fish value chain], the last three meetings that we went to him and asked him whether he is working along the value chain, he said no. Meanwhile, practically he is working along the value chain. Because he deals with the fishermen and with the processors. The fishermen, when they catch [fish], they supply it to the processors and then the processors supply it to traders. So practically, he is working along the value chain, but because he doesn't know the concept, he thinks he is not. Something of that sort. So, I think there are other things going on along the value chain but you wouldn't know until you are being taken through the value chain concept, before you realize that you are really working along the value chain." (2010_2: 173)

In order to attract policy-makers' interests, public attention and acceptance, the approach was framed as a "new" concept. Reframing it according to global discourses of UN agencies, development organizations and CAADP served to legitimize investments and interventions drawing on the approach. Policy-makers and development consultants were deeply entangled in the "power-laden processes of repetition and legitimation, competition, and cooperation" (McCann 2013: 20). Globally traveling market concepts turned into policies are influential imaginaries that are translated to other sites and places. There, as the Ghanaian example demonstrates, they are adopted and increasingly proclaimed as *the* recipe for economic development.

The politics of policy alignment

Agriculture contributes significantly to the economies of most African countries, yet few of them have been able to capitalize on the sector's considerable potential for development through modernization and industrialization. Therefore, an enabling environment had to be created to "remov[e] internal value chain and institutional constraints" in Ghana (UN Economic Commission for Africa 2013: 14). In an OECD development report (OECD 2012: 29), it is argued that trade must be mainstreamed in agricultural policy and development policy. Yet, how did the market-oriented approach find its way into the Ghanaian policy framework?

In 2002, the Ghanaian Ministry of Food and Agriculture (MoFA) developed its first Food and Agriculture Sector Development Policy (FASDEP I) (Fynn 2011), which provided a guideline for the modernization of the agricultural sector (Ministry of Food and Agriculture 2007: vii). Herein, the role of PPPs for managing agribusiness clusters was highlighted. After a few years of its implementation and the development of sub-sector policies, FASDEP I, was revised to integrate and reflect learned lessons and to react to changing needs of the sector. Two developments led to the review: First of all, PSD approaches of the early 2000s were built on publicly subsidized service delivery and were complemented with "stand-alone projects" funded by donors (ibid.: 14). Yet these approaches were considered insufficient by MoFA: Donor projects phased out, so that little consistency was provided. Second, and related to the first point, at the beginning of the 2000s Ghana's agriculture policy was largely production-oriented. A review of the national Ghana Poverty Reduction Agenda (GPRS I) revealed that poverty could not be addressed if the economy did not grow. The modernization of ''poor smallholder agriculture'' (ibid.: 1) remained focused on improving and extending production, not markets. The consultation process gained pace in 2004-2005. It included a sector review workshop and inputs from inter-ministerial teams and experts. A draft was proposed to MoFA and development partners, which was distributed at workshops to include the views of a wider cross-section of stakeholders (Government of Ghana 2013). Development consultants accompanied the policy revision process of FASDEP I in 2005-2006. They recall that the anchoring of the value chain approach in MoFA was exhausting: "The MoFA staff as well as university professors were at first very hard to convince… they didn't believe in the value chain concept (…) The technocrats in the ministry were against market-oriented development, [as] they feared [that] their production-oriented thinking was taken away" (2013_10: 10-11).

In the shift from production- to market-oriented thinking, ministers and political decision-makers such as MoFA directors "who were very powerful at the time" (2013_10: 35) had to be convinced. They opposed the approach, since the application of the value chain framework targets cross-sector coordination, and there had been no attempts or projects for decentralization at the district level. Local development consultants were hesitant to apply economic analysis and thus further rejected the reforms. When "value chains came into the discussion" (ibid.: 22), "[a]ll sectors had to respond to this change in national policy and agricultural orientation. MOAP [GIZ-funded program for market-oriented agriculture] piloted the value chain concept, and then worked and pushed for changing mindsets on agriculture" (ibid.: 10-11). In 2007, the revision process was accomplished with the introduction of FASDEP II, in which it is stated that

> "a value chain approach to agricultural development will be adopted with value addition and market access given more attention. Efforts will be intensified to build capacity towards meeting challenges of quality standards in the international market, with focus on increasing productivity along the value chain (…) To improve productivity along the value chain will contribute to poverty reduction." (Ministry of Food and Agriculture 2007: 17, 27)

The government's development strategy as outlined in FASDEP II represented a break with the previous national policy agenda. It was based on growth-inducing policies, sustainable resource management and PSD promotion with the overarching goal to attain middle-income status by the World Bank. It emphasized the integration of smallholders at the bottom of value chains, as argued in an report by a Ghanaian economist: "It is interesting to note that the central theme of the recently revised Food and Agricultural Sector Development Policy of MoFA is the adoption of the value chain approach starting at the smallholder or outgrower level" (Owusuansah 2008: 13). The policy reform, hence, had not gone unnoticed.

The shift in the agricultural sector policy led to further policy reforms (Table 4). The Medium Term Agriculture Sector Investment Plan (METASIP, 2011-2015) builds on the agricultural performance targets of CAADP under NEPAD and operationalizes FASDEP II by determining sector-wide measures for the development of the agricultural sector. It is maintained that "a platform for private sector and civil society engagement with several ministries, departments and agencies" will be established (ibid.: 54). Hereby, linkages between value chain participants, and between public policies and private partners, are reinforced. Besides the development of rural infrastructure and the promotion of cash crops, METASIP specifies that two selected agricultural value chains shall be developed in each agro-ecological zone of Ghana in order to promote food security and income growth. Concrete targets include furthermore the increase of yields by an average of 50% by 2015, enhanced productivity of all operators along the value chain and improved access to markets. In the 25-page document, the development of value chains is referred to 67 times which shows its perceived relevance as a model for economic growth (Ministry of Food and Agriculture Ghana 2010). A "Joint Sector Review" of MoFA and GIZ states that "a value chain approach to agricultural development in Ghana has policy support at all levels - sectorial, national, sub-regional and continental" (Fynn 2011: 11).

Table 4: Policy landscape around value chain development in Ghana

Time-line	International Policy Framework	National Policy Framework	National Agricultural Sector Policy	Important landmarks beyond
1987-1995		Structural Adjustment Programme I-III	Medium-term Agriculture Development Programme	
1996		Ghana Vision 2020, 1996 - 2000		
1997				
1998			Accelerated Agricultural Growth and Development Strategy	
1999				
2000				
2001				
2002		Ghana Poverty Reduction Strategy I, 2003-2005	Food and Agricultural Sector Development Policy I	
2003	Comprehensive Africa Agriculture Development Programme			
2004				
2005	ECOWAS/NEPAD (ECOWAP/ CAADP) Action Plan, 2005-2010		Revision of Food and Agricultural Sector Development Policy I, 2005-2006	
2006		Growth and Poverty Reduction Strategy II, 2006-2009		

Time-line	International Policy Framework	National Policy Framework	National Agricultural Sector Policy	Important landmarks beyond
2007			Food and Agricultural Sector Development Policy II	First discussions about value chain approach in university curriculas
2008				
2009	Ghana signs Comprehensive Africa Agriculture Development (CAADP)		Medium Term Agriculture Sector Investment Plan, 2011-2015	Value chain practitioner forums 2009, 2011, 2012
2010		Ghana Shared Growth and Development Agenda, 2010-2013 National decentralization policy		
2011				Joint sector review about value chain development in Ghana
2012				
2013			Implementation of fiscal decentralization process, 2013-2014	Midterm-review of Metasip
2014		Ghana Shared Growth and Development Agenda II, 2014-2017		

Source: Own draft

The incorporation of the value chain framework in Ghana came along with a conceptual shift. While international donors, who had from the beginning on accompanied the policy reforms, advocated a focus on pro-poor based growth, this orientation was lost along the way. In the Joint Sector Review, the purpose of value chain development is defined as follows: "There are four basic principles for value chain development: i. the starting point is the market (…)" (Fynn 2011: 4). Hence, the idea of value chain development to "increase the incomes of the poor through promoting their involvement in market-oriented production" (Humphrey, Navas-Alemán 2010: 18) has been replaced by an exclusive focus on the market. The introduction of the framework in Ghana shows that policies are not stable concepts or fixed arrangements (McCann, Ward 2013: 8). Policies are assembled differently in each new setting, and they respond to particular interests and purposes: Markets come first in Ghana.

Anchoring value chain thinking in academia

Following its institutionalization in the Ghanaian policy framework, the value chain approach was introduced into academic curricula. Around 2006, at the time of the FASDEP I revision, MoFA initiated together with an international development agency a project that aimed at incorporating the topic in agronomics departments and programs at Ghanaian universities. A participant of the introductory course on value chain development recounts that the market-oriented perspective was welcomed by the academic community: "it was readily received by the broader academia as a necessary means of protecting our agriculture" (2015_1: 1). However, at the beginning there was no common understanding of the term, as another lecturer admits:

> "People are now using the term 'value chain' vaguely and it's because at the university they were not teaching value chains. (…) Now, we assure that we have the same understanding of what we mean by value chain. Only when we have programs at the universities, courses, so that people have really an understanding of what it is. But as for now, as you said, people call anything value chain. I believe it's not right. Let's get a proper understanding." (2011_4: 19)

Study curricula were revised in order to match the policy shift. A national value chain committee was formed with professors in Tamale, Accra, Kumasi and Cape Coast who were all willing to develop courses on value chain development in their respective universities. Since "what they [professors] were teaching was from the 1980s" (2013_10: 42-43), acceptance for adopting the approach into academic curricula was high. GIZ worked through its MOAP program with MoFA and universities to develop curricula both on value chain development and on food safety and quality assurance, i.e. on capacity development. Another format was the two-week short courses on value chain development targeted at practitioners. Instead of a theoretically oriented academic course, it was a practically oriented advanced vocational training offered by the University of Kumasi. While no specific course on value chain development is taught at the University of Legon in Accra, a professor associates this framework with a broader recent shift towards market-orientation at his university:

> "Now, if you look at trends, departments that do these kinds of studies you see they are now called 'agricultural economics and resources'. Some are called 'department of agriculture and resource economics', others 'agricultural economics and agribusiness' (…) We teach our students managerial economics, we teach them accounting, fundamentals of agribusiness, marketing... all these put together is what we call 'agribusiness' at the department." (2013_9: 39)

The introduction of market-oriented approaches to agricultural development has led to the establishment of "agribusiness departments" in universities. These politics are about the power to create new meanings: What has been previously called "farm management" is transformed into "agribusiness" whereby agriculture is transformed into a value-enhancing and market-driven sector. Re-labeling academic departments is about the "politics of value": It extends the outreach of markets into every sector of society, even into education systems, in the Global South.

Creating the consultancy value chain

The scope that a global policy regime achieves can be measured by taking a look at those actors who mobilize it. In a highly interconnected world, development agendas not only circulate, but "interact with historical-cultural formations of identity, rights, and development, which are then in turn "globalized" through advocacy chains" (Mosse 2013: 232). The circulation of a policy model is channeled through particular techniques and passed along by consultants, some traveling with the model, while others learning about it at their work place. They all constitute what one interviewee has called the "consultancy value chain" (2010_1: 184). It is a network of international and local development practitioners who contribute their services at various stages of the value chain. The stages of such advocacy chains evolve simultaneously to the value chains that they assess, as a technical consultant and a zonal agricultural manager in Ghana mentioned:

> **Interviewee2:** We have regional implementing consultants [RIC] and below them are technical and training service providers who we call TTSPs and they are being supervised by the RIC.
>
> **Interviewee1**: It's actually a longer chain! The CMC prepared the training documents.
>
> **Interviewee2**: Yeah, we have the CMC - Central Management Consultants - who prepare the materials. Those are international consultants.
>
> **Interviewee1**: And then we review these things with the help of local professionals. We reviewed it several times and when finally we were satisfied with the training material, we found other international consultants to implement it. And when they took it - they are confined to this northern region - they in turn found much lower consultants, local consultants, trainers to implement the training documents under their supervision, so we have the CMC supervising, we have MiDA [Millennium Development Authority] supervising, we

> have the RIC supervising, but the TTSPs are holding the chalk on the chalk board and teaching (laughter) (…) That's the consultancy value chain. Indeed, that was a long chain (2010_1: 171-185).

While value chain participants seek to link up with one another as to enhance the overall performance of a value chain, development consultants create a parallel system in which they seem to interact (only) with other consultants who work at adjacent departments or levels. The emerging knowledge infrastructure facilitates exchange between consultants. Over time, the infrastructure becomes bloated, so that the consultancy chain needs to be cut off, as it does hinders a lean coordination and functioning. Yet, for the innumerable programs now working on value chains, many facilitators are required to explain the concept to farmers. Where to find and recruit people with knowledge about value chains?

> "We are working with what we call facilitating agencies, who we have recruited, they are private consultancy firms (…). And then we contract them for a season to do this work in A, B, C, D districts. The next thing is that within the Ministry of Agriculture we do what we call the trainer of trainers. (…) We've taken some of the regional directors or at least some of the young enterprising extension or district officers, we train them, take them through the model, let them test the field and then they can now also go to the frontline staff of the ministry and the technical officers and also let them imbibe a value chain concept. And then, they explain [it] to farmers at their regular meetings, so w ith time, a lot of people will begin to understand when you say "value chain", they understand what it is." (2010_3: 35-36)

A public official illustrates the different steps of knowledge mobilization. Meanwhile, a sophisticated infrastructure of experts has evolved. One element therein are field schools in which technical staff approaches smallholders and teaches harvesting practices, the appropriate application of fertilizers, the grafting of seeds and GAP. The basics about dynamics of markets are also part of field schools, whereby shifting prices and demand can be explained to farmers and thinking in terms of value chains is enhanced. The promotion of closer linkages among participants in value chains requires a sound collaboration with external institutions, which can in turn create an enabling environment for smallholder market access and opportunities to invest. These workshops take place regularly, particularly during the cultivation season when smallholders need assistance most urgently. Smallholders often do not get in touch with global ideas beyond these encounters and forms of training (Chapter 8).

There is a timely dimension regarding the input of international consultants and field staff in development programs. The executive director of a development program of the value chain in Ghana illustrates the changing role and input of consultants by using the metaphor of a soccer match. During the first phase of the match, everybody is playing soccer on the field. Then, in the second phase, the (international) staff assumes the trainer position and thereby acts "at a distance", while leaving the direct interaction with smallholders in the field to local practitioners. The coordination is put on an institutional level, while the expertise on value chain development "travels" to public officials, local consultants, academic staff and further support services providers. In the third and last phase, the training of (local) trainers, the staff withdraws completely from the operative level. Hence, consultants increasingly see themselves as supervisors of the game. The role of the project staff hence changes over the different program phases, with an increasing focus on training for local experts: "We must anchor this knowledge by training advocates for the sector in different institutions. They can push the cashew sector forward. We mustn't keep it at the level of the project, but instead build it into institutions" (2014_14: 18-20). This endeavor can be described in Callonian terms (Callon 1986) as the moment of enrolment in the context of translation processes.

In Ghana, the inscription of the value chain approach has gone far indeed. At the time when I was investigating its political and economic outreach in Ghana, I arranged a meeting with a senior consultant working with MoFA at the regional level. As usual, he handed out his business card at the beginning of our conversation to me. Holding it in my hand, I read his job description: "Value Chain

Specialist". As his job title had drawn all my attention, the question of how he ended up sitting there talking about value chains imposed itself:

> "[The] first [time] I understood the position of a value chain specialist was advertised, that time I was too comfortable with Technoserve and I didn't respond to it. But I think the first people that were recruited - their CVs went to Rome - were those that they thought didn't have sufficient to say and teach. So it was re-advertised and then, one of my directors encouraged me that I should apply for it. So I applied for it the very closing day and then I was called, I responded to the interview and I think they finally accepted that I should be the value chain specialist. That's how I ended up in this chair." (2010_3: 48)

The market-oriented approach had created its own profession. The job description as advertised by the FAO in Rome had no clear profile for a value chain specialist. One becomes a value chain specialist only by "long experience" in a particular sector, I was told. The opinions on what a value chain specialist is and has to do diverge: From a (workshop) facilitator (2010_2: 146), to a person who is "responsible for linking up with all value chain actors" (2013_39: 10), to a person who constitutes an information node in the value chain network, who coordinates meetings, supports the formation of farmer associativity as well as the creation of norms (2013_26: 22).[20]

The formation of value chain experts encourages the entrepreneurial subjectivity of individuals who collectively organize processes of knowledge management within local economies (Rose 1992). Whether the "value chain specialist" title signals the creation of a new profession or whether it is just an appealing label in the current value chain "boom" remains questionable. What it reflects indeed is

[20] In Peru, an expert on value chains is linked to a particular value chain. He or she oversees the activities along the chain and in a sector and coordinates it from the national level. For instance, „there is an expert for the potato value chain. He considers the potato value chain at the national level, and reflects what can be done with this value chain from the political, technical, consultancy perspective in order to create alliances, achieve agreements and contracts between different economic agents and make chain diagnoses" (2013_17: 139-141).

the emergence of a sophisticated infrastructure around the formation of experts on value chain development and hence the performativity of this market model. An emphasis on embodied agents of change makes valuable contributions to helping unpack diverse geographies of economic globalization (Larner, Laurie 2010: 219). Behind the seemingly technical issues regarding trainings initiated and conducted by development practitioners lies the broader effort of creating subjects that follow the principles of market-oriented development.

Advocates of value chain development in Ghana

All prominent donor organizations operate development programs in Ghana. According to the Agriculture Sector Group that was initiated by MoFa, Denmark (DANIDA), France (AfD), Germany (GIZ, KfW), the Netherlands (SNV), Japan (JICA), the United Kingdom (UKAID) and the United States (USAID) are among Ghana's most important bilateral partners in development cooperation, that provided a budget of about 117.37 million of a total budget of 221.55 million GHC (Ministry of Food and Agriculture Ghana 2015). Multilateral assistance stems from the World Bank, the EU, the African Development Bank and United Nations agencies like FAO, IFAD and WFP, while contracting partners and NGOs include CARE International, Engineers without Borders, Acdi/Voca, Practical Action and Technoserve. An overview over value chain programs is provided in Figure 10. Compared to Figure 9, which illustrates the program timeline for Peru, the length of programs varies as much, yet the number of programs is constant and still growing in Ghana contrary to the trend in Peru.

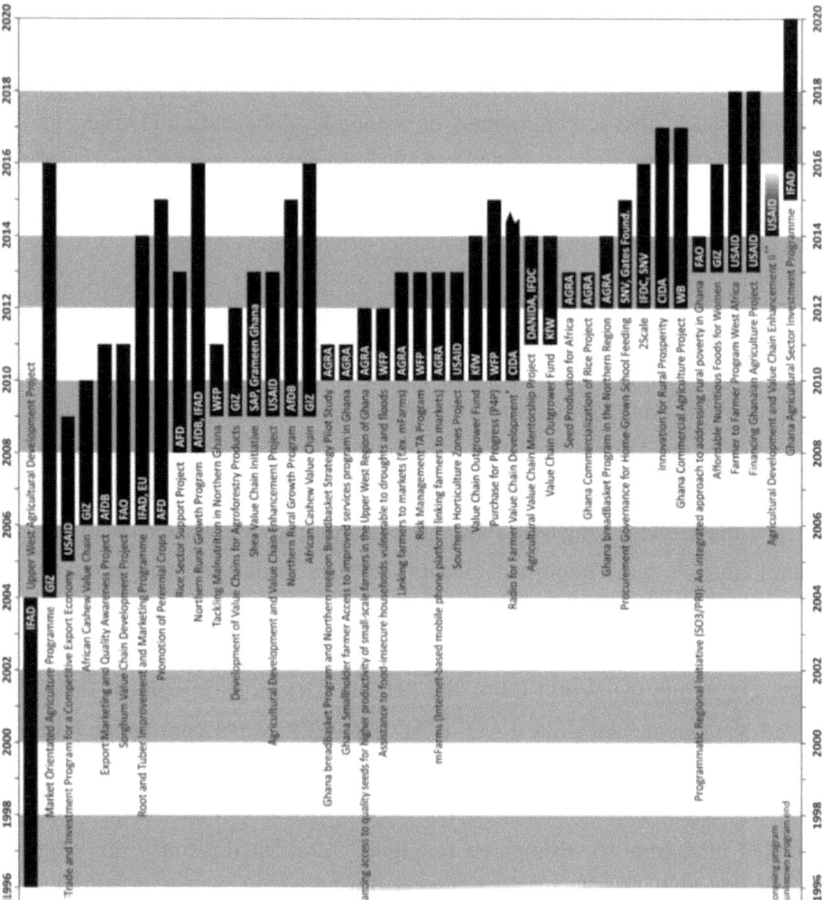

Figure 10: Value chain development programs in Ghana
Source: Own data collection and own draft

Bilateral development cooperation

The American development agency USAID has cooperated with Ghana for many decades and has funded agricultural value chain improvement projects that have been implemented by partner organizations such as Acdi/Voca, Technoserve and Chemonics. In Ghana, USAID and acts through the Millennium

Development Authority, which manages and oversees a bilateral grant of 547 million USD of the Millennium Challenge Account (MiDA 2015) and the overarching Feed the Future Program (Feed the Future 2015). Ghana has hereby been provided important financial resources for the transformation of the agricultural sector by targeting increased productivity of high-value food crops to supply local and international markets. With the World Bank, USAID is currently running the Ghana Commercial Agriculture Project (GCAP, 2012-2017) which promotes viable PPPs, increased private sector finance and better access to land for female smallholders. It applies mobile applications to manage land tenure and facilitate land registration for smallholders (USAID 2015). From 2009-2016, USAID supports the Agricultural Development and Value chain development (ADVANCE) program which is implemented by the partner NGOs and contractors ACDI/VOCA and the local ACDEP. The program targets the mitigation of constraints and risk reduction along selected value chains and has supported more than 30000 farmers through leveraged investments in rice harvesting equipment, soybean planters and threshers (ACDI/VOCA 2015a). ACDI/VOCA has also run the Accelerated Microenterprise Advancement Project (AMAP) from 2002 to 2012. It promoted economic growth for smallholders and poor communities and achieved improved performance and competitiveness of micro and small enterprises (MSEs). In a 2011 issue of the USAID's newsletter "microlinks Connections", the project's achievement in establishing the value chain framework in Ghana was strongly emphasized (ACDI/VOCA 2015b).

Apart from the bilateral American development partnership, the enhancement of value chains is promoted by many other donor organizations. In interviews with local development practitioners, professors and entrepreneurs, development cooperation with Germany is considered particularly influential on the policy-making process by practitioners of various international and local organizations in Ghana. It applies a holistic approach that

> "is based on value chain development, looking at the market opportunities and following through from farmer to consumer. Linking stakeholders of the value chains and distributing value added equally

> are central to the German development approach. Quality assurance along the Value Chain and adequate volumes to satisfy consumers' needs are also crucial." (Ministry of Food and Agriculture Ghana 2015)

The German Development Cooperation Agencies GIZ, PTB and KfW are actively engaged in the support of value chains for market integration of producers both on the operative side through technical assistance and consulting services and through financial support. The general objective of German development cooperation in the agricultural sector is to improve the income of rural populations by supporting small-scale farmers and local value-addition, thereby enabling value chain participants to compete in national, regional and international markets. From 2004-2016, GIZ is implementing the Market Oriented Agriculture Program (MOAP), which was one of the first initiatives to introduce the Value Chain perspective in Ghana. Advisory services in the political realm have contributed to focus on a value chain approach in policy-making. Meanwhile, policies consider actors at all stages of the value chain so that the government is currently in the process of developing an integrated, Ghanaian version of the model. Key achievements include not only increased living incomes and the creation of jobs, but also less measurable indicators such as gender participation and improved access to finance/markets (Ministry of Food and Agriculture Ghana 2015). Hence, the program pursues an integrated approach: on the macro level, it fosters political dialogue and provides consulting services to institutions; on the meso level, it strengthens the cooperation and supply of public and private services; and on the micro level, it promotes the competitiveness of smallholders, processors and retailers as target groups of the program. Another important project is funded by the German Development Bank (KfW), in cooperation with the French Development Bank (AFD). The Outgrower and Value Chain Fund (OVCF) is a refinancing vehicle that promotes value chain linkages by providing financial support for medium and long-term loans to commercially viable value chains through the banking sector. This fund has drawn upon a capital stock of 35 million EUR since its creation in 2009. Herein, outgrower schemes are perceived as suitable instruments to integrate smallholders into value chains and strengthen linkages between value chain participants. Further initiatives target the strengthening of smallholder agribusiness and chain linkages in cocoa, food crops and cashew; the African Cashew Initiative being among the most prominent programs.

The Dutch development organization SNV proposes an innovative and particularly contextualized approach to market integration through one of its several operating programs in Ghana, the Ghana Home Grown School Feeding Programme (GSFP, 2005-ongoing). Aimed at an improved governance of the school feeding supply chain, which embraces business relationships between caterers, traders, and farmers, domestic food production is to be boosted and retention increased. Hereby, not only locally grown foods are strengthened but also gender equality is focused on, since private sector businesses are typically run by women (SNV 2015b). SNV also tackles land tenure issues to the extent that these are linked to food security and value chain development. This issue is particularly apparent in the Ghanaian North, where property rights and land tenure have constituted an obstacle to sustainable value chain development due to restricted access to land and constrained disposition over the cultivation of crops.

The government of Ghana has engaged in a partnership with multilateral agencies in the realm of value chain development. As one of its largest programs for agricultural development, MoFA manages a 105 million USD fund for the ''Northern Rural Growth Program'' (NRGP), that aims to integrate excluded and poor populations in Ghana's North into global, national and local markets. The IFAD, a specialized UN agency, finances the ongoing program that started in 2009 which shall contribute to increasing rural households' income on a sustainable basis. The program focuses on commodity chain development in northern Ghana, rural infrastructure development and access to financial services (Ministry of Food and Agriculture Ghana 2015).

Value chain committees and the role of practitioner forums

A key market device to foster value chain linkages is the creation of platforms for value chain participants from input dealers to representatives of farmer groups, processors and traders, and public entities, research and financial institutions. These are called mesas técnicas in Peru. In value chain committees, sector intervention strategies are developed, common action points are identified, stakeholder activities are coordinated, information is exchanged, and responsibility of each participant is enhanced through the creation of trust and transparency in chains. A senior consultant in Ghana elaborates on issues that are particularly relevant for the creation of institutionalized coordination mechanisms between value chain participants:

> "Among actors in the value chain, trust, transparency, people still…the attitudinal change is there because information is key, if I have information and you don't have, I can take advantage of you. But then the result is just short lived because eventually you found out that because of your lack of information I cheated you (…) But we want a long-term relationship rather than short-term benefits so that's also key. So these are about the three things that we call papers on and we discuss. Then of course we are going to talk more also about the institutional topics: Who is going to house this secretariat? How is this secretariat going to be financed? If there are some issues that government needs to be looking at, how are we going to put that together and confront government with these issues for the Ministry of Agriculture or the Ministry of Trade and Industry to look at in their policies? We shall also be doing that. So the essence of the practitioners' forum is to harmonize our practices, okay? And build synergy in our projects." (2010_3: 29-30)

Apart from the creation of sector-specific dialogue platforms and institutions, various organizations that promote value chain development in Ghana aim at harmonizing their approaches in a national "Value Chain Practitioner Forum". Such a forum was organized three times by MoFA and NRGP in 2009, 2010 and 2012. The purpose was to create an opportunity for all participants to say where they are, what they are doing, to learn from those who are already using the value chain approach and to collaborate as partners to move value chains forward (NRGP 2009). These forums have contributed to creating and gathering expertise together and to actively creating – rather than finding – successful policy models and circulating best-practice lessons.

"Ghanaizing the approach": The local version of a global model

In settings of increased exchange and mobility between mobile development consultants, local experts and policymakers in Ghana, global models are themselves undergoing a conceptual and ideological transformation. While prominent manuals for value chain development are considered a roadmap for action that can be followed, the introduction and inscription of the value chain approach in Ghana differs from such "universal" models as described in the manuals. Acknowledging that frameworks are implementable as long as they take account of the sociocultural, political as well as institutional contexts in which they touch ground, a senior planning officer highlights that "[t]here must be a Ghanaian value chain approach. Not one with any label that is imported. Because in the end, it must be something homegrown" (2014_4: 35). Hence, a "ghana-ized" (2013_10: 31) version of the framework serves as a guideline for trainings on value chain development, as a senior advisor argued. Commodities were prioritized according to local needs, existing infrastructures and specificities of all Ghanaian regions based on three criteria: food security, income generation, and market competitiveness. Five features were key in the processes of policymaking and implementation of the value chain framework in Ghana:

First, the majority of development programs based on the framework carry the "value chain" label prominently in their title, which stands in contrast to the decreasing use of the label in Peru. While many programs draw on the framework as a method, others literally raise the framework to become a blueprint for development – to name just a few: "Agricultural Development and Value chain development" (USAID), "Radio for farmer value chain development" (CIDA),

"Shea value chain initiative" (SAP and Grameen) and the "Sorghum value chain development project" (FAO). The plethora of programs and funding organizations reflects and reinforces the visibility of the approach. It has materialized in the creation of a value chain specialist profession, its incorporation in economics curricula at various Ghanaian universities, value chain practitioner forums and national, regional and district value chain committees. The prominent uptake and integration of the discourse on value chain promotion in FASDEP II in 2007 has boosted the anchorage of the model in Ghanaian society and exemplifies the proliferation of the discourse on pro-poor growth in the Global South.

Second, while in Peru, climate change mitigation the sustainable treatment of biodiversity play a prominent role in policy-making and agricultural development strategies, in Ghana, the focus of value chain programs is narrowed down to the market alone. It would certainly be wrong to assume that climate change is not a concern for development organizations in Ghana. At the same time, other program emphases such as the transfer of technology appear more urgent. Since economic actors have little or no access to financial and other resources, including modern technologies, the role of technology transfer with the introduction of ICT systems has become a major issue of development programs such as the Alliance for Green Revolution in Africa (AGRA)-funded program "Linking Farmers to Markets (FTM, 2010-2013) or USAID's initiative "Mobile Solutions Matter for Land" (USAID 2015). Both offer information services to farmers and serve as stabilizing links in the market-development nexus. Since the vast majority of farmers use mobile phones and smartphones, the most direct and easy way to communicate with them is via digital technologies. Development actors from abroad but also private firms are experimenting with different means how to reach smallholders and assist them at the time during harvest time, when they are out in the field, and at the time of post-harvest. Service providers have developed mobile applications and SMS services that inform farmers about market prices, weather forecasts, information on soils and the application of fertilizers and represent a powerful communication tool for businesses, projects, NGOs and governments to connect with farmers (Chapter 8). Some technologies allow agro-dealers to record all supplies bought from distributors as well as sales to customers and thus calculate their remaining stocks. Transparency creates trust in markets and hence is a central market device.

Third, a development practitioner outlines the outreach of the introduction of the value chain framework in Ghana, which goes hand in hand with a profound transformation and modernization of the agricultural sector: "What we are now preaching; is [no less than] a new attitude towards agricultural development" (2010_3: 1). The enrolment of public agencies and support for the institutionalization of the value chain approach is important both in Peru and Ghana. What a senior consultant in Peru had argued did not hold true more generally: He claimed that "in Ghana, the 'global' version of the value chain manual has asserted itself. To me it seems that in Ghana the approach is much more private-sector-oriented, not really being of interest to the public sector" (2013_16: 240). In both cases, the market-oriented approach encountered at first skepticism and resistance. In Ghana, skepticism was not based on ideological reasons, but administrative efforts that needed to be undertaken to institutionalize it, as the length of the FASDEP II reform demonstrates.

Its incorporation required a change in mindsets that affects society and culture at various levels. It concerns gender issues, land entitlement and property rights, as well as education and literacy, which cannot be separated from this broader shift. Land entitlement, for instance, remains a contentious issue because of the traditional chief system which is prevalent particularly in the Ghanaian North: "Most of the north is a patriarchal society", a senior consultant in Ghana mentions, "[a woman] cannot decide on her own when she wants to acquire land. She has rights to her father's land until she is married. (...) Sensitization to the chiefs and other power blocks is essential. Yet, getting an official title to land is not a very common practice" (2013_7: 31). Although at first sight, the introduction of market-oriented thought patterns and agricultural practices might seem unrelated to deeply anchored sociocultural conditions, these factors must be equally addressed in strategies for agricultural development, including workshops, program emphases, and the creation of apt instruments.

Fourth, the variety of local dialects and languages impacts the diffusion and outreach of the market model and the facilitation of workshops in Ghana. Multiple translations are required: First of all, farmers must learn to speak the language of markets, or must achieve "business literacy" (2013_7: 25), as a consultant in the Ghanaian North emphasizes:

> "Of course, some farmers - most of them - are illiterate. But then we also recognize that at least someone is literate in the household. We want to transform the farmer's community into a literate farming community. If you are not alphabetically literate, you should at least have business literacy. [That means] you are able to keep an eye on your cost."

This involves a shift in agricultural practices with an orientation towards quality management and a reflective use of fertilizer. Facilitators must also translate the essence of the value chain perspective from English to local dialects, whereby they have to switch into symbolic language, illustrations and periphrases since there are no words and direct translations in most of the local dialects. A zonal agricultural manager and a program officer describe the translation process as follows:

> "They call the chain 'zuolugey'. That's a chain. 'Anfaani' is actually value. So they say 'Anfaani Zuolugey', ahaa, almost literally, it is a chain with value, you know. I hear that very often among the groups, the farmers." (2010_1: 141-143)

> "Most of them understand what value chain means. When I say 'value chain', they understand. When we were training them, what we did, was we used symbols and other things. Perhaps you see a farm, maybe, let's say, an input dealer and you have all the inputs. It is showing the arrow, you show it to them, so this is termed as value chain from one point to the other. So we all consider it as value chain even though they don't really know much. They are illiterates but they know what value chain is all about, if you ask them." (2010_2: 177-178)

Linguistic barriers are common, but are solved by pragmatic means through the facilitators. Although this aspect is not problematized in manuals, the multiple translations from English into local dialects and from illiteracy into business literacy assume an important amount of time in field schools and farmer workshops on value chain development. Communicating the essence of the market-oriented approach assumes an important role in sites where alternative words and representations as well as new modes of calculation must be found and introduced.

Fifth, the creation of sustainable linkages in value chains requires transparency and trust along the entire chain and beyond, when funding institutions come on board. This involves technical assistance including regular visits to farmer villages, participation in district meetings, the mutual elaboration of contracts as well as the provision of tools to farmers, such as weighing scales. The latter are key to sustainable relationships, because they enable the farmers to weigh their products, which was previously done by intermediaries and out of their sight, and was thus a source of mistrust and cheating.

> "The issue of trust is always a problem, no matter what you do. Sometimes it is not easy for [the farmers] to disclose certain information. That is the reason why they often cannot go into contract farming. Because when the prices increase and they realize that what my contract person is offering is not enough, they do not follow the contracts anymore." (2013_5: 33)

In Ghana, banks have traditionally withheld from providing funds to smallholder farmers, being described as "risk averse, especially when it gets to agribusiness" (2014_21: 46) due to a lack of knowledge about the sector. In order to "change that mentality" and "bring them on board" (2011_4: 62-63) instead of seeing themselves outside the chain, the German KfW created the Value Chain Outgrower Fund. This is a refinancing vehicle which provides medium and long-term loans to commercially viable value chains through the banking sector. Funds are channeled through financial operators to the groups and technical operators so that a close cooperation becomes the condition for success for the fund. Thereby, accountability and trust between farmers, financial operators (banks) and off-takers (bulk buyers, processors and exporters) have considerably improved.

Conclusions

This chapter has provided insights into the process of circulation and inscription of value chain thinking in Ghana by following the "consultancy value chain" (2014_6: 10) which takes a decisive role in the policy revision process. The approach has gained wide recognition and appeal among policy makers and public officials. This is shown by its inscription into policy agendas, university curricula, and the creation of value chain committees. Since the early 2000s, a plethora of development organizations and programs have engaged in the enhancement of selected commodities and drawn on the GVC approach as a guideline for action. As an effect of the mobilization of such "traveling rationalities" (Craig, Porter 2006), which are channeled through a global actor networks, the framework has been linked to specific agendas: The global model has created localized versions, as could be shown in the "Ghana-ized" version of the GVC framework. Today, the approach is considered as a seemingly all-encompassing panacea for the integration of the Ghanaian economy and society into global markets. The market rationale lends itself as an overall recipe for wealth, poverty reduction through value chain integration, gender equality through the insertion of women into the formal workforce, digital inclusion through mobile market information systems, public consultation of farmer's voices through the creation of farmer-based organizations, the promotion of (business) literacy through field schools and farmer trainings, and the revaluation of farmer groups through formalized linkages with agricultural banks. Ghanaian society has become a laboratory for the experimental testing of markets via the implementation of value chain models by development practitioners and international institutions alike.

7. Commodity circuits

> "Value chain development is a collective work: It's an effort, and you keep thinking about it: you bang your head, you fall, you come back on track." (2013_21: 143)

The framing of goods, people and ideas in GVCs requires time, money and collective efforts. Setbacks and resistances, as the development practitioner mentions, are part of this endeavor as much as successes, and they appear in the form of socio-institutional, legal, and technological obstacles.

My research on two particular value chains and trajectories of commodities thematically lines up with an impressive body of work proposed by human geographers and sociologists who have investigated the spatiality of commodity chains more broadly (Hughes, Reimer 2004), geographies and politics of food chains (Jackson et al. 2006; Jackson 2002) or closely followed particular commodities (Cook 2004).[21] Scholars have investigated circulating commodities, transnational linkages between value chain members, and the developmental effects for regions and smallholder farmers (Maertens 2006; Schipmann 2006). Yet what is lacking in many of these studies is an engagement with the ontological trajectory and transformation of commodities, including the adjustments between traveling things and human agents, ongoing dynamics of movement and stability, and the processes that, first of all, enable commodities to be identified as such. Such a perspective on the "biographies" of things and the politics of value surrounding their valuation has been proposed by anthropologist Arjun Appadurai (1986). He does not fall into the trap of assigning commodities an a priori value (Callon, Çalışkan 2005: 386). Instead, he argues that a thing trans-

[21] The broader body of work that addresses the chain of activities from production to consumption of a commodity has also been subsumed under the notion of "commodity studies" (Bernstein, Campling 2006). Yet, commodity studies have "no common purpose, object of analysis, theoretical framework or methodological approach" (ibid.: 240), which is why any attempt to review this broad field is necessarily partial and selective.

lates into a commodity only at the moment when it becomes a clearly defined object of economic value (Appadurai 1986: 3). Although he applies a political economic perspective, he goes beyond a Marxian production-related perspective on the historical and material features of commodities. More specifically, he considers things as changing their ontological status as they move along preordained paths of commoditization.[22] However, Appadurai's approach refrains from an engagement with the practical materiality of things.

An analysis of the "socio-geographic trajectories" (Castree 2003: 274) of economic goods as they travel along with economic agents, norms and regulations attends to the dynamics rather than seeking to pin commodities in time and place. This is the point of departure for my research on the Peruvian inka nut or sacha inchi value chain. [23] I focus on the contingent and ongoing processes of translation of the economic good without losing grasp of the surrounding politico-institutional, technological and knowledge infrastructures. This research involves journeys to Lima and the Peruvian Amazon, i.e. the sites of constructing the value chain. The journey raises ontological questions around the previously "unqualified" status and economic value of a plant and food for local consumption. Treating commodities as analytical matters of concern in their own right can only be achieved by following them to the sometimes messy sites of enactment, production, and transformation. It is only then that the above mentioned quote from the consultant in Peru can be fully understood and grasped.

---

[22] Commoditization and commodification mean different things: Commodification stems from Marx's body of thought and still has a certain connotation, while commoditization is associated with business literature (Rushkoff 2005). Both refer to processes by which goods are assigned economic value. Yet commodification points to a social critique of labor conditions involved in this process. Since the late 1990s, attention is drawn to the "natural" dimensions of commodities which disentangled the notion commodification from its Marxist association. However, to the present day, much imprecision prevails in the use of "commodity", "commodification", and "commoditization" (Castree 2003). Mosse, for instance, refers to commodification as the "extension of markets in all spheres" (2013: 237). In this book, I use the notion of commoditization to unveil the politics of value that are part of the translation of a good into a commodity by shifting the regard to the actors involved and its political, institutional, and social outreach.

[23] Sacha inchi are two words in the local language Quechua, one meaning "tree" or "bush" and the other "nut". Common terms are "sacha inchi(k)", "maní del inca" or "maní del monte". For a discussion of the terminology, see Valles (1993). In English, it often translates into "inka nut".

Global encounters or the economy of attention

International fairs are sites where mobilized models about markets and development touch down to gain fuel and traction. One international fair for organic foods has developed into a particularly prominent nodal point for the promotion and presentation of agricultural goods, which target niche markets. These products may be unknown to the larger public before being promoted as "superfoods," which has become a label for foods that are said to confer remarkable health benefits.

The Biofach is the most important international organic food fair which takes place every year in Germany. Roughly 42000 trade visitors from 134 countries came to the fair in 2014 (Biofach 2014) to learn about new developments in the rapidly growing organic food and clothes market. Certified organic products were offered by 2265 exhibitors from 76 countries including SMEs and export firms, for-profit farmer associations, and related development organizations. Among these exhibitors, the vast majority trades with already widely established vegetables, nuts, fruits, oils, and cereals or clothes which are then represented and marketed in an innovative way. My interest was different, however. I was eager to see how a formerly unknown product, which had only recently been translated into a "qualified" economic good on global markets, was presented in front of international buyers. I identified eleven, mostly Peruvian, SMEs which traded with a widely unknown product at the Biofach: sacha inchi. Being promoted either as a cosmetic ingredient within high-end skin products and lotions or as an alimentary product in the form of snacks, oil, flour and pasta, it attracted the attention of international buyers and visitors on this occasion. In the Biofach magazine, a full-page advert for sacha inchi figured on the first page, with discussions about its nutritive value. What made sacha inchi attract that much attention at the fair? Conversations at the Biofach reveal insights into the entrepreneurs' strategies of promoting a barely known product on global markets.

Context 4: Marketizing exotic nuts at the Biofach

At an international fair as the Biofach, firms try to position their stands right in the middle where everyone passes along catchy and appealing product displays. But how to attract the attention of international exporters, European traders and firms for a new product among the variety of firms and already established products? Some stands are situated within the halls of European export promotion agencies, which might turn the attention away from the origin of the product and the enterprises. Other stands are on their own, where more attention goes towards the product itself and its history.

A typical dialogue: Every conversation at the sacha inchi-trading stands revolves around the health aspect, i.e. the beneficial nutritive values of sacha inchi. Firm representatives mention the high content of omega 3, 6 and 9, and the diverse beneficial nutrients of sacha inchi to interested passers-by. Several are skeptical about the "miraculous food" that many of them never heard about. 'Who are the exhibitors already trading with? Who are they selling to?,' the passers-by want to know and note it down. The second set of questions addresses the geographical origin of the product: Are the supply chain members rather "close" to European markets? Does the transportation require a long time? Rarely does a conversation touch the political interest and aspect of protecting Peruvian biodiversity, which was an important point in the conversations I had in Peru. What counts in this setting, logically, is a marketing strategy that posits sacha inchi as an outstanding new product on global markets and in a standardized format with neatly packaged and appealing bottles, bags and cans that fit the desires of end consumers.

An example of a European firm that imports sacha inchi and trades it on European markets: One stand particularly draws the visitors' attention to the health-promoting benefits of the product through colorful bright product information sheets, flyers and books that are on display. It stems from a Swiss firm that trades with products derived from sacha inchi and processes the seeds in Switzerland since the late 2000s. The founder relates that the first years of business were very challenging. The investments in making the product known to European consumers and attracting attention to a food that faces particularly high bureaucratic hurdles were challenging in two ways. First of all, high costs awaited the firm - several hundred thousands of Euros for the marketing alone. Second, much time was needed until the "Novel Food barrier" (for an explanation keep reading this chapter) was finally surpassed. The target markets are in Europe, with Germany as the most promising market, and a future potential expansion to the Chinese and Russian markets. Besides the oil that they offer as pure sacha inchi oil or in a blend with sesame and avocado, they sell snacks, a type of powder and pasta made of sacha inchi flour.

Although the entrepreneur notices my knowledge about the product, its origin and the composition of the value chain, she repeatedly stresses the benefits of consuming sacha inchi and the bright future that lay ahead of the product on European markets. Her employee promotes the product in a managerial, bank-like fashion. Anticipating the skepticism of price-conscious European visitors to whom he counts me, he breaks down the price to one plate: "One serving of sacha inchi pasta costs the consumer 1 EUR - indeed not even – 0.85 EUR, since it is very nutritious and the portions are smaller than in servings of conventional pasta. (…) We are selling the pasta via the serving." He knows his business and translates the product into quantifiable servings, breaks the price down to a size that fits the individual European consumer. No comment about pro-poor impacts to farmer communities in Peru. The conversation turns around business, health and wealth for the European consumer, "that's all that counts". The next market trend is "beauty and health", he reasserts. "Once the European consumers know what sacha inchi is, they will buy it and the market will explode". And "as burn-out is the number one disease among hard-working managers", there is "a big potential market for the omega 3, 6 and 9-rich product. Beyond its nutritive value, the taste is also good", I am told. When I ask the founder why she started to invest in sacha inchi, she relates in an enthusiastic manner that it has always been her dream to sell a Peruvian product that she has known from her childhood to bring it to European markets. She tells the story of her son consuming it while he was sick. And how much he preferred the taste of sacha inchi oil to fish oil. (Field note, 2014)

The Biofach is a site in which the maturity and potential of a product can be measured. The observations illustrate how unknown products are promoted to respond to the demands of targeted groups: demanding, health-conscious consumers who are looking for innovative certified niche products find a promising product in sacha inchi. Sacha inchi seems to fit the zeitgeist and increasing concerns for health and ecological aspects, fair labor conditions, and an interest in exotic foods. At the Biofach, it is promoted as an Amazonian superfood, vegan, organic, protein-rich, apt for cosmetic use with a revitalizing effect on the skin, and, on top of that, already used by the Incas. The appealing marketing story relates it directly to health-related concerns. It is proclaimed to be of benefit to people with elevated cholesterol levels and contribute to weight loss, whereby a balanced diet can be achieved. At the same time, one's social conscience is served as entrepreneurs recall its pro-poor effects. Indeed, juggling with consumer's health-awareness combined with pro-poor discourses proved to be a powerful marketing device (Table 5). How was sacha inchi detached from its original setting, qualified, aligned with international norms and ontologically reconfigured as a promising product for international consumers? Which market agencies were involved in preparing sacha inchi to "take off", as a Biofach magazine put it?

Back to the roots of Amazonian superfoods

Subsumed under the notion of "bioprospecting", the search for new sources of compounds, genes and plants which can be transformed into new products is of strategic importance for global pharmaceutical, cosmetic and food industries (Powell, Chavarro 2008: 114). Development organizations similarly share an interest in exploring market niches that may facilitate market access to formerly excluded groups. Amazonia lends itself for such a research, as it is considered the world's most important center of biodiversity in which several crops for global agriculture such as cocoa, cassava, potato and rubber were first domesticated. Down to the present day, several plant species with promising economic value remain little-known and virtually neglected by science and commerce (Krivankova 2007), so that their exploration and commercialization presents a potential for the Peruvian economy and its positioning in global markets. One example of such a species is plukenetia volubilis (Figure 11). Better known as sacha inchi, the plant was already grown and consumed by Pre-Inca civilizations 5000 years ago. The Incas knew about its beneficial nutritious characteristics and used sacha inchi oil in a mixture with flour so as to make a cream that refreshes the skin.

Figure 11: Sacha inchi cultivation in Northern Peru
Source: Own photos (2013)

The geographical center of the cultivation of sacha inchi is located in San Martín in Northern Peru, a transitional region between the high Andes and Amazonia which is widely covered by tropical rainforest. The promotion of sacha inchi gained center stage in San Martín for political reasons: It fits the current interest in biotrade promotion (further explicated below). Value chain development is part of UNCTAD's global BioTrade Initiative which supports activities of "collection, production, transformation, and commercialization of goods and services derived from native biodiversity under the criteria of environmental, social and economic sustainability" (UNCTAD 2015), and hence, legitimizes interventions into agricultural and economic development:

> "The BioTrade Initiative sees the strengthening of value chains as a critical element in facilitating the implementation of good practices related to the sustainable use and conservation of biodiversity and in promoting the equitable sharing of environmental, social and economic benefits among value chain participants." (UNCTAD 2007: 30)

Sacha inchi has also become prioritized in the Regional Development Plan of 2008-2015 (Gobierno regional de San Martín 2008: 152-156) and thus on its way to become an identity-reinforcing national nut. It figures as a substitute to replace the formerly wide spread and lucrative coca cultivation for the illegal drug trade. From 1985-1992, violent acts of insurgency by the Shining Path dictatorship that agitated Peru affected the region (Muñoz 2006; UNODC 2011). The technological development of licit crops stagnated until the end of the 1990s when agriculture in the region was re-oriented towards crops such as rice, citrus fruits, plantain, cocoa and coffee with the support and establishment of an increasingly stable and democratic regional government (Dirección Regional de Agricultura San Martín 2012: 40). Down to the present day, the agricultural sector in the region is financially and technologically underequipped. For these reasons and the related high incidence of rural poverty, many programs from the government in cooperation with international development organizations promote agricultural development to achieve higher productivity, better quality management and thereby enable smallholder farmers to upgrade their position in national and global markets.

In the wake of increasing political and economic stability, regional entrepreneurs became interested in the cultivation and commoditization of sacha inchi in the mid-2000s (cf. Context 5), and development agencies soon followed them in an effort to create pro-poor value chains that enable smallholders and SMEs to access global markets. Within a few years, nine sacha inchi-trading SMEs were established in the region out of which five operate according to biotrade principles (Mesa Técnica de Sacha Inchi 2013). With the financial support of public authorities and the international development community, these started to promote the product at international and national food fairs such as the Biofach (GIZ 2013: 32). In 2004, the first firms started to extract sacha inchi oil which accounts for 90% of sacha inchi exports (Juarez Nima 2007: 41). The following fieldnote illustrates an entrepreneurs' perspective, his reasons for taking the risk of trading with sacha inchi – and an insight into the setting in which sacha inchi is grown.

Context 5: Investments into exotic nuts

Manuel*, an entrepreneur whom I accompanied several times on field visits, owns one of the processing firms in the region. He first got in touch with sacha inchi in 2006 when his neighbors were throwing away the fruit of their sacha inchi plants which grew as weeds in their backyard. They had no idea what to do with the "weeds" in their courtyard, which they occasionally used in their diet, yet not on a regular basis. Manuel became interested and searched for more information about this plant which he had seen growing wildly in patches not only in his neighbors' backyard but also in the fields around Lamas, a village in the Peruvian province of San Martín, which is known for its annual festival with dances and music of the indigenous communities. While searching for further product information, he met the biologist Juan Acosta*, a regional biologist and sacha inchi expert who was eager to attract public awareness to native plants of the Amazon. Providing scientific information about the species, Juan Acosta oriented them to Lamas, where Manuel settled down to develop a small business and engage in agricultural development. There, the lands dedicated to sacha inchi cultivation outnumbered those of neighboring provinces. Manuel mentioned that his decision to invest into sacha inchi was impacted by existing scientific data provided to him by Juan Acosta which indicated promising economic potential: Sacha inchi grows on roughly any kind of soil; there are no pests nor plant diseases known in the region; post first harvest, plants continue to fruit so that they can be harvested every twenty days throughout the year; the cultivation provides employment for farmers in the region; the existing biological and morphological studies promised added-value if functioning chains were constructed in the first place. Being trained as a construction engineer in Lima, Manuel had no previous connection to or knowledge of sacha inchi. His decision to create a sustainable and socially respectful business that engages with rural communities in the Amazon region was based upon the interest to "invest in our Amazon", which meant for him investing in regional economic and technological development via the trade with a barely known product. (Field note, 2013)

At first, sacha inchi was studied only for its biological qualities by regional experts (GIZ 2013: 32). As such, it had no economic value ascribed to it. The moment that entrepreneurs became interested, the features of sacha inchi had to be qualified in new terms to fit the demands of global markets. The Callonian distinction between a good and a product grasps this ontological shift: While a "good" refers to a "result or, more precisely, to a moment in that never-ending process" of transformation and valuation (Callon et al. 2002: 197), a "product" corresponds to the continuing processes of production, circulation and consumption. Hence, the process of commoditization led to the valuation – or indeed, re-valuation – of sacha inchi in economic terms. Through various investments, sacha inchi was rendered calculable.

Commoditizing sacha inchi: Entanglements of science and politics

The endeavor of constructing spaces of calculability for sacha inchi requires three components: material investments, instruments of calculation and economic theory. The setting-up of a socio-technical infrastructure for the commercialization of sacha inchi was conditioned by technical, monetary, social, procedural, and scientific investments in which not only the product itself but also those human actors who were involved in its processing were transformed and ontologically reconfigured. Both human and material agency engaged in the tuning (Pickering 1995) or aligning (Callon, Muniesa 2005) process to gradually bring about the reality that the value chain framework describes. The entities that were continuously "drawn together", as Latour calls it (1986b), become meaningful only within a network of actors and devices. As Callon argues, "translation involves creating convergences and homologies by relating things that were previously different" (1981: 211). Rather than a straightforward process of market construction, the realization of these steps proved to be conditioned by "dances of agency" (Pickering 2010), i.e. experimental trials that lacked orientation at times and required posterior (re-)adjustments.

Enrolling support through the mesa técnica

One of the early initiatives to bring order and stability into the emerging value chain is linked to the creation of an exchange platform for entrepreneurs, producers, public authorities and service providers. The so-called mesa técnica was born out of the initiative of entrepreneurs in the region in 2006. The regional government charged one of its employees to coordinate, assess and assist this institutionalized body, surveil the implementation of the Regional Export Plan and create sustainable links between public and private actors. It is a

> "dialogue forum that facilitates, promotes and brings together all regional value chain participants in order to generate an exportable good with added value that allows to improve the livelihoods of the involved actors in the process of regional development, based on the respect of BioTrade principles, economic viability, equity of opportunities and benefits and in harmony with the environment." (Guzmán 2013: 9)

Regular monthly meetings and a bi-annual encounter with all members build the foundation for enhanced cooperation. It is the only platform for the sacha inchi industry and serves as a reference for other value chains at the national level due to its innovative format and dynamics.

Each actor group is seen to benefit from the exchange: The mesa técnica provides a voice to the roughly 1000 organized smallholder farmers in the region, which is still small compared to the already institutionalized value chains like cacao with 40000 organized smallholders (GIZ 2013). Entrepreneurs can source information as to where producers are located and what needs they articulate. The regional government sees in the mesa técnica a space in which all chain participants put forward their necessities whereupon the funds for value chain development can be oriented and distributed. Research institutions and service providers can develop their lines of work based on the challenges and achievements in the field that are put forward in the discussions. Through the mesa técnica, value chain participants can formulate a common strategy for the development of the sacha inchi industry so as to make it more competitive and transparent and thus prevent misunderstandings due to diverging interests and priorities.

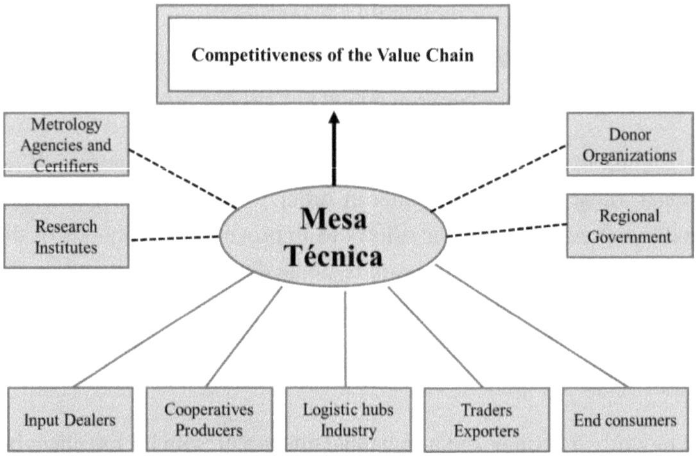

Figure 12: The mediating role of the mesa técnica
Source: Own draft

Every two years, the members of the mesa técnica gather to exchange information and share achievements in innovation, associativity, sustainable development, research, and quality management. In 2013, a total of 90 entrepreneurs, producers, representatives of the regional government, and representatives of public institutions reviewed the achievements of the seventh anniversary of the mesa técnica. The mesa técnica presents itself confidently as a dialogue platform which strives for the

> "development and competitiveness of this value chain since 2006 and which has successfully brought together entrepreneurs. It strives for enhanced service provision, access to finance, the establishment and compliance with standards and the improvement of the political and regulatory framework." (Invitation to the 4th encounter of value chain participants and interested public, November 2013)

A regional project manager and consultant proudly recounts the evolution of the mesa técnica into a powerful and widely recognized rule-setting body: "We have started off with this chain from scratch in 2006. And from there, it is a huge achievement that the mesa técnica is in the position where it is now" (2013_20:

231). What has been achieved since the creation of this platform? From 2006-2011, 29 out of 38 agreements that were listed on the operational plan of the mesa técnica have been accomplished (Mesa Técnica de Sacha Inchi Región San Martín 2012). Among the achievements are a compilation of studies on sacha inchi, a fact sheet with information on the scientific features of the plant, a sheet comprising all regional producers' data, the commitment to and realization of field schools and capacity building, the elaboration of outgrower schemes between businesses and producers, the achievement of organic certification for some producers and SMEs, and the participation and intervention in national and regional fairs.

Certainly, there have been harsh negotiations and competition among members of the mesa técnica. This should not be a surprise, given the fact that market-making is an "on-going experimental process" (Callon 2009: 543) that involves a series of trials of strength in which human and non-human actors vie with one another and hence try to enroll allies to advance their own aims (Latour 1988: Part II, Irréductions). Not all members share and exchange information, so there remains a certain level of reticence among those who have continuously done so. A consultant confirms that in times of falling prices due to lower demand, competing entrepreneurs hold back information about their activities, since

> "in the last year we had meetings taking place behind closed doors [without the regional government]. This is what the entrepreneurs asked us [development consultants] to do. The entrepreneurs accused each other of taking away the other's producers, of not sharing important market information... But this is the logic of competing firms. And we cannot stop them from discussing these issues because we need these forms to compete. This is the asset of the chain. We need the logic of competitiveness along the logic of collaboration." (2013_21: 89)

Moreover, and despite the achievements of the institutionalized mesa técnica, the involvement of all members and the implementation of common strategies for action cause constant discussions, as one entrepreneur argued:

> "As the regional government does not show any signs of real support, this mesa técnica is built upon few legs. Hence, the future of the mesa técnica is uncertain. It is all the more important that they [the government] listen to our entrepreneurial perspective. We firms have a commitment and contracts to comply with – that is a reality and an opportunity. But there is an opportunity cost that we are not capitalizing upon because we are not working in an articulated manner." (2013_32: 11)

It is no surprise that conflicts arise as the reasons for each member's participation differ as well. Constant efforts are required to keep the mesa técnica active and functional. As the relations become closer and the sacha inchi industry becomes more institutionalized, regular meetings and exchanges become less important. Only in times of crisis – plagues, lower demand, unfair competition or monopolization – will the value chain participants sit together to discuss solutions and find compromises to these issues. The process of enrolment involves "group multilateral negotiations, trials of strength and tricks that accompany the intéressements and enable them to succeed" (Callon 1986: 211). Enrolling new market agencies means persuading them to engage in a common roadmap for action in spite of potentially diverging interests. Yet, "how do they align?" a consultant formulated in a question which he then answered right away:

> "When supporting agencies and institutions such as the state enter, they all have their own interests. They come with a program, as government, etc. (…) and the idea is that in this space they can generate alliances, get to know entrepreneurs and producers, ally with others and duplicate the efforts. The most important: locate themselves to determine what will be their role in the process of enhancing the value chain." (2013_21: 85)

What should have become clear is that the establishment of the mesa técnica and its gradual institutionalization has led to enhanced cooperation, exchange and political support through public attention. Its formation marks a significant shift towards sector organization and has achieved a stable position in the value chain.

Scientists at work in the framing of value

For an "unknown" product to enter global markets, information has to be provided that defines the product qualities. Research institutions generate scientific studies that are used to legitimize interventions, policy shifts or uphold a marketing strategy. Circulating knowledge about the plant as generated by scientists is combined with embodied knowledges of mobile development consultants so as to draw the "exotic" plant of the Peruvian Amazon into the center of value chain promotion.

The scientific interest in sacha inchi noticeably precedes investments from private actors or other institutions, as one of the few reports on the sacha inchi value chain confirms, which features a timeline of the establishment in San Martín (GIZ 2013: 32). In the mid-1980s, for the first time, bromatological and biomorphological analyses of sacha inchi were conducted by American scientists of Food Science of Cornell University. They indicated that sacha inchi seeds are an important source of omega 3, 6 and 9 and rich in proteins (Hazen, Stowes and 1980, cited in INIA 2006:4; Juarez Nima 2007: 16). The interest in the plant stemmed from foreign researchers and focused on defining the qualities and features of the plant. Gradually, Peruvian research institutes started to research the species as they received funds to study the species (Zegarra 2008). The rising investment in research about the product correlated with an increasing interest in exotic plants from the Amazon region. In 1993 and 1996, further evaluations of the crop were realized by INIA, a regional research institute located in Tarapoto, San Martín (GIZ 2013: 32).

Table 5: Scientific assessments of sacha inchi

Studies realized about sacha inchi and their key take-away	Source
Sacha inchi consumption has beneficial effects for vision	Bhargava et al. 2013
Sacha inchi is purported to fight depression, reduce cholesterol levels, prevent heart disease, and aid in diabetes management	Fanali et al. 2011 Gorriti et al. 2010
Essential fatty acids protect your central nervous system (the brain and spinal cord) from neuro-degenerative disease	Fotuhi et al. 2009
Preliminary research indicates that sacha inchi may be of some benefit to people with elevated cholesterol levels	Garmendia et al. 2011
Sacha inchi is unusually high in tryptophan, an amino acid essential to the production of serotonin (a nervous-system chemical involved in regulating appetite)	Sathe et al. 2012
The consumption of sacha inchi strengthens the entire cardiovascular system	Simopoulos 2002

Source: Own draft

While the initial interest in analyzing the biochemical composition of the plant was scientific, meanwhile these studies were used to legitimize its promotion for economic, ecologic, health and further purposes (Table 5), including food security or pro-poor development claims.[24] In the political realm, its promotion was associated with socioeconomic development, as public authorities argued that many smallholders with small land property could live on the cultivation of sacha inchi which generates regional employment. The interest thus shifted towards the marketable assets that are of interest to consumer demands and expectations.

[24] Scholars from interdisciplinary and transnational backgrounds have studied sacha inchi – for its morphological or chemical features (Betancourth 2013; Bondioli et al. 2006; Dostert et al. 2009; Gorriti 2013, 2010; Gutiérrez et al. 2011; Krivankova et al. 2012), its potential for disease prevention (Hanssen, Schmitz-Hübsch 2011) and the economic value or export potential (GFU n.d.; GIZ 2013; Krivankova 2007; SIPPO 2012).

Biotrade and the politics of value chain development

Every year, the Peruvian Ministry of Agriculture publishes a list of prioritized value chains at the national level. In 2013, prioritized value chains included coffee, cocoa, plantain, potato, yellow maize, oranges, rice, quinoa, avocado, palm oil and cotton. Sacha inchi figures as a "prioritized" commodity at the regional, yet not at the national, level. Therefore, financial resources and support are limited..[25] Biotrade targets market niches for an affluent and ecologically-oriented, health-aware international clientele that is willing to pay for additional certifications. A development consultant praises biotrade as the crucial value-adding component for sacha inchi commercialization:

> "Our public-private partnerships are the best evidence that biotrade works. We have experienced it. Manuel, the founder of a regional processing firm, invited us to accompany him on a monitoring visit and he told his visiting clients from abroad the following 'I am an entrepreneur working according to the biotrade principles and I respect the rights of my suppliers, the smallholder farmers, and their ancient knowledge, as well as the economic value of their work'. Another local entrepreneur brought his buyers from Texas to small communities and very poor villages, he walked with them along the streets and the buyer remained astonished when the local entrepreneur told him 'I came here last year and the houses were rustical and made of adobe. Now you see houses of noble materials, they have television, you can see the antenna. This all is related to sacha inchi and biotrade.' So, what happened? The relationship with his client from Texas strengthened, as the local entrepreneur told me that he had received a touching letter in which the client expressed his appreciation for the work with poor communities. So it shows as well that biotrade has indeed not only strengthened the commercial link-

[25] Nevertheless, the Peruvian government recently launched a public investment program for enhanced competitiveness of the sacha inchi value chain in San Martín. The 5.9 million PEN (= 1.9 million USD) project promotes research on the technologically-induced genetic improvement of the seeds for local research institutions such as INIA (Dirección Regional de Agricultura San Martín 2012).

ages between the entrepreneur and the producers, but also between the entrepreneur and his foreign clients." (2013_21: 151)

This extract from a conversation with a consultant illustrates the symbolic value that is ascribed to biotrade in the local setting by development consultants. Indeed, following biotrade principles generates additional costs for the entrepreneurs in this early stage of the value chain emergence. The general manager of a medium-size sacha inchi firm in San Martín admits that the commitment to biotrade was initially not a voluntary decision: "We did not know what biotrade really was nor what conditions it involved, nothing of that. Common sense dictated that there were no real alternatives" (2013_32: 186). Entrepreneurs engage in biotrade principles because they consider biotrade as key to developing the sacha inchi value chain. It helps them to promote the product internationally and relate to the goals of environmental sustainability, poverty alleviation and economic growth.

Standards and the making of an economic good

Apart from scientific assessments, entrepreneurial interests and strategies for its commercialization, for a product to access global markets it must comply with or alternatively produce around itself a set of norms and regulations. In the words of a Peruvian consultant, "the commercial success of a product depends on many factors. Besides its proper potential, it requires a formal and legal framework that enables access to those markets towards which it is directed" (Guzmán 2013: 43).

In the current "economy of qualities" (Callon et al. 2002), the rise of standards has reached enormous dimensions (Busch 2011). Everything from goods to labor, time, bodies, environment and health is qualified and quantified, measured and certified. Consequently, various public and private standards have emerged on different geographic scales over the last years that prescribe quality parameters, many of which address global trade (e.g. Nadvi 2008). This development does not seem to be an exclusively contemporary phenomenon. At the beginning of the 20th century, the economist Thorstein Veblen had argued that

> "[m]odern industry has little use for, and can make little use of, what does not conform to the standard. What is not competently standardized calls for too much of craftsman-like skill, reflection, and individual elaboration, and is therefore not available for economical use." (Veblen 1904: 11, cited in Morozov 2012)

Whereas standards have always played an important role in the manufacturing of machinery and technical equipment, the importance of standards in the food sector is a recent phenomenon. Producers and SMEs in the Global South who want to grasp opportunities in globalizing and globalized markets struggle to comply with increasingly complex product and process quality requirements imposed by firms and institutions from both public and private sectors in the Global North (Lee et al. 2012; Busch 2008). Transnational trade is built upon sophisticated infrastructures and governing entities, which is why a new product like sacha inchi must be reconfigured and made to fit the scientific, legal and industrial regulations of global markets. A standard is defined as "a document established by consensus and approved by a recognized body that provides, for common and repeated use, rules, guidelines or characteristics for activities or their results, aimed at the achievement of the optimum degree of order in a given context" (Kellermann 2011). More broadly speaking, standards are governance systems, as they determine the value of procedures, things and infrastructure.

Since the late 1980s and early 1990s, with the introduction of Ecolabels and standards for organic food, there has been an incessant rise in standards, most of which relate to economic and environmental quality or social equity. Within roughly two decades, more private food-related standards have emerged at the global scale than in the previous five decades combined (Giovannucci 2008: 2).[26] Although standards are often taken for granted, their influence should not

[26] While public standards focus on consumer protection, food safety and trade facilitation, private standards are imposed by buyers and usually require higher norms than public standards. Some-

go unnoticed: As ontological devices they build realities by valuing things over other alternatives. Vivid debates address the new kind of governance that is produced through standard-setting regimes and how it affects a new social contract that evolves between state, firms and NGOs (Giovannucci, Ponte 2005). The rise of standards leads to the reconfiguration of the role that the state plays: Accreditation bodies and standard-setting agencies increasingly assume the role of states, since decisions along international supply chains are driven by these rather than governmental regulations (Higgins, Lawrence 2005). The proliferation of standards in the global agrifood system has generated an intransparent and complex system of international and national, public and private, process and product as well as legally binding and voluntary standards. For higher-value agricultural food products, private standards compliance is essential for accessing markets. The most wide-spread private standards are those of the International Organization for Standardization (ISO), GlobalGAP and Good Manufacturing Practices (GMP), HACCP (Hazard Analysis at Critical Control Points), Fair Trade and Organic. The International Organization for Standardization (ISO) is the largest nongovernmental and global regulatory institution that exerts global governance as a standard-setter (Murphy, Yates 2009) and publishes up to 1500 standards per year with more than 20000 standards in total, while only some relate to the agrifood sector. The effects of standards on producers are not negligible. Producers in the Global South have to meet an increasing number of standards to export to target markets in Europe, the US and Asia. Not only are the costs of living up to such standards becoming certified high, but it is also the organization and structure of GVCs more broadly that determines the conditions for small-scale farmers in terms of market access, poverty reduction and overall agricultural development (Lee et al. 2012; Henson, Reardon 2005).

In the case of the sacha inchi value chain, the mesa técnica has pushed forward standardization processes. Members of the mesa técnica founded the "Technical

times private sector standards like Certified Organic are adopted by states as regulations, which is the case in several European countries as well as the EU. Process standards refer to labour conditions, the use of resources or wages along the entire cultivation and manufacturing process, whereas product standards refer to the features of the final product.

committee for the standardization of sacha inchi" in 2008 in cooperation with national research institutes, export firms, standard agencies, the Ministries of Agriculture and of Export Promotion. It promotes the standardization of products made of sacha inchi and exerts an influence within a complex international and national quality management infrastructure. The making of Peruvian technical standards for sacha inchi involves multiple steps: From an interest and request expressed by consumers and industries overseas as well as by policymakers in Peru; to an assessment by scientists about the biochemical qualities and nutritional value; to an alignment with international standards and regulations such as Global GAP, Ethical trade, Fair trade and the organic certification; to an approval or rejection by the national committee for standardization and audit (Indecopi-CNB) as a Peruvian technical standard. Several standards were established for sacha inchi in Peru between 2009 and 2012, which have been accredited at the national level. They include requirements for the processing of sacha inchi oil, GMP and GAP for the cultivation of sacha inchi, requirements for the processing of sacha inchi snacks, a traceability standard and a guideline for the interpretation of the first technical requirement (Sato 2013). These provide the national regulatory frame of reference for product quality and innocuousness according to which sacha inchi must be processed and thus enhance trust, transparency and traceability in trade relations with (international) buyers.

An exceptional resource of power was created with the standardization of sacha inchi. The Peruvian standards for sacha inchi-derived products and processing have developed into internationally recognized requirements for the cultivation and production of sacha inchi-derived products, even if they have not (yet) been recognized as ISO norms. Certification and standards are by no means natural components of the global trade system, but should be considered in the Foucauldian sense as means of regulation which govern the conduct of market actors (Fourcade, Healy 2007: 14.20; Rose, Miller 1992). In a biodiverse-rich country as Peru, various products do not have "normative antecedents", as a technical officer claims (Indecopi 2011). They must therefore be made to fit standards or become the departure point for the establishment of new standards and norms.

While national norms are usually aligned with supra-regional and international norms, there are cases such as Peruvian asparagus, which has become an ISO standard, and the fruit Lúcuma (Indecopi 2011), for which the Peruvian technical standard has become recognized by Andean countries. In the case of sacha inchi, there was simply no pre-existent norm, as an expert on accreditation systems in Germany relates:

> "Sacha inchi is a good example [for a standard from the Global South], because it is associated with two Peruvian norms that do not have any international norm which they refer to. Sacha inchi basically only grows in Peru and the Amazon basin. (…) These norms were developed in Peru. And for Peru, in order to regulate the processes, producer-supplier-relationships, the conditions for processing particular products, and the parameters for qualifying and improving the value chain." (2013_34: 70)

Standards, after all, are not only devices that, once accomplished, enable access to global markets. They create new frontiers due to high costs and require technical expertise. To the present day, few countries in the Global South have been able to produce internationally recognized standards. Knowledge transfer remains for the vast majority, as the quote demonstrates, linked to a unidirectional flow from the Global North to the Global South. Sacha inchi is no exception, yet it is particular as it is both cultivated and entirely processed in a country of the Global South.

Quality management in value chains: Who decides over quality?

Workshops and field schools tackle the issue of quality management in value chains. They address questions of standardization, metrology, accreditation, and production and processing practices. Since quality management is a cross-cutting issue that requires enhanced cooperation of public and private actors, it can be applied to all levels – regional, national, and international – and sectors – health, environment, social responsibility, food safety, and sustainability.

I had the chance to participate in a workshop in Northern Peru organized by a development organization and an internationally operating metrology institute in which guidelines for the enforcement of sacha inchi standards were developed that enhanced its competitiveness at the national and international level. Entrepreneurs from San Martín, Lima and Europe, farmer committee representatives, certifying authorities, representatives of research institutions and public officials from the regional branch of the Ministry of Agriculture gathered to discuss quality-related concerns. A fieldnote provides insights into the workshop setting, topics of debate and the state of commercialization:

> The first day, the agenda foresees an introduction into the topic of norms and standards. The participants are told to write down which norms and regulations are relevant for the sacha inchi value chain. We, that is the workshop facilitator and I, order the post-its and put them on the pin-board: international, national and regional standards, voluntary; private and public ones, including norms such as organic trade, HACCP, ISO or GlobalGAP. After the identification and classification of various types of regulations, we talk about challenges that each node in the chain faces. Small groups of participants are formed which represent different chain nodes. The groups are told to research specific requirements for engaging in trade with the US, Japan, Europe or Central America and link it to existing bottlenecks in the chain. Back in the plenary discussion, we converse about the requirements of international buyers and what they look for when they start trading with new business partners. Among the participants are international buyers who relate their experiences with the transformation of the raw commodity – sacha inchi – into oil. "Adding water in the fusion process is important to prevent the product from dehydrating", a European businesswoman says. "The water is eliminated in the filtration and decanting process and passes through another process of refinement. This involves a process of deodorization when volatile compounds are released and the oil is neutralized." None of the participants objects, until shortly afterwards the CEO of a processing firm in Lima voices doubts and turns the discussion into a vivid debate. 'It does not work that way here.

> Our oil must not and cannot pass through a process of refinement – then it would not be any more natural, extra virgin oil. And this feature helps us a lot to market and sell the product. Our oil has low peroxide value, therefore we simply do not need this process'. (Field note, 2013)

Different understandings of quality co-exist as to the processing, as the intervention of the Peruvian entrepreneur reveals. There is no common rule that prescribes how sacha inchi oil should be processed. Peruvian entrepreneurs have made their experiences with sacha inchi, while the European businesswoman is closer to the target markets. She brings her experience in to the marketing and expectations of end consumers. It is a juggling act between local knowledge, global market demands and profit calculations. Yet, who defines quality in a sector where standards are just being developed?

A conceptualization of quality that relates to cognitive, intersubjective, and normative aspects is necessary at that point – in practice as well as in theory. The idea of quality is completely sidelined in neoclassical economics. This stands in stark contrast to French convention theory (Boltanski, Thévenot 2006), which places quality at the heart of understanding how market exchange works: Through conventions, the coordination and qualification of people and things among different actors is facilitated (Boltanski, Thévenot 2006 [1991]). This lens offers a better conception of quality in markets: The parameters of competitiveness are cognitively assessed depending on the system that is used to justify evaluation and action. Over time, different valuation mechanisms are set in place according to which goods are qualified (for a critical discussion, see Gibbon, Ponte 2005: 164-170). The judgement of quality is neither certain nor stable and always open for contestation. It remains bounded to cultural, institutional and social valuations.

> On the second day of the workshop, we focus on the analysis of the quality infrastructure in the Peruvian sacha inchi value chain. The international expert of the Metrology Institute who closely cooperates with INDECOPI [Peruvian institute for standardization and ac-

> creditation], stresses the need to comply with international accreditation systems and calls for more investments to align with these requirements. To illustrate his point, we leave the workshop venue for a visit to a nearby processing firm where we can follow the transformation process of sacha inchi into oil. Counting among the larger firms in the region, the managing director has invested in a range of certification programs, including the organic certification to export to the US and the EU. Before entering the fabrication sector of the rather small firm, we are asked to follow the hygienic regulations by putting on a hairnet. We then enter the hall and see several employees selecting what is classified as "good" sacha inchi from the "bad". A few meters further, two young men de-shell big pots of sacha inchi by hand and put them on an outspread plastic blanket lying on the bare floor. This selection by hand is the usual procedure all over the region. We then proceed into the next room where three steel machines stand. While the managing director explains how the sacha inchi proceed from one machine to the next and what happens at each step of transformation, I take a closer look at these machines. They have stickers on them, indicating that they are accredited by the international norms. The "stainless steel" machines press the nuts and out comes a liquid oil shining like gold. It makes the room smell intensely of sacha inchi. The machines seem easy to handle. One can understand the process by standing next to them: from the de-shelling of nuts, to the press, to another press and to the stainless-steel tanks. No heating up, no adding of preservatives or ingredients. Meanwhile, I talk to the expert from the metrology institute who is also carefully watching what stickers are on the machine. He seems pleased with what he sees. (Field note, 2013)

The visit of the processing firm shows how value chain development is interpreted in practice and how it becomes effective in the product transformation process. Processing firms in the region are adapting to international requirements: Hygienic standards are applied and machines are internationally accredited. And yet, there remains much to do to meet the expectations of international consumers.

The attention shifts towards distributed forms of agency that are at work in the increasingly standardized market for sacha inchi. Regarding Foucault's understanding of disciplinary institutions and how they construct subjects (Foucault 1991), we can observe how a sophisticated disciplinary apparatus emerges that controls not only the exterior of tools and agents but also the interior of their decisions and valuations: First, quality standards and accredited technologies govern entire value chains and market agents. And second, local practices and global norms are increasingly entangled which creates intermediary zones where different practices and modes of valuation meet. Such zones are technological in the widest sense and can be distinguished in three complementary types: metrological zones, infrastructural zones and zones of qualification (Barry 2006: 239). While the introduction of metrological systems conditions the acceptance of common forms of measurement, a technically and logistically sophisticated quality infrastructure leads to common standards, criteria and qualification measures. These intermediary zones not only structure commercial relations, but exert normative force upon market subjects and devices (ibid.: 241). New forms, practices and subjects arise as well as contestation. Questions arise as to how practices and processing norms would look without the influence of internationally traveling development experts and their comprehensive methodologies and guidelines for action. Or how does striving to comply with international norms reinforce spatially determined relations of power as they ascribe supremacy to a certain type of practices and norms? While responses to the first issue must remain speculative, the second question can be tackled by following the sacha inchi value chain to its beginnings.

The role of trust in a world of standards

The proliferation of certifications has an effect on every agent and node in the sacha inchi value chain. This current shift comes along with a set of questions that development consultants and field staff are confronted with every day: How to convince farmers, the backbone of agricultural value chains, of the importance of complying with international norms and certifications? How to make them realize the importance of calculating the appropriate fertilizer quantities and measure their cultivated land area based on geometrical or GPS indicators when they have never learned to do so or even heard about it? How to explain that the market is not an abstract phenomenon with a steady demand and supply or stable prices? Every value chain is as strong as its weakest element. Hence, every segment's input and commitment is needed for a proper functioning of the whole system. Without having the farmers apply GAP and further norms, the sacha inchi value chain cannot properly function.

Beyond formal economic theories, the introduction of technical standards – ranging from formalized agricultural production practices to processing methods and proper storage facilities – affects the everyday practices and living environment of smallholder farmers. For field staff of regional firms, the advisory in GAP or organic cultivation methods is a time-intense procedure and includes several visits to farming communities and conversations with producer associations. It requires the establishment of long-term relationships. And yet, trust seems to be relegated a secondary role in today's global economy where standards seemingly replace the former, as a senior consultant in Lima argues: "The generation of trust…certainly, trust can exist in small entities, in small territories. But to the extent that markets expand and become more global, this topic of trust must be compensated for securities [through standards]" (2013_16: 395-396). This, however, is different in the case of the recently emerging sacha inchi value chain. The creation of relations based on trust is crucial, not only, but in particular in the early stages of markets in the making. A consultant and member of the mesa técnica recounts that

> "[w]e as mesa técnica went as far as presenting the entrepreneur to the producer. And then we said to the entrepreneur: 'Well, here we leave you, now you have to arrange it with them [farmers]. You have to work together to reach a commercial agreement. If you have reached a commercial agreement, then you can come back to us and we from the mesa técnica and the institutions that support the value chain will put several services at your disposition: the IIAP will tackle all that has to do with research, we will work on capacity de-

velopment, but you need to gain the [farmer's] confidence!' That's a topic of the private actors, we do not intervene in that. Through the commercial agreements, prices were fixed, minimum prices and a safe haven price. Generally, the transaction goes by the market price, but the experience with the price fall in the case of the sacha inchi value chain in 2006-2007 provoked a great crisis. In that situation, the producers cut down their plantations. In the agreements, it is now stated that once the price falls, the enterprises settle on a safe haven price up to which they will buy from the producers. This helped to regain the confidence of producers who once again started to put seeds." (2013_21: 57)

Due to fluctuating prices, relationships among value chain members have been compromised. Commercial agreements have consequently been established, which both parties have to sign. Long-term rapport with farming communities through frequent visits and technical support as well as the introduction of "safe haven" prices grants producers planning and revenue security and prevents them from engaging in practices such as side-selling. Despite such commercial agreements, side-selling remains a powerful practice: At the time of harvest, traders appear who offer higher prices for sacha inchi, so that producers are incited to sell their products to unknown traders. Beyond the concern with trust-building, side-selling can be seen as a calculative practice, which orients actions and decisions according to shifts on global markets.

An account of a visit to a rural community in Northern Peru allows insights into a formalization process, which modifies relationships between entrepreneurs and producers. It illustrates how farming practices are gradually aligned with the exigencies of international certifications on global food markets.

Context 6: Organic certification and the creation of order in markets

A regional processing firm, InkaGo*, and its suppliers are in the process of achieving the organic certification for sacha inchi. Complying with international standards is costly for SMEs. It involves a long process as firms need to adjust their own processing norms while ensuring that smallholder farmers adjust farming practices to the requirements of the certifiers. Once the certification is achieved, it holds the promise of higher value-added for all chain participants.

Vistoso is a small village with approximately 70 families which is located 45 minutes by motorbike from Tarapoto. Like many villages in the region, locals are mainly reliant on agriculture to make a living. The access to Vistoso is difficult since there is only an earth road in bad structural condition that connects the village to neighboring villages. Every two weeks, an InkaGo extension worker visits the producers to train and assess the producers. This time, I accompany Koki, the regional coordinator and zonal head of InkaGo. Usually, he works from his office in Tarapoto, but since the procedure of organic certification requires complementary field visits and advisory services for the producers, Koki assists his colleagues in the field.

Upon our arrival, the villagers are called to gather for the sacha inchi committee meeting by microphone. Five of the sixteen sacha inchi smallholders in the village attend the meeting. Koki recalls the rules of clean storage and GAP to the farmers by reading out aloud the principles of the "Cuaderno del productor ecológico", the farmer's handbook. After the short gathering, the five assessors of InkaGo split up to visit and check the "chacras", the farms and lands of the smallholder farmers. I accompany Koki to several farming huts, Koki sits down together with each farmer and goes through the handbook, showing how to fill in the required data - the borders of land on which they cultivate sacha inchi, the date of the last weeding, the price that they received for their and record the information on the seed variety, the date of the first seed placement, and the cultivated crops on neighboring lands. Koki runs through a questionnaire and makes sure the farmers know what they are supposed to do (Figure 13). The questions that Koki asks the farmers about dates of seeding and harvesting seem to be difficult to answer for the farmers, as they do not use calendars. Instead, they count the number of sunrises as an orientation as to what should be done for their crops throughout the year. Koki explains that the certifiers will soon visit the community and check if the conditions for organic certification are fulfilled. Therefore, not only must the chickens be raised separately from the drying sacha inchi kernels in order to ensure hygienic norms. The farmers must also measure the size of their lands, since every cultivated area must be mapped and documented. With one farmer, we step out of the hut in order to draw a map of the estimated cultivated area. It is not as easy as it seems at first, since sacha inchi is cultivated along with other crops in hilly terrains where land has not been measured before. Our map remains an estimate based on the stretch of a rope around some trees, which is far from properly assigned geometrical measurements. When we get to the last requirement in the farmer's handbook, Koki reads out aloud that no chemical products must be used. In a region where sacha inchi has traditionally grown without the use of any chemical pesticides, this point raises more questions than it provides clues: The farmers have not spent a thought on applying chemical treatment to the only recently commercialized plant, and in any case the plant has proven to be resistant and strong. Our visit ends at the farmer's huts with the mutual signature of both parties: Every producer signs the contract that Koki holds in his hands that – together with the signature of the certifying authority – turns them into a group of certified and formal market agents. (Field Note, 2013)

Figure 13: Signing agreements for organic farming
Source: Own photos (2013)

It is not surprising that the implementation of global requirements for organic certification calls for local adjustments and contextualized solutions (Context 6). It starts with the regional varieties and requirements for organic certification: In this case, it is the European organic certification that shall provide access to European markets. Obtaining this certification in Vistoso is not a question of reducing and eliminating the use of chemical fertilizers, as proposed by the farmer handbook. Local farmers have never used fertilizers for sacha inchi cultivation in the past. Its cultivation has always been organic. It is a paradoxical situation in which the documentation of an always existing status quo marks the difference and produces effects as to the value added that can be obtained. The introduction of seemingly mundane equipment and devices such as record-keeping books, accounting techniques and even ropes that are used for measuring lands bring about new ways of doing agriculture. They assume a mediating role in translating international standards and norms into the language, practices and living space of sacha inchi farmers. And they create what local consultants refer to as "order in markets". A practice or a fact which can be put into numbers, figures or words is valued over its undocumented and unmeasured counterpart. Documentation and fact-building becomes a resource of power. Record-keeping books are not only passive devices, but generate new practices and therefore alter market agencies.

Considering the standardization and certification regime which holds sway in the Peruvian agro-export sector as a depoliticized one that functions as a way to flatten the playing arena of the market would miss an essential point. Standardization is closely linked to the exertion of (political) control (Loconto, Busch 2010). It is the attempt to frame and regulate the activities of market agents in the Global South. Not only are new calculable objects created, but these may also become the object of economic calculation themselves (Callon 1998a). This attempt, however, remains necessarily incomplete: Efforts at framing always provoke overflows (ibid.: 150). These include, for instance and as explored above, side-selling of market agents who do not comply with formerly signed agreements but do instead respond to dynamics within markets. Thereby they resist and oppose the ever more regulated and formalized market exchange imposed upon them. Trust, after all, remains important in a world of standards.

When markets resist

Despite various investments into the modelling and design of market infrastructures, the outcomes of framing efforts in markets are controversial. Framing is a scientific practice which is open-ended, as the example of sacha inchi shows: First of all, the goals of scientific practice are imaginatively transformed versions of its present. Scientific practice must be understood here in its broader terms, including the activities of economists "in the wild". Development practitioners have from the beginning on targeted export markets, imagining a prosperous future and market potential for sacha inchi and the associated market agents. Second, these goals emerge in the real time of practice. Market-making is a deeply practical endeavor in which various market agencies are involved and in which they meet to create order, rules, discuss and negotiate. Beyond all modeling, and this is the third and last point, goals are being reconfigured throughout practices when they intertwine with material agency. In this intertwining of humans and materials, active and passive forms of contestation arise (Barry 2001; Dunn 2005).

The promotion of the sacha inchi value chain was from the beginning oriented towards export markets, while the national market had been sidelined by donor organizations and entrepreneurs. This exclusive orientation had various reasons. One decisive factor was the little knowledge about sacha inchi in Peru and the products' nutritive value. International consultants envisioned high demand or at least high potential on global markets for sacha inchi-derived products. Entrepreneurs in Peru expected export markets to provide higher value added to producers: "Why Europe? Because the money comes from Europe" (2013_15: 87). This assumption had severe effects on the development of the sacha inchi value chain. Regulations for "new" foods, when they enter global markets, were largely ignored (cf. next section).

First of all, the global orientation of the sacha inchi value chain strategy was done without due regard to producers, which proved to be fatal for them and the emerging value chain. Without being trained in GAP or equipped with farming techniques or technological devices, producers were not ready at first to comply with export requirements and international quality standards. Moreover, most farmers were unorganized. They were more vulnerable for not having an organized body in which they could express their needs and challenges:

> "There is not a sufficient supply of sacha inchi in terms of quality and quantity that permits to be competitive in international markets. (…) Only very few producers are organized in associations or committees, and if so, they are not yet consolidated nor strong in terms of entrepreneurial thinking. (…) Moreover, a limited export culture and global strategy for the future that would include capacity development and good commercial practices based on values." (2013_21: 33)

At first, smallholders' farming practices did not comply with international standards, which hampered access to global markets. Besides weak associativity of producers and unstable product supply and offer, an "export culture" was missing among farmers who were required to apply an "entrepreneurial vision" (Juarez Nima 2007: 48). According to the local consultant, the Foucauldian entrepreneurial self lacked enforcement.

Local SMEs faced equally challenges in meeting quality criteria of international markets. Private certification schemes present entry-barriers to global markets due to their technical complexity and the financial investments required to fulfil them, as a local consultant states: "If you ask firms what they think about the costs for certification, they tell you that it is a strong sacrifice (...) but neither the US nor Europe provides access to you without certification" (2013_21: 139). Certainly, complementary certificates allow for the capture of extra value for smallholders and exporters (Ouma 2010). However, complying with them is tied to a long-term perspective for local SMEs, as the managing director of a local processing firm explained. He was incensed about the analytical approach of development consultants, which remained far from the necessities of market agents on the ground:

> "I imagine all those looking at the value chain methodology and their global perspective... it is for those who remain in their office, gathering papers, not going out to meet the people in the field, not getting dirty hands with the real necessities of the farmers. And now [in the new practitioner manual] they found out that we entrepreneurs need a business plan – really, how funny! – I know what I need: Capital to improve the infrastructure and optimize processes. Only that! The rest of the magic formulas only hold on paper." (2014_1)

Training was introduced for farmers, while "alianzas estratégicas" – strategic alliances – were formed between regional firms and producer organizations. Gradually, cooperation between chain members was enhanced: Investments into field schools, the exchange of information and best practices stabilized the emerging market order.

When the market becomes political again

Sacha inchi presents a perfect example to illustrate the challenges involved in introducing "unqualified" products to global markets. The efforts of development practitioners, Peruvian policy makers, and service providers for making the value chain comply with international requirements had focused on European markets. These, however, seemed to be in vain, because of a market access barrier that impeded the import of sacha inchi on European markets. Until 2013, sacha inchi could not be imported as a product for alimentary consumption in the EU. A senior consultant who worked for a sacha inchi value chain program recounts that

> "when the program started, we had a more or less clear idea. Theoretically, some protectionist measures turned up in the national market, so our strategy was to export. The global market is huge, the prices were attractive and it meant a significant contribution to poverty reduction and livelihoods improvement of those whom we wanted to support. But when we started to work, we did not realize that in those spaces and territories which we had selected as target markets, sacha inchi could not prosper." (2013_20: 191)

Under the Novel Food regulation of the European Commission, sacha inchi was considered a potentially dangerous "novel food" (cf. Context 8). Accordingly, it had not been used for human consumption to a "significant degree" in the EU before 1997 when the regulation came into force. The only exception to this regulation was sacha inchi oil which was exclusively destined for the cosmetics industry (APISI 2010: 15). Similar barriers restricted its exportation to other international markets as well, including the US and Japan where respective regulations exist. In the US, the Food and Drug Administration deals with consumer safety and market entry requirements through the "Generally Recognized as Safe" (GRAS) regulation (US Center for Food Safety and Applied Nutrition

2014; ITC 2014), while in Japan, the food regulation Fonshu (Vera 2014; Krigbaum n.d.) limits access to new foods. These latter regulations were nevertheless not as limiting and longstanding as the case for the European market proved to be. In the beginning, entrepreneurs were not aware of the technicalities of the Novel Food Regulation and were ready to fulfil any requirement. Yet they gradually learned about the costs that the procedure would involve:

> "We are what could be called 'at the foot of the mountain'. That means: We are ready to provide whatever [document] we are asked to hand in. We have invested a lot of money obviously, we have sent analyses, etc. But we have been doing this for 5 years now. (…) We did not know about the Novel Food barrier, and we thought, we can overcome it. We presented a draft, but I understood that information was missing that we could not provide. It was going to cost a lot more. This is when everything slowed down." (2013_32: 77)

In order to overcome the regulation and achieve the authorization for free trade with the EU, the innocuousness of the product had to be proved. This set in motion a chain of activities and investments by Peruvian public institutions and firms that aimed at overcoming this barrier (cf. Context 7): A dossier was prepared that included information about the historical use of the novel food sacha inchi in the country of origin, referential dates as to the process of elaboration, statistical figures about the production and national consumption, and research confirming that sacha inchi's composition and properties were safe for human and animal consumption (Guzmán 2013: 62-63). The compilation and commission of the comprehensive dataset made the dossier very costly.

Context 7: Sacha inchi and the Novel Food regulation

After I had returned from my first field research in Peru, I remained fascinated by the case of sacha inchi and its commercialization process. Not having been trained in law around international trade before, I did intense research on existing non-tariff barriers and trade regulations in the food sector that restrict the entrance of particular foods into the EU. I talked with food and consumer law associations in Brussels and Berlin, conversed with French entrepreneurs on the challenges and procedures of promoting sacha inchi, went on international fairs with enterprises that sell sacha inchi products and studied various documents that I could find on the internet on that case. Bits and pieces of the accreditation process were gathered from various sources.

Novel foods are defined as foods and food ingredients which were not consumed in the EU to a significant degree before the adoption of the Novel Food Regulation (European Commission 12.2013b). In 1997, with the entry into force of Regulation (EC) Nr. 258/97 on novel food ingredients, the authorization and use of novel foods and food ingredients was harmonized in the EU. Following an impact assessment in 2008 commissioned by the EU, the novel food regulation was updated with the objective to reduce the considerable length for the authorization procedure (3.5 years on average) and increase the efficiency, transparency and application of the safety assessment and authorization system. However, it was only in the end of 2013 that the EU Commission presented a revised legislation on novel foods. One of the major changes consists in replacing the current system of individual authorization by generic authorizations and by a fully centralized application procedure. SMEs are expected to benefit in particular since the proposed measures will reduce administrative burden (removal of current double risk assessment) and the length and cost of the authorization procedure for the food industry (18 months).

The proposal states that „the measures will also facilitate EU market access for traditional foods from third countries by setting up a simplified and more proportionate procedure“ (European Commission 12.2013a). By December 2013, around 150 firms and associations had applied for approbation, with 70 novel foods being authorized for use in the EU. Two examples of products that have successfully passed the Novel Food regulation illustrate the lengthy accreditation process, which lasted from 2 (Baobab fruit powder) up to 6.5 years (Chia dried fruit pulp). After all, access for novel foods to EU markets remains limited. Economically speaking, procedures for market access of a special food that take more than three years are not profitable to petitioners (Gerstberger 2011).

To apply for approbation, companies have to present a safety assessment report to an EU-country-specific authority. Comprehensive documentation of the product and its benefits comes along with high financial costs. The latter point remains the critical challenge for most Peruvian SMEs.

The first dossier was handed in via French institutions in 2005, but an authorization to import was not given at that time, due to insufficient available information according to the European Commission. Various initiatives followed this initial attempt to overcome a political regulation that had rendered almost futile the market-making efforts in Peru: Farmer field schools were intensified so as to comply with GAP and further certifications, PPPs, and commercial agreements were set up between value chain members and agricultural practices and processing procedures were adjusted to fit international norms. The product became certified as organic and thus as a high-value commodity for which it was more difficult to find Peruvian consumers.

Paradoxically, sacha inchi oil had already been imported into the EU. At the “World Edible Oils” competition which takes place every year in Paris, it had been awarded the gold medal in 2004 for its outstanding organoleptic qualities. Not only once, but many times – in 2006, 2007 and 2008 as well (van Helvoirt 2014). It was awarded at other occasions such as ANUGA in Germany 2005 as one of the top innovations in the 2006 “International Trends and Innovations Directory” (GIZ 2013: 32). These early European awards for sacha inchi-derived produces should surprise, given the fact that gourmets in France had not only tasted it – despite the Novel food regulation – but approved it and even considered it the best among all gourmet oils. For sacha inchi oil to be accepted to these fairs, it had obviously passed the necessary tests. Market access was hence provided to some market agents while barriers for other market agents, the very producers of the product, remained.

In 2010, the “Association of Industrial Producers for the Commercialization of Sacha Inchi-derived Products” (APISI) was founded for the purpose of gathering scientific studies with technical information about the product’s features. Video conferences were held between the Peruvian Ministry of Export Promotion, the

Peruvian ambassador to France, as well as representatives of French public and private institutions from academia to consumer protection agencies (APISI 2010). Moreover, workshops were organized in which market analyses were prepared and conducted. A new dossier was handed in by Ireland in 2009 under the equivalence procedure, in which the physical and chemical properties of sacha inchi oil were compared to virgin linseed oil. The EU did not react to the submitted dossier for several years. Another pilot dossier was prepared by APISI, the Peruvian Ministry of Foreign Trade and Tourism and GIZ in 2010 (ibid.). Meanwhile, technical standards had been developed by the Committee of Standardization in Peru.

The standardization process of sacha inchi in Peru generated the conditions under which the non-tariff barriers of the Novel Food law could gradually be overcome (Guzmán 2013: 44-45). Eventually, the legal approval for trade with sacha inchi-derived food products was obtained at the beginning of 2013. In the Peruvian case, the costs for applying and overcoming the Novel Food regulation amounted to more than 300000 USD (APISI 2010). These were split among the Peruvian Ministries of Trade and Tourism and of Export Promotion, APISI and European counterparts which campaigned for the abolition of the import barrier of sacha inchi. Hence, the bureaucratic and juridical procedures for the application were entirely financed by the petitioners. A senior consultant in Peru criticized the administrative system of the EU for not differentiating foods that fell under the scope of the Novel Food regulation:

> "Certainly, it is a protectionist barrier. The problematic issue with this is that the Europeans put genetically modified products in the same basket as natural ancestral products such as sacha inchi and yacón. When we were working for the biotrade program, we did an inventory and information gathering before the European Parliament in order to prove that native products coming from Africa, Asia, and Latin America were different than genetically modified products." (2013_16: 422-424)

Whereas the non-tariff barrier for sacha inchi-derived food products with countries of the EU until 2013 remained valid, imports of sacha inchi to Switzerland already started in the mid-2000s. Despite its small market size, it represented an "open window to the fortified castle" (2013_20: 235). Under similar administrative as well as financial efforts, exports of sacha inchi-derived alimentary products to the US and Japan were meanwhile approved. And while sacha inchi has been formally approved access to markets of the EU under the Novel Food Regulation, one restriction remained: Trading partners needed to present their dossiers on a case-by-case basis. The access is "not only product-specific, but producer-specific" (2013_34: 86). This means that every producer must file his own application and pay for the market license. Novel foods, however, also incite interest from third parties, which claim particular rights to them (Context 8).

Context 8: Who owns novel foods?

Another attempt to hamper access to global markets emanated from a French firm in 2006. It tried to secure a market for itself by applying for a patent for trade with sacha inchi. The firm maintained that it had not only "invented" the application of sacha inchi oil for cosmetical purposes but that it had moreover discovered its nutritive, calming, hydrating, anti-age, and purging effects. French and international NGOs and the National Peruvian Anti-Biopiracy Commission claimed that the patent filed by the firm is the "negation of existing traditional usage of sacha inchi extracts by several Amazonian people for cosmetics, alimentary and therapeutical purposes" (ICRA 2009: 1). The enterprise, under pressure from Peruvian and French institutions as well as broad media attention, withdrew its request in 2009 which it had filed for the use of sacha inchi. How can one interpret this bold move by the French firm?

Once a new product enters global markets, interests from different institutions and firms are voiced that attempt not only to position the product on these markets, but to capture and maximize market share for themselves. While product and process standards are one basic feature of global markets that aim to harmonize production practices and guarantee consumer safety, they do not tackle the issue of property claims and impediments to competition. This is the moment when regulatory institutions and political actors that are in charge of controlling market transactions and dynamics must intervene in order to enable "fair play" among market agents.

Conclusions

The geographical, physical, commercial, and ontological trajectories of sacha inchi are as diverse as the market agencies who are involved in the translation procedure. Markets are not simply mechanisms of allocation, but must be considered as sociotechnical agencements in which value is assigned to all kinds of things in motion. In this chapter, I have argued that the calculability, i.e. the temporarily achieved qualification and standardization of a commodity, is a conditional feature of global markets. Only through the qualification and assignment of economic value are goods enabled to circulate beyond political and spatial frontiers.

These attributions of worth are contested, since market-making is far from being disconnected from the political and juridical realm. The case of sacha inchi shows that global markets are full of power struggles. These are at work especially in so-called frontier regions (Mitchell 2007) in which things and agencies are being (re-)framed through a market-oriented logic. In the course of such translations, various interests are voiced and at times they clash at different levels:

First of all, interests and plans within development practitioner circles must continuously be aligned and re-adjusted. The sacha inchi value chain development program was re-oriented to target not only export markets, but also the national market. This was necessary due to international market barriers, which kept sacha inchi from being traded on European markets. Paradoxically, a European development organization had oriented the value chain towards markets to which – for a long time – it did not have access. Second, these legal barriers were eventually removed after vivid contestation by European NGOs, public agencies and Peruvian firms. In this chapter, markets were shown to represent not only "places where the quality of goods is tested and evaluated" (Eymard-Duvernay et al. 2003: 12, cited in Ouma et al. 2013: 233). In fact, markets are places where *different* estimations and classifications of economic or alternative value co-exist and interfere: Sacha inchi had been awarded the gold medal in international competitions several times in Paris at the World Edible Oil Competition. Europe's most critical gourmet cooks had qualified its (nutritional) value and taste long before the lift of the Novel Food regulation. Yet it took until the beginning of 2013 to be officially accepted for importing into the EU. And third, companies voiced interests and tried to patent the new commodity for its outstanding nutritive value and characteristics, aiming to safeguard exclusive rights on its trade. This attempt was ultimately rejected by European institutions. It shows, however, how increasing attention for goods alters their appeal, economic value, and the ambivalent interests expressed by all kinds of market agents.

The conflict over market boundaries occurs in a highly politicized sphere where battles are fought out concerning the role and scope of responsibility of institutions, public agencies and firms. It is a constant struggle of market agents with diverging interests. Power must not be considered an a priori resource, as Latour (2005b: 64) notes: "Power, like society, is the final result of a process and not a reservoir, a stock, or a capital that will automatically provide an explanation. Power and domination have to be produced, made-up, composed." Its production occurs at different sites and moments between market agents who are constrained by material, social, or technical limitations. The next chapter addresses relations of power which are connected to the disciplining of farmers in Ghana.

8. Framing farmers

> "One broken nut is half the value of the [whole] nut. You cannot lose any whole kernel. That's the special thing about the cashew kernel: Everyone's being crazy about the whole nuts." (2014_21)

This chapter tells another story about marketization. It deals, once again, with nuts – although in a different setting, Ghana, and with a different nut, the cashew nut..[27] Cashew nuts are far from being "novel foods" on global markets: The existence of a global cashew price confirms this. Cashews have recently started to be cultivated for commercial purposes in Ghana (Context 9). For a long time, they exclusively served the purpose of providing shade in Brong-Ahafo, i.e. Western Ghana, with its hot climate (Figure 1). Since the early 2000s, development organizations in cooperation with international retailers started to invest in the cashew value chain. Cashew apples and kernels were consequently harvested for food consumption on export markets. The aim was to reorganize the West African cashew industry to make it globally competitive. The recent interest in the stabilization of the cashew value chain in West Africa is due to at least four factors: First, flourishing export markets promise a steady demand. Consumption is rising in Europe and the US, and remains high in India where cashews are part of the diet. Second, the effects of cashew cultivation for regional economic development are important. Cashew harvesting is labor-intensive and mostly carried out by smallholder farmers (88%) (Cashew Report 2010*: 8), the key target group of development programs. Third, cashew farming contributes to food security because it is harvested in the lean season of all major staples like maize, yam, plantain and millet. And fourth, in the last five years, commodity prices for other nuts such as shea nuts strongly decreased, while the global cash-

[27] In fact, cashew is a seed and not a nut. Yet, as cashews are widely considered and labelled as nuts, I refer to cashews in this book as nuts as well.

ew price soared to an "all-time high" (Fernandes 2014). Consequently, some firms and buyers have started to invest into cashews.

The cashew nut is a special product, as the quote from the Ghanaian entrepreneur reveals: Its economic value decreases remarkably when the kernel is broken, which does not apply for other types of nuts. This is why particular attention must be paid to the processing of the product. In this chapter, attention is drawn nevertheless not primarily to the transformation of cashews, but to the targeted actors of value chain development programs: cashew farmers. Indeed, economic goods cannot be valued and framed without cognitively and materially equipped market agents. Market-making is not simply about mobilizing adherents, but also about fitting them into sociotechnical agencements. The stabilization, coordination, and collaboration in GVCs is enabled only through market agencies that are equipped with calculative agency (Barry, Slater 2002). From a Foucauldian perspective, this involves a (trans-)formational process in which individuals are subjected to a form of self-reference and reference to others through particular forms of rationality and technology of governing (Barry et al. 1996; Bührmann 2005; Peters 2001). In the course of "subjectivation", a calculative self emerges, whose actions, feelings, and modes of thinking are conditioned and driven by values and attitudes as responsibility, accountability, and efficiency. "Social engineering", as Callon aptly puts it, has "the same terms of reference as technical engineering and, like it, it has to be organized formally" (2009: 536). Development programs for value chain development attempt to shape and orient farmers' practices and procedures according to the expectations of international consumers. Creating farmer agencies that qualify goods and perform GAP is a condition of "success" in value chain interventions.

Wenchi, the hometown of cashew

Let me start with an encounter with a cashew farmer in the Brong-Ahafo region who had invited me to sit down in the backyard of his house to listen to his story of cashew cultivation. He starts the conversation by recalling that the place where we sit, Wenchi, "is the hometown of cashew" (2014_22). He had already decided to go into cashew in 1992 having been a taxi driver in the region. 40 acres (= 16 hectares) is the actual land size on which he cultivates the crop. Since it was family owned land, he did not have to pay for it. In 2004, he was awarded the status of "National Cashew Farmer" by MoFA. What had turned someone, who quit school before secondary education, into a successful entrepreneurial cashew farmer?

In 2000, the farmer was a founding member of a then small farmer union, which was supported by international development NGOs. Its purpose was to enhance the bargaining power of cashew farmers to sell their products. The association was lifted to the state of a formal association in 2006. Meanwhile, it represents 3000 farmers, is Fairtrade-certified and covers five districts in the region. It is indeed the biggest and most formalized of its kind in Ghana and has its own constitution, with annual audits and sub-committees that administrate and coordinate activities under an executive council. All members are local farmers and have to pay a monthly membership fee of 1 GHS (= 0,23 USD). The money is reinvested, for instance, in the establishment of warehouses, on the base of a democratic vote. What do the farmers gain by joining the association? The association strives for the improvement of productivity of its members, the alignment with GAP and enhanced quality management. Most importantly it gives a voice to the otherwise underrepresented farmers' voice in committees and decision-making entities at the regional level.

The farmer association has recently emerged and has already achieved an outstanding level of organization. Without the shaping of entrepreneurial market agencies, it would most probably not have risen to become a reference model for farmer organizations at the regional and also the national levels. A study of the conditions under which it came into being directs attention to the transformation of farmers into responsible trading partners.

Context 9: The cashew industry in Ghana

Africa as a whole produces about 45% of global cashew production, while Brazil, India and Vietnam are major producing countries. Ghana has developed into a hub for cashew processing in West Africa. Most firms are located in the Brong-Ahafo Region, where cashew has become one of the main cash crops. Less than 10% of raw cashew production is processed in Africa before being exported to the major processing countries India and Vietnam, from where it is transported to the target markets – the US, the EU and India itself. Until now, a mere 2-5,5% raw cashew nuts (RCN) are processed in Ghana due to logistical bottlenecks in chains, lacking access to credit for farmers and quality issues (Cashew Report 2010*). The remaining more or less 95% are exported as RCN mostly to India (MOFA Nyarko 2013). Nevertheless, Ghana provides a business-friendly environment for international buyers, as it does not raise export taxes on cashew, compared to the Ivory Coast, where high export taxes apply. This has transformed cashew into the second-largest non-traditional export crop in Ghana just behind cocoa.

The government of Ghana together with its development partners, NGOs and the private sector contributed in diverse ways to the development of the cashew value chain. Cashew cultivation in Ghana took off in the 1960s from the Central and Greater Accra Regions and spread into Brong-Ahafo, Northern, Upper East and Upper West Regions. While the industry suffered a setback due to the absence of governmental policies to support the development of an emerging industry, it was identified as one of the major non-traditional commodities for export in 1983 under the Economic Recovery Program (Ministry of Food and Agriculture Ghana 2013).

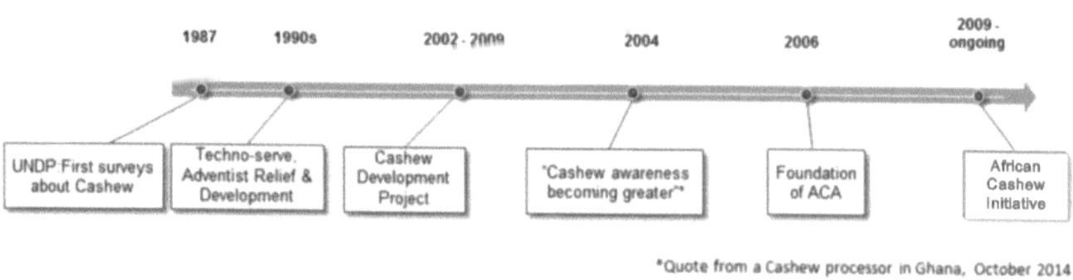

Figure 14: The promotion of cashew production and trade in Ghana
Source: Own draft and own research

Figure 14 shows that the economic use and trade with cashews in Ghana was from the beginning on tied to international players: UNDP supported product research in the 1980s, while NGOs such as Technoserve, promoted cashew as an export product in the early 1990s. The real breakthrough for the cashew value chain came with Ghana's membership in the continent-wide business association African Cashew Alliance (ACA) and the African Cashew Initiative in Ghana.

From scratch: Organizing farmers as market agents

The existence of demand and supply or the availability of goods are not the only conditions for the construction of markets: First of all, market agents must be defined who can engage in trade relations and get their products on the market. How to find trading partners when there is no identifiable "pool" of market agencies?

The making of the cashew value chain in Ghana's central cashew cultivation region reveals insights into how market orders are gradually constructed. Figure 15 illustrates the stages that farmers need to pass through until they reach the "business stage". While the illustration to the left is part of a presentation of a development agency about value chain development in Ghana, the sketch to the right was drawn by a Ghanaian interviewee during an interview to explain the steps that farmers run through in order to participate in formalized relations. The sketch demonstrates the power of images that circulate among practitioners: They are used and diffused in various situations. Such images not only illustrate processes, but actually act upon practitioners: The value chain illustration performs the world it intends to represent.

Figure 15: The formalization of commercial linkages in value chains
Source: Practitioner slide and practitioner draft* (2013)

The identification of agents who engage in trade relations marks the set-up of value chain development. The case in Ghana revealed that is not a trivial process. For the community population size and the number of households, only an outdated census of the Ghanaian government existed, which did not help the international firm TOFFEL* to identify their suppliers. For a duration of two years, TOFFEL field staff passed every farming community and conducted a farmer census of the cashew farmers in the region – around 21000 – with their name, a picture, an assigned number, farmland and household size, and intercropping information. Hence, the registration of farmers constitutes the first step.

Second, once farmers were registered, they had to organize themselves in associations. Single farmers can barely "survive" in value chains: Their supply is limited, and often, they live in remote locations which are difficult to reach for firms. For a better organization of farmers, a warehouse was built in which the farming community can store bags of cashew. It has made the trade in cashew nuts with smallholder farmers appealing for both international and local buyers. A “contact farmer” was elected as spokesperson out of each farming community.

The third step refers to the set-up of contracts and accountable farmer-based organizations (FBOs). This procedure builds on trainings and investments into the “construction” of competent market agencies. Beyond technical knowledge on cultivation methods, farmers were incited to consider “farming as a business”, instead of the previously prevailing “giving culture” in which “farmers wanted everything for free” (2014_19), as a local buyer explains. I will discuss the related behavioral and attitudinal transformations in detail below.

The fourth step refers to a nationwide organization with cooperatives acting at the national level which can claim their rights, such as the association of farmers in Wenchi which still strives towards having a voice in national and international cashew boards and institutions, as they already exist in Benin and Ivory Coast (ACA 2014). It participates in the establishment of a Master Development Plan for the cashew sector in Ghana, which was put together in 2013, but which has not yet been signed.

Disciplinary practices

Certainly, the formalization process around cashew farmers is a process in which farmers do not only group together and find common interests. It requires from them the ability to document and record all practices and activities in a written, often standardized format. Farmers must keep an eye on their costs, time, inputs and outputs, if they want to engage in commercial relationships. New technological devices allow traceability of the production processes. Internet and Communication Technologies (ICT) not only alter the practices, but also the very subjects who use them. Through such interventions into value chains, the conduct of farmers is gradually molded into an entrepreneurial form. Taken to an abstract level, the “making” of market agencies requires manifold investments that lead to “artificially arranged or contrived forms of the free, entrepreneurial, and competitive conduct of economic-rational individuals" (Burchell 1996: 23). In what follows, I engage with the above-mentioned procedures that are part of equipping farmers with the cognitive and calculative skills to become formalized market agencies.

Measurements and record-keeping

Development practitioners, MoFA and buyers offer field schools for cashew farmers in which farmers learn to measure land, qualify products, quantify in- and outputs and record their own activities..[28] In such farmer community training, farmers learn to calculate their production costs. For the preparation of lands and the introduction of new saplings, exact data on land size and soils are required. Yet, how is land being measured when there are no tools at hand? A rope serves as a substitute for alternative measurement devices, whereby a 10 x 10 meter spacing between the cashew trees, resulting in 100 trees per hectare, can be calculated. In order to distinguish the newly planted cashew saplings from other weeds and plants, a stock with a black plastic bag is put besides the small plant (Figure 16). Not only is a proper spacing between the cashew plants ensured, but also the land size of each farmer: Formerly undocumented land is measured and can consequently be registered.

[28] During training on GAP, farmers learn about land preparation, farm sanitation, such as clean storage practices and farm maintenance, and harvest and post-harvest methods, including proper drying methods for storage.

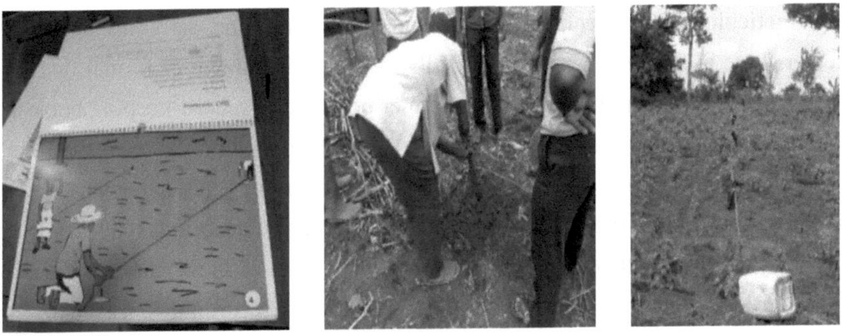

Figure 16: Measuring and qualifying lands for cashew cultivation
Source: Own photos (2014)

Training is provided throughout the year. However, during the season it is difficult to gather the farmers, as they spend their days out in the field. Copies of the illustrations are handed out to farmers for them to carry with them. As illiteracy rates are high among farmers – according to a local buyer, more than 70-80% of farmers in the region are illiterate – illustrations form an important part of the training, as much as demonstrations by the facilitators (Figure 17). Facilitators are advised to explain these to farmers and demonstrate the functioning of GAP. Besides such training, radio programs, text messages, and online programs serve to pass on market information and practical tips to farmers.

Figure 17: Calculation and documentation tools for cashew farmers
Source: Own photos (2014)

The meticulous documentation and calculation of farming activities occupies center stage in trainings and more broadly in the establishment of formal linkages between farmers and buyers. Each farmer possesses a record-keeping book in which all activities are documented (Figure 17). The community keeps "Farmer Pass Books" and records the in- and outputs of farmers. A technical advisor stresses that through these books "we are able to tell the quantities that they [the farmers] produced, that they sold and the incomes that they made out of it" (2013_5). Beyond its use for facilitators and buyers, recording tools empower farmers since "initially, farmers were selling at any price to get money out of it, but when we introduced the record-keeping book, they realized that they had to write something down and see if they really made profits or not" (ibid.). Particular mechanisms have been installed through which farmers are incited to record their activities. For instance, in order to be awarded the title "National Farmer" on "National Farmer's Day" by MoFA, farmers have to disclose all required information, as a MoFA advisor explains: "If you don't have a record keeping book, there is no way that you can ever become the best farmer" (2013_5). Record-keeping books play an important role in equipping farmers with the calculative devices to participate as full-fledged market agencies in value chains. Another such tool is the weighing scale. At first sight, there is nothing special about a scale that is used for measuring products and associating prices to these. Yet, the scale is entangled in a process which has previously occurred behind closed doors. The scale was hitherto subject to cheating by middlemen who manipulated scales in order to pay lower prices to farmers. Farmers had to supply their products to middlemen, as they were the only persons that farmers were in contact with. Since the moment that TOFFEL provided a scale to the community, farmers observe the weighing process and can assess the measurements themselves.

The introduction of land measurement practices, record-keeping books and weighing scales has changed farming practices. It has empowered farmers to participate more equally in commercial relations as such devices provide transparency about the activities along the chain.

Accountability through contracts

At the core of market-making processes are translation procedures in the course of which farmers become accountable market agencies. Buyers have set up various mechanisms and infrastructures that render farmers responsible for their actions, among which contract agreements are the most common.

These can only become effective when a set of valuations are put into place that facilitate the qualification of the product (cashew) and its origin. Buyers have organized training in which they explain to farmers the role of accounting and of compliance with previously agreed terms and conditions. This involves focusing on "how to read contracts [in order to] make sure the farmer understands" (2014_19) every single point in the contract. This is similar to what Callon explains at the example of the making of research agreements between a researcher and a commercial partner: "[T]he aim of the contract is to frame the interaction in as unambiguous a way as possible and/or formulate an agreement on any procedures which may have to be implemented" (Callon 1998a: 256). The measurement of the cashew kernel forms part of the contracts. Making sure that the cashew kernel is well dried is a condition for buyers to engage in trade, because the degree of moisture in the cashew kernel conditions the final product quality. A measurement system helps to calculate the defectives. A rule of thumb estimate foresees a three-day sun-drying process to ensure good quality. Buyers conduct quality tests on the basis of the kernel outturn ratio (KOR): They cut the texture of the cashew kernel, calculate the ratio of the weight of whole kernels in relation to the total weight of kernels recovered after shelling, and subsequently decide whether they buy products or leave them. Only a moisture degree of up to 8% is acceptable. If this moisture level is exceeded, the products are sent back to the farming community. Farmers are accountable to comply with these quality requirements that have been set up by international buyers, processors and institutions such as the ACA.

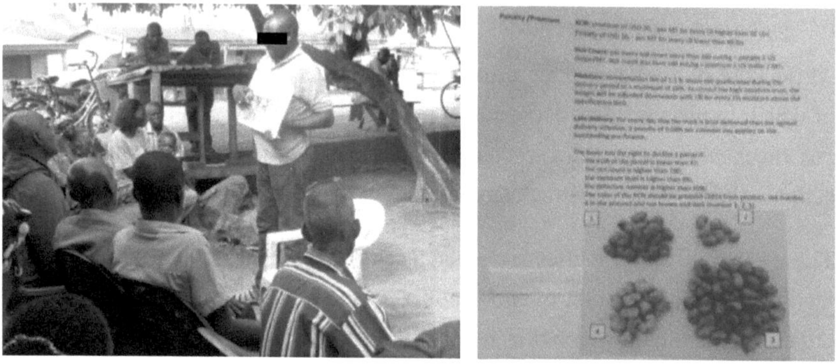

Figure 18: Training in quality management and kernel selection
Source: Own photos (2014)

Contracts need to be clarified and discussed in the presence of farmers, yet they still take on a life of their own as they are circulated and interpreted by all contract participants (Figure 18). A buyer admits potential challenges since "in Europe, a contract is a contract. In Ghana, the contract is just a piece of paper" (2014_19). What he refers to is side-selling: Farmers do not necessarily act according to contracts which they previously signed. In times of high demand, as happened in 2014, farmers may neglect contracts and sell their products to unknown buyers who offer higher prices.

Firms have set up means to prevent such behaviors. Loyalty is rewarded. In group training, farmers who do not live up to contractual agreements are exposed by the facilitators. Certainly, it is not only farmers who do not comply with contracts: the same occurs in the case of buyers who cheat farmers by paying them lower prices than appropriate, or by workers in cashew factories who do not show up or live up to contractual agreements. A signed agreement turns into a long-term commitment: This must be gradually internalized and put into practice.

Traceability via living laboratories

Various investments made by buyers and development organizations into financial, technological, and institutional infrastructures enable farmers to participate as autonomous market agents in trade relations. As Callon and Caliskan aptly argue, "the more an agency is capable of complicating its own calculation by linking it to a large number of other prices (thus transformed temporarily and locally into prosthetic prices), the higher its capacity to determine the terms of the exchange" (Callon, Çalışkan 2007: 35). Recently, ICT have developed into prosthetic devices: They guarantee transparency and traceability along value chains by providing current market information to all value chain members – independent of member's spatial (im)mobility or financial equipment.

Recently, the international software firm Cashcom* has developed a mobile application for cashew farmers in partnership with the donors of the African Cashew Initiative. The software allows traceability among value chain members. Warehouse staff on the ground can make use of a geographical information system (GIS) that displays farmer contact data, farm size and location, tree inventory and information about prices, and makes it easier to forecast and optimize the collection of the harvested cashew nuts. Farmers receive a receipt at the end of the cashew season with an overview of how many sacks of cashew nuts they have sold and at what price. It enables them to keep records, and simultaneously fosters trust by providing traceability between farmers, processors and buyers. Everybody is guaranteed to be paid the right price.

Along with the introduction of the application, a "living laboratory" has been installed in Ghana. It is a literal laboratory in the Latourian sense for the testing of market technologies. In the piloting phase, 300 farmers and 5 purchasing stations have been included in the experiment, with more than 100 tons of RCN being traded via the mobile application system. The living lab methodology enables also mobile money transactions. As its name indicates, it is not developed behind closed doors in academic laboratories where scientists run through all the potential errors before the technology is put into the field. Instead, it is directly tested on the ground. Feedback can be injected by users at every stage of the implementation. The program research advisor claims that "it is not enough to run through a program from A to Z in a laboratory. Expectations were often miscommunicated and false prioritizations were undertaken, but the prioritization itself is subject to change" (2014_7). End-user workshops serve to validate and control results for cashew sales and logistics, design and functionality of the software application and raise stakeholder awareness of the potential of ICT while the experiment is already put into place.

Through the tracking system of Cashcom, new forms of calculative agency emerge: Farmers gain insights into the entire production process and price dynamics at all times. This improves their negotiation power and position in value chains. And through the instauration of the living lab methodology, they can determine the direction of the market experiment, as every user can give feedback. Farmers can act as experts in that they (can) link knowledge to political power in distinctive forms.

Disciplining has its limits

Value chain interventions have disciplinary effects upon market agencies. Technologies, contracts and all kinds of new reporting practices modify the linkages between market agents, and the agencies themselves. Nevertheless, farmers are not passive subjects who are infiltrated by a market rationale. First, not everything can be framed and disciplined (Callon 1998b: 26). And second, framing endeavors involve both accommodation and resistance of calculative subjects, technologies and the collective agency that is produced when they are entangled with one another (Pickering 2010). Development organizations attempt to shape farmer's behavior: They will "first think as entrepreneurs, then learn as entrepreneurs and finally perform as entrepreneurs" (World Bank Blog 2015). Yet what happens if they do not or cannot live up to such requirements? A committee in which all value chain actors are represented, sanctions them:

> "[Y]ou leave that to the district value chain committee. It is more or less the inter-professional body. All actors have their presentation day, they screen members: Whether you are sociable, or whether you disturb [the] business." (2013_7: 29)

The committee decides over the funds and loans that farmers can apply for at banks. It is thus a powerful institution that surveils farmer's access to credit. But it need not go as far as leading to being formally excluded from the district value chain committee. There are various levels of exclusion for not fulfilling the norms and standards that govern markets. On the one hand, farmers do not necessarily underperform on purpose. Many farmers are illiterate and struggle with adopting new documenting practices. They may have signed documents without grasping their content and outreach. Still others simply cannot participate in this new market logic that holds sway in Ghana: They do not own the lands on which they farm, due to the system of traditional chieftaincies which persists in Ghana, in particular in the Ghanaian North. Property titles, however, are a sign of empowerment and enable farmers to upgrade their position in GVCs (Soto 2003).

Open and unregulated markets for cashew nuts in Ghana can put value chain linkages at risk, without one singular source of agency to which the turmoil can be attributed. In the cashew season 2013-2014, "a lot of chaos" made value chain members "do whatever they have to survive" (2014_21), as a local entrepreneur claimed. The market for cashews overheated due to persistent droughts in nearly all major cultivation regions, mostly in India, but also in West Africa. The Ghanaian cashew industry faced "high demand, high prices, short supply" (2014_21) of RCN according to a local processor. A trade regulation of Ivory Coast caused short supply of RCN in Ghana: In the end of 2013, the Ivorian government passed a law which prohibits trade in RCN with Ghana via road, while it permits trade through the port. For many years, cashew trade between both countries had been flourishing. The Ghanaian cashew industry relied on RCN imports from Ivory Coast, Togo and Burkina Faso. Ghana's economy depends on RCN imports as it has many processing plants, yet cashew production is not high enough to use the facilities to the full (cf. Essel 2014). In this situation, "the Indians", as Asian buyers are called in common parlance by Ghanaian farmers and processors, were in such shortage of supply that they themselves visited cashew farming communities during the season. They passed each farmer's house and offered high prices as well as the direct collection and transport of RCN. This affected the relations and previously convened agreements between cashew associations and local processors. Moreover, farmers were not complying with the process of properly drying the cashews because of the short supply and strong demand. According to an entrepreneur, "farmers don't even dry correctly. Because of the high demand of the Indians, they do not do it the proper way. Much side-selling is going on. This is why high prices distort the market" (2014_19). The cashew farmer, whose story was related at the beginning of this chapter, maintained that due to worsening relations with local processors "the chain is broken" (2014_22). Processors blame "the Indians" for distorting prices and sidelining quality enhancement practices and the farmers for selling to international buyers. Farmers blame local processors for paying low prices that force them into such negotiations. What does this situation demonstrate? Market agencies may be equipped with all the necessary calculative devices and competencies, yet attempts at framing remain subject to change and external dynamics. After all, farmers and all market agencies act in dynamic spheres where diverging interests are expressed that clash from time to time.

Conclusions

Attempts to frame both commodities as economic goods and farmers as entrepreneurial agents are at the core of value chain development programs. Such programs intend to endow market agents with the cognitive and practical competencies that allow them to qualify and valuate things. In this chapter, the case of the cashew value chain in Ghana served to illustrate the various attempts and procedures to frame farmers as accountable, responsible and disciplined market agents. It revealed at the same time that disciplinary attempts necessarily remain experimental: Farmers are not passive agents, but may "resist" market orders at any time: Despite an increasingly sophisticated apparatus of contracts, reporting systems and instruments, attempts to transform agents remain ongoing trial-and-error processes. These market experiments must be seen in the context of what I call the broader *experimental interventionalism* that currently floods the Global South. While value chain development programs aim at improving the overall performance of value chains and propose various tools to reach these goals, such endeavors are only temporary, and they require intense efforts of buyers, farmers and development practitioners: Struggles occur along the way and behind closed doors that do not find their way into program assessments and evaluations.

Through a triangulation of perspectives, I attempted to provide a broader understanding of the construction, circulation and framing of markets. A marketization perspective served to highlight the procedures at work that allow farmers to become entrepreneurs. Why did I choose such a broad conceptual mixture? First of all, governmentality studies taken alone tend to sideline the practical struggles as well as the material devices that work in and on markets. In contrast, Callon's performativity approach assigns material arrangements and technologies a predominant role in markets. However, it cannot account for anything that lies outside of the economic sphere, because it opposes the "embeddedness argument" (Dumez, Jeunemaitre 2010b: 27; Muellerleile 2013; Mukhopadhyay 2014). This means that it rejects the idea of social structures or institutional frameworks in which markets gain momentum. Its strength lies in highlighting the conditions, infrastructures and processes that enable market models to become powerful. Pickering's argument provides a valuable addition to this conceptual umbrella: He provides a framework that allows one to frame market-making as ongoing practical accomplishments and "dances of agency" (Pickering 2010) that stabilize, but also resist attempts at framing. The making of (market) agencies is not only entangled in materials, but enacted through practices.

9. CONCLUSION: MARKETS GOING NUTS?

Certainly, it is legitimate to ask what practical insights and recommendations for action research into the making of GVCs provides. Inspired by Yarrow's ethnography on development politics in Ghana, I reframe a provocative question he poses in the beginning of his book (Yarrow 2011: Preface x) and apply it to my research project: Why (only) philosophize about marketization when urgent problems, such as persistent poverty, require concrete action? My answer to this question is that *describing* and *enacting* are two related spheres. This claim is highly consequential: Only through detailed descriptions *of* and investigations *into* the emergence of market orders and rationales can a broader understanding of ongoing marketization be achieved. Researching and discussing the "how" of market-making allows it to be subsequently acted upon. Theory, accordingly, must be considered as a form of action.

The insights gained through the investigations in Ghana, Peru, and along the paths of GVCs have inspired me to draw up the research program of *associational politics of markets*. Based upon eight constitutive prisms, I have carefully analyzed and explicated how developmental markets take shape and become effective in society at large. My research problematized three conditions: first of all, the interdependency between market models and "real" markets. Second, the outreach of circulating policies and concepts inscribed into all kinds of devices, infrastructures, and institutional arrangements. And, third, the practices that enable the transformation of things and people into market agencies.

The research has led me to different sites of market-making, including development organization headquarters, international food fairs, production, and processing factories, farming communities, conference venues, and offices of public officials in Lima and Accra. First-hand observations were made of centers of calculation, i.e. the sites and practitioner networks from where value chain models are being conceived and mobilized. Markets were read and interpreted from a "mobilities" perspective: The research was conducted "on the move" and along policy pipelines and equally drew attention to the procedures and emerging structures rather than assume the existence of stable market entities.

In what follows, I lay out the key findings and assessments developed in the course of investigations. In the beginning of this thesis, I claimed that markets, development, politics, and the associations between them constitute the core research concern. These notions provide the structure for this conclusion as well: First of all, a concluding definition of what I understand by markets will be provided. Second, I demonstrate how sociotechnical associations around value chains constitute collective agency. Third, I discuss the developmental effects of market-oriented interventions in Ghana and Peru. Fourth, I tackle the question whether such interventions bring about the performativity of the GVC framework. Finally, I discuss why the framework has become a prevalent model for economic development throughout the Global South and beyond. Brought together, these interrelated claims and observations shed light on markets – how they emerge, stabilize, and how they are subjected to resistances and drawbacks. Hence these overarching notions provide the grounds for the study of traveling rationalities which make marketization a real and potent force.

Markets: From facts to artifacts

> "In our efforts to make sense of current political-economic events, we have moved from analyses of globalization to analyses of neoliberalism, but our labels continue to obscure the details and complexity of the processes involved." (Larner 2003: 509)

Markets, in the form of GVCs, involve the formation of complex technological zones, which forge linkages between producers, consumers, buyers, regulatory bodies, and standard-setting agencies. In such zones, one rationale prevails: the competitiveness rationale. Just as much as geographer Wendy Larner issues a warning not to settle for the simple adoption of terms and concepts without questioning their meaning and modes of application, one should not join in simplistic rejections that reify these either. Both ways lead to an essentialization of the matters of concern that need to be investigated. Consequently, I refrained from approaching the rise of market-oriented development policies as a problem in need of an answer. My research started from a different angle and demonstrated that markets are more *arti*-fact than fact: The etymological origin of the Latin verb "facere" (to do, to make) helps to clarify what is at stake: Markets are not simply there, but are carefully designed "by experiment, by intellectual work, and by observation that is normally technologically mediated and typically is disciplined and goal-oriented rather than haphazard" (MacKenzie 2009: 8-9). The Latin word "ars" is translated as both art and science. Markets, hence, are no incidental effects, but they are consciously constructed like a piece of art.

Development practitioners aim to enhance the coordination of activities between backward and forward linkages in value chains and to adjust practices so as to comply with international standards, norms, and regulations. While pro-poor oriented development is a pervasive claim in market-oriented interventions, all practical efforts go into the creation of competitive infrastructures and market environments. This is also reflected in internal shifts in the organization of the development community (Chapter 4): While technical advisors and program managers in international development agencies were until the 1990s mostly trained as agricultural engineers, they have been replaced by agronomists. Thereby, economic rationales extend into such organizations. Development organizations meanwhile have their own permanent offices integrated into national ministries and thus act no longer from the outside and through temporary programs alone. They have become part of the national political and advisory system. Thus, they broadly inscribe market-oriented agendas like the value chain approach into cross-cutting agendas, policies, and practices. Based on the observations and insights from the field, markets are an empowering political rationale, agencements that materialize in models and all kinds of techniques and instruments, and third, they represent the institution that seems to rule societal engineering (Carrier 1997: 22-37, cited in Boeckler, Berndt 2012: 199). Their construction requires ongoing human, technical, and material investments.

From associations to collective agency

Much associational work goes into the construction of markets, as the increasingly sophisticated infrastructures around value chain development illustrate. Linking up market agencies must not only be understood metaphorically, but also literally, as it is promoted in workshops that address value chain development. Reconstructing the associational dynamics of markets requires researchers to explore the social lives of globalizing policy models, traveling market agencies, and economic goods. Such an endeavor embraces a flexible array of methods including documentary analysis, interviews, formal and informal conversations, distant observation, and close participation at different sites and conjunctures, which can fruitfully be combined – i.e. associated – with one another.

International development consultants are revealed to be central nodes in the network that emerges around market-oriented development. These experts convey mobile knowledges and move between public and private sector as well as international, national, and local institutions. In fact, consultants both translate policy goals into practical interests, but also practical interests back into policy goals (Mosse 2005: 8). Consultants convey their messages in the form of imagery, "simple" terms, and illustrative learning material to farmers; they use "scientific" language in manuals, flyers, and evaluation reports to procure cooperative forms of consensus by donor agencies and policymakers; and they conduct economic market analyses and put together technical market information for entrepreneurs. This is what Tania Li (2007) calls the "rendering technical" of political strategies: By translating interests into different institutional languages, they enroll support of various actors and tie them up in their programs and agendas. Thereby, they create the conditions in which common strategies for development become effective: Topics of concern are framed within political agendas – rural development, biotrade, sustainable economic growth, and gender equality – and thereby rendered legitimate and are widely accepted.

Inscription devices play a crucial role as a (re)source of agency: Manuals become meaningful when they are mobilized by consultants in workshops or reunions (Chapter 4). They travel physically as documents and digital files, as well as in embodied forms, practices, and knowledges with consultants. Consequently, manuals become a roadmap for action for various actors and institutions, as a development consultant in Peru maintains:

> "So how do you implement the value chain model in practice? This is the working plan for the enhancement of a value chain. It translates into a roadmap for the government official or for any actor who wants to start assessing and supporting a chain, a board of chain participants, to start the work (...) I as a technical advisor, I go to the board meetings, where the value chain participants discuss. And I am there, amongst them, I am the advisor. Always with the road map in my hand. I walked in those meetings, always with the printed road map, and asked: What is missing here? And I told them: 'You need this road map!' (pointing to the imprint)." (2013_21: 94)

Consultants make wide use of the manual as it plants the steps for implementation. If manuals are considered technical devices, then it can be concluded that technoscience (Pickering, Guzik 2008: 297) stimulates sociotechnical interdependencies to proliferate. It is through such devices that traveling knowledges, models, experiences, ideas, evaluation reports, and policy papers take shape and turn into Latourian immutable mobiles. Once diverse human and non-human elements are associated with one another, they become powerful sources of action and agency. Put differently, market agencies gain significance only in relation to one another.

Development: From "jungle warfare" to market-oriented agriculture?

Due to shifts in current development policies, scholars have come to question whether the mobilization and proliferation of value chain development is either a "tool for development or a neoliberal device" (Fernandez 2014). Being aware of the risk of inflating the value chain framework as an abstract imaginary by arguing in favor or against it, it is nevertheless necessary to reflect upon its practical and performative effects on economic development and society: Indeed, (pro-poor) development is not just a conceptual apparatus but also an institutional one which has real effects in social life through reports, policies, programs, and projects (Ferguson 1990: 73-74): The development consultant in Ghana cited at the very beginning of this book referred to it as the transformation of the archaic agricultural sector in Ghana ("jungle warfare") into a competitive market-driven field (2013_7: 33-35).

A snapshot into a rural sacha inchi farming community in the Peruvian Amazon makes possible a micro level assessment of the effects of human, technical, and financial investments into the sacha inchi value chain (Chapter 8). The observation of the houses allows a first evaluation. The farmer chairman's house is made of brick and has recently been renovated from the in- and the outside. Beforehand, it was built out of adobe, the only affordable fabric for many farmers in the region. Within a year, the prices for sacha inchi have risen due to completed organic certification and rising demand. Moreover, the productivity of the community has grown due to the installing of a shelling machine in the chairman's backyard that separates kernels from shells. From the perspective of entrepreneurs, two achievements are particularly valued. On the one hand, the setting up of contractual agreements and a "safe haven price" have enhanced trust and improved relations with farming communities. On the other hand, the creation of the mesa técnica of sacha inchi has increased the capacity to act upon and influence policy-makers, public entities, standard-setting bodies, and academic institutions in terms of collaboration in the transformation process. Stabilized infrastructures for production and trade, higher prices, market-oriented production, and enhanced cooperation between market agents were the results of interventions into the sacha inchi value chain. Meanwhile, sacha inchi is exported not only to the US, Canada, Japan, and Australia, but also to the EU, where previous trade restrictions and import bans have been leveraged through collective efforts. Hence, for the duration of the program, the results were encouraging.

The experience of the Ghanaian cashew enhancement program reveals that a business-driven supply chain management approach has been put into practice which aims at shaping entrepreneurial farmers (Chapter 8). In order to reach global competitiveness, farmers were first identified, grouped together in organizations, linked to buyers and research centers in matching funds and PPPs. The focus of training on value chain development is on quality management, enhanced research on new saplings, productivity increase, technological development, and product diversification of cashew nuts. This case differs from the Peruvian case, since infrastructures for cultivation and product transformation did not have to be established from scratch. Global demand for the product already exists. Yet this crop was used for a different purpose than for commercialization until recently: The huge old cashew trees provided shade in otherwise shadeless areas with a tropical climate. Progress through cashew value chain development programs can be measured not by the fabric or size of the farmer houses but, for instance, by the existence of community warehouses. These are usually equipped with a weighing scale, which enables farmers to surveil the measuring process: Thereby, farmers are empowered with regard to intermediary buyers, who often cheated while measuring the supplied bags of cashew. Through the installing of central community warehouses, middlemen lose their privileged access to farmers. In matching partnerships, international and a few national buyers and processors engage directly with farming communities. They invest in infrastructures such as warehouses, registration, and the training of farming communities. In the midterm, the number of value chain intermediaries decreases, which benefits farmers.

Development practitioners have invested in sophisticated evaluation apparatuses, yet the long-term effects on various groups, practices, levels, and institutions are difficult to estimate. Indeed, the purpose of this book is not to evaluate the effectiveness and outreach of such interventions, but the capture of perspectives of various chain actors and the study of the "post-program state" reveals important insights. The sacha inchi value chain was left destabilized in Peru after the program end: Former value chain promoters such as the regional government lost their fervent interest in promoting this value chain. Although it does not necessarily mean the death of the value chain, because infrastructures have already been set up, it reveals that (development) politics is not only about contextualized solutions, but strategic interests. To what degree can socioeconomic development be traced back to value chain programs? Is there a place for development in discursively pro-poor yet factually profit-oriented business strategies? How should development models, programs, and agendas be shaped as to make them sustainable? Answers will be contested and can only be elaborated through contextualized analyses. After all, the value chain approach does not provide a universal panacea for development, but is a tool that can further development, depending on its integration into institutional infastructures and the ideational topics associated with it.

From a model of the market to markets of a model

> "The achievements of the value chain concept are broad. More than being simply a reality, the concept can be considered as an academic perspective that helps to interpret it, as well as a methodological instrument for the analysis and organization of the streams of relations and activities that a product passes through until it reaches a consumer." (IICA 2006a: 21)

Value chains are at once an analytical model of the market and a methodology for constructing (inclusive) markets. The circulation and rise of the GVC framework has revealed itself as an exemplary case for how an economic model becomes a powerful source of action. Through its incorporation into policies, laws, workshops, and university courses, the GVC approach "created" the discursive and material conditions that it originally (only) purported to describe. That confirms what social studies of finance and marketization have long argued: Economics does more than simply describe an external reality that is not affected by economics. Nevertheless, these scholars tend to focus on the sphere of economic agents and calculative devices alone. This conceptual argument must be extended, however, to a broader claim about the power of economic models to reach out into society. By studying markets exclusively through the lens of (economic) calculation, algorithms, and calculative devices, Callon misses the point that market-making is an inherently political-institutional process (Callon 2007b). Callon's performativity thesis cannot help to answer the reasons for the rise of value chain thinking, but it helps to investigate how the model is inscribed at all levels of society. I have outlined in Chapters 4-8 that market-making involves, modifies, and generates (political) power and subjectivity over time (Mukhopadhyay 2014: 204). The role of "[t]he wider institutional parameters of economization (e.g. property rights) which possibilize the emergence of calculative agencies by opening up the space of calculability" (ibid.: 184) must be included in the investigation: The state-induced, or at least state-supported, transition to market-oriented economic development and agricultural growth based on the GVC concept generates a societal shift which cannot be described alone by explaining how an economic actor gains autonomy from the wider social context. Hence, the performativity of market models to bring about the phenomena that they describe must be understood not in economic terms and agency alone. Public policy plays a key role in rendering value chain development effective.

After all, has the value chain approach become performative? Yes, as I have argued based on such a broader understanding of performativity. Nevertheless, as I have illustrated as well, is resistance to market-oriented reforms and institutional transitions not unusual. In the case of the Ghanaian Ministry of Agriculture, resistance manifested itself in the rejection of the shift from a production- to a market-oriented approach to agricultural development. Only over time, acceptance of the new paradigm became significant within the Ministry of Food and Agriculture (Chapter 6).

Despite its astonishing uptake by policy actors, the GVC approach has not trickled down to all target groups. When asked about the meaning of value chain development, farmers both in Ghana and Peru did not understand, but simply replied by asking what a value chain is. Technical consultants do not necessarily draw distinctions between the development-oriented GVC approach and business-driven approaches towards agricultural development (Chapter 4). If there is no understanding or awareness of the matter at stake as such – value chains for development – then it would be exaggerated to speak of a full-fledged performativity of the GVC approach known as "Barnesian performativity" (MacKenzie 2006: 15-25). Attention should not focus on the remaining gaps between theory and reality and unrealized actions for value chain development that could suggest a failure of theoretical economics and models to "perform" their worlds. Instead, the regard should turn towards the force of global capitalism to continuously inscribe itself into economic systems: Despite recent calls for a reform of the global market system, international organizations and development institutions keep in place an economic system that promotes market-oriented development as a path to poverty reduction. UNCTAD has acknowledged in its Trade and Development Report 2014 that markets need regulations and institutions to make them free and accessible for all, which does not mean departing from the longstanding market rationality. Instead, it implies a steering towards institutional approaches like the value chain approach, which combine market development with the state support and institutional arrangements, and helps to reinforce the market rationale (see next section), instead of proposing a departure from it.

Yet, why has the value chain approach been so successfully circulated after all? What made it become *the* blueprint for economic development in several countries of the Global South? Global policy regimes are both flexible and resilient when they travel in various forms and embodied knowledges which make them easily adaptable elsewhere. A consultant framed the reasons for success of the GVC approach in Ghana as follows:

> "It wasn't so much some master minders, it was a kind of combination of popular economic thinking which made it visible along with better marketing from people who believed in it at the post-levels" (2010_7: 88).

Politics: From flexible frameworks to performative politics

Global models of the market become effective only when they allow spaces for interpretation and flexible adaptation. The framing and promotion of value chain thinking as a "global best practice" (Peck, Theodore 2015: 224) both by critical development studies and orthodox Washington-Consensus-oriented policy-makers indicate the ease with which some policy models, despite diverging motivations and interests, are appropriated by organizations. In this case, a critical analytical model was translated into a market-making policy and proved to be open to reinvention not least by some of the very forces it was designed to counteract. I have reconstructed the mobilization process of the GVC regime and proposed an analytical framework for the study of policy mobilities (Chapter 4). The concept was first disembedded from its original "setting" in critical sociology, then enwrapped in an inspiring invention narrative as a policy and development tool that tackles both pro-poor development and business-oriented efficiency and productivity management. This founding narrative has been raised to mythical status in academic and practitioners circles and international institutions while being equipped with a comprehensive toolbox of material (and replicable) practices, from manuals, learning formats, refined rules, institutions that transcend local contexts to deliver similar results in various places (Chapters 5 and 6).

Although everybody seems to be talking (about) value chains (see quote at the very beginning of the book), the GVC framework has not been translated into a universally homogeneous set of guidelines for action. Under the vague conceptual umbrella of value chain development, interpretations and adaptations of the model take on a life of its own once they touch ground in new settings. As such, the value chain framework became effective in Peru when it was linked to the UNCTAD-funded BioTrade initiative for the sustainable use and management of natural resources. The promotion of the sacha inchi is related to a concern for biodiversity and thereby encounters wide acceptance and legitimization among policy-makers and the wider public. In Ghana, the framework has evolved into an increasingly vague notion that is linked to agricultural development at large.

Sociocultural factors play a prevalent role herein, such as historically entrenched rights over lands, gender issues around agriculture and the role of trust in engaging in commercial relations. It becomes clear that at the moment of inscription, the approach is already devoid of any radical agenda to transform core-periphery relations from below or profoundly alter systems of resource distribution or allocation mechanisms, despite the fact that it was originally intended to promote pro-poor oriented approaches to development. They are translated into "technical" language, based on compromises, and are subject to pragmatic amendments.

My research on the circulating GVC framework has outlined in detail that it has, and how it has, become an immutable mobile. It is a model that is simultaneously "mobile but also immutable, presentable, readable and combinable with one another" (Latour 1986b: 6). What makes it so powerful is that it enables coalition building around one idea: market-oriented development. As such, the GVC approach, or some version of it, has been rolled out in countless aid programs around the world. The framework is caught in between a globally traveling fix and its flexible variants that gain momentum on the ground.

Coming back to the initial question at the head of this conclusion, in which I emphasized the usefulness of reflecting on the means and modes of marketization, I conclude this thesis with a discussion of the political dimension and effects of this research. Politics must be understood here in the ontological sense. Even the selection of the GVC framework as research topic is political. Through our case study selection, we as researchers draw attention to, and also delimit, who and what is part of market networks, who is involved in the mobilization of policies and who incorporates them into political discourses, institutional settings and power structures.

I have analyzed the processes that lie behind and are caused by the proliferation of value chain models. These include ontological reconfigurations and attributions of value and economic worth. Commoditization processes constitute the heart of markets: Things and market agents are qualified, measured, detached, standardized, valuated, and linked to powerful discourses and policy agendas. Both the framing and commercialization of sacha inchi as an economic good and the reconfiguration of farmers into accountable market agencies illustrate processes in which the social and natural worlds emerge. If, at the macro level, "the great divide between economics and politics, economy and society is (…) the outcome of a long historical project of separation" (Cochoy et al. 2010: 141), the separation of economic goods and agents from their contexts is its equivalent in micro scale processes of market-making. The market infrastructures for the sacha inchi value chain were co-constructed and built up from scratch by a broad array of economists "in the wild". Together, they create new sociotechnical entanglements, hence, new agencies. The plant that was once considered as a weed in the backyard of smallholder farmers in the Peruvian Amazon region is meanwhile valued as a protein-rich, vegan and organic "superfood" that figures as the latest innovation and trend oin international food fairs.

Such transformations, and thus marketization more broadly, have political effects. Translation – the process whereby products and agents are ontologically re-arranged and configured as market agencies – involves assembling seemingly different entities: For instance, sacha inchi value chain development in Peru links rural economic development in the Peruvian Amazon and biotrade to global specialty markets for novel foods, and then demonstrates that they are able to work together, that they have similar interests, and may become allies (Barnes 2002: 491). Opening the "black box" of markets contributes to enriching both the academic study of markets as well as public discussion in relation to them. It is a matter of destabilizing unquestioned economic orders and imaginaries of the world, whereby other worlds can become possible (Gibson-Graham 2008). The performative character of our own research practices must be problematized as well: We study and discuss specific concerns whereby we make things visible that may have been framed differently, or completely sidelined, by other researchers. We need to acknowledge and critically question our own analyses and practices, as they are part of bringing a new reality – here, the power of market models to create their own worlds – effectively into being. Every research agenda is hence political, yet not in narrow ideological terms.

After all, why is this chapter labeled "Markets going nuts"? It is obviously related to my empirical research which is based on the transformation of two types of nuts into economic goods – sacha inchi in Peru and cashews in Ghana. Strictly speaking, both are known as nuts, although neither is a nut: They are seeds. This detail does certainly not affect the broader concern of the research program of *associational politics of markets*. It goes beyond an analysis of the sites, manufacturing processes, and the economic value that is ascribed to commodities traded in GVCs. By focusing on how commodities and value more broadly emerge, materialize, institutionalize, and circulate, this book has not only explicated, but it has rendered explicit the nuts and bolts of marketization rather than simply assuming that markets are a given.

APPENDIX

List of interviews, conversations and e-mail exchange

Interview Number	Date (and place)	Interviewee	Affiliation	Format	Language
2009_1*	September 2009 Accra	Consultant, program manager	Development organization	Interview	English
2009_2*	December 2009 The Hague	Consultant, program manager	NGO	Interview	English
2010_1*	September 2010 Tamale	Consultant, zonal agricultural manager	Development organization	Interview	English
2010_2*	September 2010 Tamale	Consultant, program manager	Development organization	Interview	English
2010_3*	September 2010 Tamale	Government employ-ee	MoFA	Interview	English
2010_4*	September 2010 Accra	Government employ-ee, program manager	MoFA	Interview	English
2010_5*	September 2010 Accra	Consultant, Compo-nent manager for value chain develop-ment	Development organization	Interview	English
2010_6*	September 2010 Accra	Consultant Chief of Party	NGO	Interview	English
2010_7*	October 2010 Tamale	Consultant Senior technical specialist	NGO	Interview	English
2011_1*	September 2011 Tamale	Consultant Agricultural econo-mist	NGO	Interview	English
2011_2*	September 2011 Tamale	Consultant Economist	NGO	Interview	English
2011_3*	September 2011 Tamale	Consultant Project Officer Rural Development	NGO	Interview	English
2011_4*	September 2011 Kumasi	Lecturer Professor	University	Interview	English

Interview Number	Date (and place)	Interviewee	Affiliation	Format	Language
2011_5*	September 2011 Accra	Consultant Senior Advisor	Development organization	Interview	English
2013_1	February 2013 Germany	Consultant Project Manager	Development organization	Interview	German
2013_2	February 2013 Tamale	University Lecturer Consultant	University	Interview	English
2013_3	February 2013	Consultant Regional coordinator	Development organization	Interview	English
2013_4	February 2013 Tamale	Consultant Regional coordinator	NGO	Interview	English
2013_5	February 2013 Tamale	Consultant	Development organization	Interview	English
2013_6	February 2013 Tamale	Consultant Farmers	Development organization and farmer association	Interview	English, Twi
2013_7	February 2013 Tamale	Government employ-ee	MoFA	Interview	English
2013_8	February 2013 Kumasi	University Professor	University	Interview	English
2013_9	March 2013 Accra	University Professor	University	Interview	English
2013_10	March 2013 Accra	Consultant Program leader	Development organization	Interview	English
2013_11	May 2013	Consultant Program coordinator	NGO	E-Mail	English
2013_12	May 2013	Consultant	Consultancy	Interview	German
2013_13	June 2013	Consultant Regional coordinator	Development organization	Interview	German
2013_14	June 2013	Consultant	Consultancy	Interview	German
2013_15	July 2013 Lima	Consultant Program coordinator	Institution	Interview	Spanish
2013_16	July 2013 Lima	Consultant University Professor	Development organization University	Interview	Spanish
2013_17	July 2013 Lima	Consultant	MinAg	Interview	Spanish
2013_18	August 2013 Lima	Consultant	Development Bank	Interview	Spanish

Interview Number	Date (and place)	Interviewee	Affiliation	Format	Language
2013_19	August 2013 Lima	Consultant Local economic development manager	Development organization	Interview	Spanish
2013_20	August 2013 Moyobamba	Consultant Regional program coordinator	Development organization	Interview	Spanish
2013_21	August 2013 Tarapoto	Consultant, lecturer	Development organization	Interview	Spanish
2013_22	August 2013 Tarapoto	Scientist	Research institute	Interview	Spanish
2013_23	August 2013 Lamas	General manager	Firm	Interview	Spanish
2013_24	August 2013 Tarapoto	Scientist	Research institute	Interview	Spanish
2013_25	August 2013 Tarapoto	Consultant Workshop facilitator	Consultancy	Interview Telephone Call	Spanish
2013_26	August 2013 Tarapoto	Technical secretary Coordinator of entre-preneurial platform	Regional Government Directorate of Agrarian Competitive-ness	Interview	Spanish
2013_27	September 2013 Colombia	Scientist	Research institute	Interview	Spanish
2013_28	September 2013 Moyobamba	Government employ-ee Regional program supervisor	Regional Government Directorate of Agrarian Competitive-ness	Interview	Spanish
2013_29	September 2013 Lamas	General manager	Cooperative	Interview	Spanish
2013_30	September 2013 Tarapoto	Employee of coopera-tive Specialist on endemic plants	Cooperative	Interview	Spanish
2013_31	September 2013 Lima	Consultant, workshop facilitator	Development organization	Interview	Spanish
2013_32	September 2013 Lima	General manager	Firm	Interview	Spanish

Interview Number	Date (and place)	Interviewee	Affiliation	Format	Language
2013_33	October 2013 Lamas	Consultant, Ex-General manager of a cooperative Farmer	Cooperative	Interview	Spanish
2013_34	November 2013	Consultant	Metrology Institute	Interview	German
2013_35	November 2013	Consultant Program coordinator	Development organization	Interview	German
2013_36	December 2013	Entrepreneur	Firm	Interview	French
2013_37	December 2013	Government employ-ee	Ministry of Export Promo-tion	E-Mail	Spanish
2013_38	December 2013	Consultant	Development organization	E-Mail	Spanish
2013_39	December 2013	Consultant Workshop facilitator	Development organization	E-Mail	Spanish
2013_40	December 2013	Consultant Workshop facilitator	Development organization	E-Mail	Spanish
2013_41	December 2013	General Manager	Firm	E-Mail	Spanish
2013_42	December 2013	Entrepreneur	Firm	E-Mail	Spanish
2013_43	December 2013	Consultant	Development organization	E-Mail	Spanish
2014_1	January 2014	Entrepreneur	Firm	E-Mail	Spanish
2014_2	February 2014 Nürnberg	Entrepreneur	Firm	Interview	Spanish, English
2014_3	February 2014 Nürnberg	Entrepreneur	Firm	Interview	German
2014_4	February 2014 Germany	Consultant Workshop facilitator	Development organization	Interview	German
2014_5	April 2014	Consultant Regional leader of value chain develop-ment	Development organization	Telephone call	German
2014_6	June 2014	Consultant Program director	Development organization	Interview	German
2014_7	September 2014	Consultant Snior researcher on empowerment of emerging markets	Firm	Telephone call	German

Interview Number	Date (and place)	Interviewee	Affiliation	Format	Language
2014_8	September 2014	Consultant	Development organization	E-Mail	Spanish
2014_9	September 2014	Consultant	Firm	E-Mail	German
2014_10	September 2014	Former consultant Development director	Development organization	Interview	German
2014_11	September 2014 Accra	Consultant	Development organization	Interview	English
2014_12	October 2014 Techiman	Entrepreneur Farmers	MoFA, firm, farmer union	Interview	English
2014_13	October 2014 Around Wenchi and Nkranza	Farmers, chiefs	Farmer union, research centre	Interview	English, Twi
2014_14	October 2014 Accra	Consultant	Development organization	Interview	English
2014_15	October 2014 Accra	Consultant Policy advisor	Development organization	Interview	English
2014_16	October 2014 Accra	Consultant, Project manager	Development organization	Interview	English
2014_17	October 2014 Sunyani	Government employ-ee Regional coordinator	MoFA	Interview	English
2014_18	October 2014 Mim	Farmers, chiefs	Farmer associa-tions	Interview	English, Twi
2014_19	October 2014 Wenchi	Managing director	Firm	Interview	English
2014_20	October 2014 Mim	Managing director	Firm	Interview	English
2014_21	October 2014 Mim	Managing director	Firm	Interview	English
2014_22	October 2014	Farmers, Chairman of farmer union	Farmer union	Interview	English
2014_23	October 2014 Accra	Finance manager, communication officer	Industry asso-ciation	Interview	English
2014_24	October 2014 Accra	Consultant	Industry asso-ciation	Interview	English
2014_25	October 2014 Accra	Policy advisor Component manager	Development organization	E-Mail	English

Interview Number	Date (and place)	Interviewee	Affiliation	Format	Language
2014_26	November 2014 Lima	Consultant t	Inter-American Institute for Cooperation on Agriculture	Interview	Spanish
2014_27	December 2014 Lamas	Entrepreneur	Firm	Interview	Spanish
2015_1	January 2015	Professor	University	E-Mail	English
2015_2	January 2015	Professor	University	E-Mail	English

* Those interviews marked with a "*" were conducted between 2009-2011 by Stefan Ouma, Peter Lindner and Marc Boeckler in the context of a research project funded by the German Research Foundation (DFG, 2010-2013) about agro-export markets and the integration of smallholder farmers into global agricultural markets in Ghana.
** When there is no place indicated, it is for reasons of confidentiality and anonymization.

Bibliography

Abdulai, A.; Crawford, G. (2010): Is Ghana a Model for Africa? 5.01.2010. In *World Politics Review*, 2010. Available online at http://www.worldpoliticsreview.com/articles/4887/is-ghana-a-model-for-africa, checked on 3/18/2015.

Abolafia, M. (1998): Markets as Cultures: An Ethnographic Approach. In M. Callon (Ed.): The Laws of the Markets, vol. 46. Oxford, Malden, MA: Blackwell Publishers, pp. 69–85.

ACA (2014): AfricasheW320 Newsletter. African Cashew Alliance (35). Available online at www.africancashewalliance.com/en/news-and-info/newsletter, checked on 6/15/2015.

ACDI/VOCA (2015a): Ghana – Agricultural Development and Value chain development (ADVANCE) Project. Available online at http://acdivoca.org/our-programs/project-profiles/ghana-agricultural-development-and-value-chain-enhancement-advance, checked on 4/2/2015.

ACDI/VOCA (2015b): Great Programs in History: Accelerated Microenterprise Advancement Project. Enhancing Performance and Competitiveness of Small Firms and Farms. The Value Chain Approach. Available online at http://acdivoca.org/resources/newsroom/features/great-programs-history-accelerated-microenterprise-advancement-project, checked on 4/2/2015.

Alexander, Jeffrey C.; Smith, Philip; Norton, Matthew; Brooks, Peter (2011): Interpreting Clifford Geertz. Cultural Investigation in the Social Sciences. New York: Palgrave Macmillan.

Alianza de aprendizaje Perú (n.y.): Formación de Facilitadores de Cadenas Productivas. Articulando Conocimientos y Experiencias. With assistance of SNV, PDRS-GIZ, IMAR-CN.

Alianza del aprendizaje Perú (2008): Mecanismos de Articulación de Pequeños Productores Rurales con Empresas Privadas en el Perú. Estudio de Casos. Edited by CARE Perú. Lima, Peru.

Allison, Simon (2014): Ghana: Is Africa's Model Republic Losing Its Shine? 04.08.2014. In *Daily Maverick*, 2014. Available online at http://www.dailymaverick.co.za/article/2014-08-04-ghana-is-africas-model-republic-losing-its-shine/, checked on 3/18/2015.

Altenburg, Tilman (2007): Donor Approaches to Supporting Pro-Poor Value Chains. Report Prepared for the Donor Committee for Enterprise Development Working Group on Linkages and Value Chains.

Alvarez, M.; Riveros, H.; Rojas, M. (2005): Orientaciones Generales para la Promoción y Apoyo a las Cadenas Agroproductivas en el Perú. Lima, checked on 3/11/2015.

Anderson, B.; Kearnes, M.; McFarlane, C.; Swanton, D. (2012): On Assemblages and Geography. In *Dialogues in Human Geography* 2 (2), pp. 171–189. DOI: 10.1177/2043820612449261.

APISI (2010): Mercados y Biocomercio: Requisitos y Barreras para la Exportación de Alimentos a China, EEUU, Japón y la UE. Estudio de Caso: Sacha Inchi. Asociación de Productores Industriales para la comercialización de productos del Sacha Inchi. Available online at http://de.scribd.com/doc/49956025/APISI-NF-Sacha-inchi-2010-DF, updated on 5/28/2015.

Appadurai, A. (1986): The Social Life of Things. Commodities in Cultural Perspective: Cambridge University Press.

Appelbaum, R.; Lichtenstein, N. (2006): A New World of Retail Supremacy: Supply Chains and Workers' Chains in the Age of Wal-Mart. In *International Labor and Working-Class History* 70 (01). DOI: 10.1017/S0147547906000184.

Ausch, R. (2000): Pandora's Hope: Essays on the Reality of Science Studies. Book Review. In *Mind, Culture, and Activity* 7 (4), pp. 312–319. DOI: 10.1207/S15327884MCA0704_05.

Austin, J. L.; Urmson, J. O.; Sbisà, M. (1976): How to do Things with Words. London: Oxford University Press (1955).

Bacchi, C. (2012): Why Study Problematizations? Making Politics Visible. In *OJPS* 02 (01), pp. 1–8. DOI: 10.4236/ojps.2012.21001.

Bair, J. (2005): Global Capitalism and Commodity Chains: Looking Back, Going Forward. In *Competition & Change* 9 (2), pp. 153–180. DOI: 10.1179/102452905X45382.

Bair, J. (Ed.) (2009a): Frontiers of Commodity Chain Research. Stanford: Stanford University Press. Available online at http://books.google.de/books?id=RGBeiTT4Ib8C.

Bair, J. (2009b): Global Commodity Chains. Genealogy and Review. In J. Bair (Ed.): Frontiers of Commodity Chain Research. Stanford: Stanford University Press, pp. 1–34.

Bair, J.; Werner, M. (2011): Commodity Chains and the Uneven Geographies of Global Capitalism: A Disarticulations Perspective. In *Environment and Planning A* 43 (5), pp. 988–997. DOI: 10.1068/a43505.

Barber, B. (1995): All Economies are Embedded. The Career of a Concept and Beyond. In *Social Research: An International Quarterly* 62 (2), pp. 387–413.

Barnes, T. (2001): Retheorizing Economic Geography: From the Quantitative Revolution to the "Cultural Turn". In *Annals of the Association of American Geographers* 91 (3), pp. 546–565. DOI: 10.1111/0004-5608.00258.

Barnes, T. (2002): Performing Economic Geography. Two Men, two Books, and a Cast of Thousands. In *Environment and Planning A* 34 (3), pp. 487–512. DOI: 10.1068/a3440.

Barnes, T. (2008): Making Space for the Economy: Live Performances, Dead Objects, and Economic Geography. In *Geography Compass* 2 (5), pp. 1432–1448. DOI: 10.1111/j.1749-8198.2008.00144.x.

Barnett, C. (1998): The Cultural Turn: Fashion or Progress in Human Geography? In *Antipode* 30 (4), pp. 379–394. DOI: 10.1111/1467-8330.00085.

Barry, A. (2001): Political Machines. Governing a Technological Society. London, New York: Athlone Press.

Barry, A. (2006): Technological Zones. In *European Journal of Social Theory* 9 (2), pp. 239–253. DOI: 10.1177/1368431006063343.

Barry, A.; Osborne, T.; Rose, N. S. (1996): Foucault and Political Reason. Liberalism, Neo-Liberalism, and Rationalities of Government. Chicago: University of Chicago Press.

Barry, A.; Slater, D. (2002): Technology, Politics and the Market: An Interview with Michel Callon. In *Economy and Society* 31 (2), pp. 285–306. DOI: 10.1080/03085140220123171.

Bathelt, H.; Henn, S. (2013): The Geographies of Knowledge Creation over Distance: Toward a Typology. 17-19 June 2013. 35th DRUID Celebration Conference. Barcelona, 2013, checked on 8/28/2015.

Beckert, J.; Diaz-Bone, R.; Ganssmann, H.; Swedberg, R. (Eds.) (2007): Märkte als soziale Strukturen. Frankfurt/Main: Campus (Theorie und Gesellschaft, Bd. 63).

Bennett, J. (2005): The Agency of Assemblages and the North American Blackout. In *Public Culture* 17 (3), pp. 445–466. DOI: 10.1215/08992363-17-3-445.

Benson, D.; Jordan, A. (2011): What Have We Learned from Policy Transfer Research? Dolowitz and Marsh Revisited. In *Political Studies Review* 9 (3), pp. 366–378. DOI: 10.1111/j.1478-9302.2011.00240.x.

Berndt, C.; Boeckler, M. (2011): Performative regional (dis-)integration: Transnational markets, mobile commodities and bordered north-south differences. In Environment and Planning A 43 (5), pp.

Berndt, C.; Boeckler, M. (2009): Geographies of Circulation and Exchange: Constructions of Markets. In: Progress in Human Geography 33 (4), pp. 535–551.

Berndt, C.; Glückler, J. (2007): Einleitung. In C. Berndt, R. Pütz (Eds.): Kulturelle Geographien. Zur Beschäftigung mit Raum und Ort nach dem Cultural Turn. Bielefeld: Transcript, pp. 7–26.

Berndt, C.; Pütz, R. (Eds.) (2007): Kulturelle Geographien. Zur Beschäftigung mit Raum und Ort nach dem Cultural Turn. Neue Kulturgeographie--Tagungsreihe. Bielefeld: Transcript.

Bernet, T.; Thiele, G.; Zschocke, T.; López, G.; Velasco, C.; Devaux, A. (Eds.) (2011): Enfoque Participativo en Cadenas Productivas (EPCP). Manual del Usuario. DFID; Centro Internacioal de la Papa; Fundación PROINPA, Proyecto INCOPA; Programa Fortipapa del INIAP, checked on 3/15/2015.

Bernstein, H.; Campling, L. (2006): Commodity Studies and Commodity Fetishism I: Trading Down. In *Journal of Agrarian Change* 6 (2), pp. 239–264. DOI: 10.1111/j.1471-0366.2006.00121.x.

Betancourth, C. (2013): Aprovechamiento de la Torta Residual de Sacha Inchi (Plukenetia volubilis Linneo) Mediante Extracción por Solventes de su Aceite. Manizales.

Bhargava, R.; Kumar, P.; Kumar, M.; Mehra, N.; Mishra, A. (2013): A Randomized Controlled Trial of Omega-3 fatty Acids in Dry Eye Syndrome. In *International Journal of Ophthalmology* 6 (6), pp. 811–816. DOI: 10.3980/j.issn.2222-3959.2013.06.13.

BIOFACH (2014): Daten & Fakten. Official Website. BIOFACH. Available online at https://www.biofach.de/de/besucher/daten-fakten/, checked on 7/9/2014.

BMZ (2015): Peru: Situation and Cooperation. Federal Ministry for Economic Cooperation and Development (BMZ). Available online at http://www.bmz.de/en/what_we_do/countries_regions/lateinamerika/peru/zusammenarbeit.html, updated on 2/26/2014, checked on 3/15/2015.

Boeckler, M. (2005): Geographien Kultureller Praxis. Syrische Unternehmer und die globale Moderne. Bielefeld: Transcript (Kultur und soziale Praxis).

Boeckler, M.; Berndt, C. (2012): Geographies of Marketization. Chapter 12. Revised edition. In T. Barnes, J. Peck, E. Sheppard (Eds.): The Wiley-Blackwell Companion to Economic Geography. Chichester, West Sussex: Wiley-Blackwell, pp. 199–212. Available online at http://www.geo.uzh.ch/de/lehrstuehle-und-abteilungen/wirtschaftsgeographie/ueber-uns/mitarbeitende/berndt-christian/publikationen, checked on 9/3/2014.

Bohnsack, R. (2008): Rekonstruktive Sozialforschung. Einführung in qualitative Methoden. 7th edition. Stuttgart: UTB (8242).

Boltanski, L.; Thévenot, L. (2006): On Justification. Economies of Worth. Princeton: Princeton University Press (Princeton studies in cultural sociology).

Bondioli, P.; Della Bella, L.; Rettke, P. (2006): Alpha Linolenic Acid Rich Oils. Composition of Plukenetia Volubilis (Sacha Inchi) Oil from Peru. In *La Rivista Italiana delle Sostanze Grasse* (Vol. LXXXIII), pp. 120–123.

Borrus, M.; Ernst, D.; Haggard, S. (Eds.) (2000): International Production Networks in Asia. London: Routledge.

Bosco, F. (2015): Actor-Network Theory, Networks and Relational Geographies. Submitted Version. In G. Valentine, S. Aitken (Eds.): Approaches to Human Geography. 2nd edition. London: SAGE. Available online at http://www.academia.edu/11641103/Actor-Network_Theory_Networks_and_Relational_Geographies.

Bourgeois, R. H.; Herrera, D. (1999): Enfoque Participativo para el Desarrollo de la Competitividad de los Sistemas Agroalimentarios. San José, C.R.: Instituto Interamericano de Cooperación para la Agricultura (CADIAC, 1).

Bowen, G. A. (2006): Grounded Theory and Sensitizing Concepts. In *International Journal of Qualitative Methods* (Vol. 5, Issue 3), pp. 1–9.

Braun, B.; Whatmore, S. (2010): Political Matter. Technoscience, Democracy, and Public Life. Minneapolis: University of Minnesota Press.

Brenner, N.; Peck, J.; Theodore, N. (2010): Variegated Neoliberalization: Geographies, Modalities, Pathways. In *Global Networks* 10 (2), pp. 182–222. DOI: 10.1111/j.1471-0374.2009.00277.x.

Brenner, N.; Theodore, N. (2002): From the "New Localism" to the Spaces of Neoliberalism. In *Antipode* 34 (3), pp. 341–347. DOI: 10.1111/1467-8330.00245.

Brüntrup, M. (2011): African Developments: The Comprehensive Africa Agriculture Development Programme (CAADP) is an Opportunity for African Agriculture. Briefing Paper. 4 volumes. Bonn, checked on 3/18/2015.

Bührmann, A. (2005): The Emerging of the Entrepreneurial Self and Its Current Hegemony. Some Basic Reflections on How to Analyze the Formation and Transformation of Modern Forms of Subjectivity. In *Forum Qualitative Sozialforschung / Forum: Qualitative Social Research* 6 (1).

Burawoy, M. (2000): Global Ethnography. Forces, Connections, and Imaginations in a Postmodern World. Berkeley: University of California Press.

Busch, L. (2008): The Private Governance of Food: Equitable Exchange or Bizarre Bazaar? Paper presented a symposium on the Private Governance in the Global Agro-Food System. Münster. Available online at http://www.uni-muenster.de/Fuchs/en/forschung/projekte/agrifood.html, checked on 5/27/2015.

Busch, L. (2011): Standards. Recipes for Reality. Cambridge, Mass.: MIT Press (Infrastructures series).

Butler, J. (1990): Gender Trouble : Feminism and the Subversion of Identity. New York: Routledge. Available online at http://worldcatlibraries.org/wcpa/oclc/19630577.

CAADP (2009): CAADP Pillar II. Framework for Improving Rural Infrastructure and Trade Related Capacities For Market Access. CAADP Pillar II Expert Reference Group. With assistance of Conference of Ministers of Agriculture of West and Central Africa (CMAWCA), USAID, DFID, SIDA, BMZ, IFPRI, checked on 3/19/2015.

Çalışkan, K.; Callon, M. (2009): Economization, part 1: Shifting Attention from the Economy Towards Processes of Economization. In *Economy and Society* 38 (3), pp. 369–398. DOI: 10.1080/03085140903020580.

Çalışkan, K.; Callon, M. (2010): Economization, part 2: A Research Programme for the Study of Markets. In *Economy and Society* 39 (1), pp. 1–32. DOI: 10.1080/03085140903424519.

Çalışkan, K. (2010): Market Threads. How Cotton Farmers and Traders Create a Global Community. Princeton, N.J. [u.a.]: Princeton Univ. Press.

Callon, M. (1981): Struggles and Negotiations to Decide What is Problematic and What is not: The Socio-Logics of Translation. In K. Knorr-Cetina, A. V. Cicourel (Eds.): Advances in Social Theory and Methodology. Toward an Integration of Micro- and Macro-Sociologies. Boston: Routledge & Kegan Paul, pp. 197–220.

Callon, M. (1986): Some Elements of a Sociology of Translation: Domestication of the Scallops and the Fishermen of St Brieuc Bay. In J. Law (Ed.): Power, Action, and Belief. A New Sociology of Knowledge? London, Boston: Routledge & Kegan Paul, pp. 196–233.

Callon, M. (1998a): An Essay on Framing and Overflowing: Economic Externalities Revisited by Sociology. In *The Sociological Review* 46 (S1), pp. 244–269. DOI: 10.1111/j.1467-954X.1998.tb03477.x.

Callon, M. (1998b): Introduction: The Embeddedness of Economic Markets in Economics. In M. Callon (Ed.): The Laws of the Markets. Oxford, Malden, MA: Blackwell Publishers, pp. 1–57.

Callon, M. (1999): Actor-Network Theory. The Market Test. In J. Law, J. Hassard (Eds.): Actor Network Theory and After. Oxford [England], Malden, MA: Blackwell/Sociological Review (The Sociological review monographs), pp. 181–195.

Callon, M. (2005): Why Virtualism Paves the Way to Political Impotence: A Reply to Daniel Miller's Critique of The Laws of the Markets. European Electronic Newsletter 6 (2), pp. 3–20.

Callon, M. (2007a): An Essay on the Growing Contribution of Economic Markets to the Proliferation of the Social. In *Theory, Culture & Society* 24 (7-8), pp. 139–163. DOI: 10.1177/0263276407084701.

Callon, M. (2007b): What Does it Mean to Say that Economics is Performative. In D. MacKenzie, F. Muniesa, L. Siu (Eds.): Do Economists Make Markets? On the Performativity of Economics. Princeton: Princeton University Press, pp. 311–357.

Callon, M. (2008): Elaborating the Notion of Performativity. In *Le Libellio d'Aegis* 5 (1), pp. 18–29.

Callon, M. (2009): Civilizing Markets: Carbon Trading Between in Vitro and in Vivo Experiments. In *Accounting, Organizations and Society* 34 (3-4), pp. 535–548. DOI: 10.1016/j.aos.2008.04.003.

Callon, M.; Çalışkan, K. (2005): Economization, Part 1: New Directions in the Social Studies of the Market. Work in Progress. Available online at www.pols.boun.edu.tr/uploads%5Cfiles%5C888.doc, updated on 2009, checked on 9/20/2014.

Callon, M.; Çalışkan, K. (2005): New and Old Directions in the Anthropology of Markets. Paper prepared for the Wenner-Gren Foundation for Anthropological Researchphi. New York, 2005.

Callon, M.; Çalışkan, K. (2007): Economization: New Directions in the Social Studies of the Market. Working Paper.

Callon, M.; Lascoumes, P.; Barthe, Y. (2009): Acting in an Uncertain World. An Essay on Technical Democracy. Cambridge, Mass: MIT Press.

Callon, M.; Méadel, C.; Rabeharisoa, V. (2002): The Economy of Qualities. In *Economy and Society* 31 (2), pp. 194–217. DOI: 10.1080/03085140220123126.

Callon, M.; Muniesa, F. (2005): Peripheral Vision: Economic Markets as Calculative Collective Devices. In *Organization Studies* 26 (8), pp. 1229–1250. DOI: 10.1177/0170840605056393.

Cammack, P. (2012): Risk, Social Protection and the World Market. In *Journal of Contemporary Asia* 42 (3), pp. 359–377.

Carrier, J. G. (1997): Meanings of the Market. The Free Market in Western Culture. Oxford, New York: Berg (Explorations in anthropology).

Carroll, T. (2012): Neo-Liberal Development Policy in Asia Beyond the Post-Washington. Consensus. Six Papers on Market Building in the Era of the Post-Washington Consensus. Edited by INFID.

Castree, N. (2003): Commodifying What Nature? In *Progress in Human Geography* 27 (3), pp. 273–297. DOI: 10.1191/0309132503ph428oa.

Cetina, K. K.; Bruegger, U. (2002): Inhabiting Technology: The Global Lifeform of Financial Markets. In *Current Sociology* 50 (3), pp. 389–405. DOI: 10.1177/0011392102050003006.

Christophers, B. (2014): Wild Dragons in the City. Urban Political Economy, Affordable Housing Development and the Performative World-making of Economic Models. In *Int J Urban Reg Res* 38 (1), pp. 79–97. DOI: 10.1111/1468-2427.12037.

CIA World Factbook (2015a): Ghana. Available online at https://www.cia.gov/library/publications/the-world-factbook/geos/gh.html, updated on 9/8/2014, checked on 3/18/2015.

CIA World Factbook (2015b): Peru. Available online at https://www.cia.gov/library/publications/the-world-factbook/geos/pe.html, updated on 9/8/2014, checked on 3/15/2015.

Cochoy, F. (2008): Calculation, Qualculation, Calqulation: Shopping Cart Arithmetic, Equipped Cognition and the Clustered Consumer. In *Marketing Theory* 8 (1), pp. 15–44. DOI: 10.1177/1470593107086483.

Cochoy, F.; Giraudeau, M.; Mcfall, L. (2010): Performativity, Economics and Politics. In *Journal of Cultural Economy* 3 (2), pp. 139–146. DOI: 10.1080/17530350.2010.494116.

Cochrane, A.; Ward, K. (2012): Researching the Geographies of Policy Mobility: Confronting the Methodological Challenges. In *Environment and Planning A* 44 (1), pp. 5–12. DOI: 10.1068/a44176.

Coe, N.; Dicken, P.; Hess, M. (2008): Global Production Networks: Realizing the Potential. In *Journal of Economic Geography* 8, pp. 271–295, checked on 9/17/2014.

Coe, N.; Kelly, P.; Yeung, H. (Eds.) (2007): Economic Geography. A Contemporary Introduction. Malden, MA: Blackwell Pub.

Cook, I. (2000): Cultural Turns/Geographical Turns. Perspectives on Cultural Geography. Harlow, England, New York: Prentice Hall.

Cook, I. (2004): Follow the Thing: Papaya. In *Antipode* 36 (4), pp. 642–664. DOI: 10.1111/j.1467-8330.2004.00441.x.

Cook, I. R.; Ward, K. (2012): Conferences, Informational Infrastructures and Mobile Policies: The Process of Getting Sweden 'BID Ready'. Working Paper, pp. 1–47. DOI: 10.1177/0969776411420029.

Cooren, F. (2004): Textual Agency: How Texts Do Things in Organizational Settings. In *Organization* 11 (3), pp. 373–393. DOI: 10.1177/1350508404041998.

Corbin, J.; Strauss, A. (2014): Basics of Qualitative Research. Techniques and Procedures for Developing Grounded Theory. Fourth edition. Thousand Oaks: SAGE.

Craig, D.; Porter, D. (2006): Development Beyond Neoliberalism? Governance, Poverty Reduction and Political Economy. London, Routledge: New York.

Cramer, C. (1999): Can Africa Industrialize by Processing Primary Commodities? The Case of Mozambican Cashew Nuts. In *World Development* 27 (7), pp. 1247–1266. DOI: 10.1016/S0305-750X(99)00053-4.

Crang, M. (1998): Cultural Geography. London, New York: Routledge (Routledge contemporary human geography series).

CTA (Ed.) (2013): Guides for Value Chain Development – A Comparative Review, CTA. With assistance of Donovan, J., Cunha, M., Franzel, S., Gyau, A. & Mithöfer, D. World Agroforestry Centre. Wageningen, The Netherlands.

Czarniawska, B. (2012): Organization Theory Meets Anthropology: A Story of an Encounter. In *Journal of Business Anthropology* 1 (1), pp. 118–140.

Czarniawska, B.; Mazza, C. (2013): Consulting University: A Reflection from Inside. In *Financial Accountability & Management* 29 (2), pp. 124–139. DOI: 10.1111/faam.12010.

Czarniawska-Joerges, B.; Sevón, G. (1996): Translating Organizational Change. Berlin,, New York: Walter de Gruyter.

Deacon, R. (2000): Theory as Practice: Foucault's Concept of Problematization. In *Telos* 2000 (118), pp. 127–142.

Delaney, J. (2013): Reassembling Policy Through Research: Reflections on Situating Policy Advocacy Through Research and Practice. In *The Professional Geographer* 66 (1), pp. 18–24. DOI: 10.1080/00330124.2012.757820.

Deleuze, G.; Guattari, F. (1987): A Thousand Plateaus. Capitalism and Schizophrenia. Minneapolis: University of Minnesota Press.

Deleuze, G.; Parnet, C. (1977): Dialogues. Paris: Flammarion.

DeLyser, D.; Hawkins, H. (2013): Introduction: Writing Creatively - Process, Practice, and Product. In *Cultural Geographies* 21 (1), pp. 131–134. DOI: 10.1177/1474474012469006.

Derrida, J. (1982): Margins of Philosophy. Chicago: University of Chicago Press.

DFID; SDC (2004): Making Value Chains Work Better for the Poor: A Toolbook for Practitioners of Value Chain Analysis. With assistance of Purcell, T., S. Gniel and R. van Gent. London: UK Department for International Development and Phnom Penh, Cambodia: Agricultural Development International.

DFID; SDC (2008): Perspectives on the Making Markets Work for the Poor (M4P) Approach.

Dicken, P. (1998): Global Shift. Transforming The World Economy. Third edition. London: Paul Chapman.

Dirección Regional de Agricultura San Martín (2012): Mejoramiento del Servicio de Competitividad de la Cadena de Valor de Sacha Inchi a los Productores en Cuatro Provincias de la Región San Martín". Resumen ejecutivo. Tarapoto, San Martín. Available online at http://www.agrodrasam.gob.pe/, checked on 6/5/2014.

Dolan, C.; Humphrey, J. (2000): Governance and Trade in Fresh Vegetables: The Impact of UK Supermarkets on the African Horticulture Industry. In *Journal of Development Studies* 37 (2), pp. 147–176. DOI: 10.1080/713600072.

Dolowitz, D.; Marsh, D. (1996): Who Learns What from Whom: A Review of the Policy Transfer Literature. In *Political Studies* 44 (2), pp. 343–357. DOI: 10.1111/j.1467-9248.1996.tb00334.x.

Dostert, N.; Roque, J.; Brokamp, G. (2009): Factsheet Botanical Data. Sacha Inchi - Plukenetia Volubilis L. Proyecto Perúbiodiverso. GIZ.

Dumez, H.; Jeunemaitre, A. (2010a): Michel Callon, Michel Foucault and The "Dispositif". In *Le Libellio d'Aegis* 6 (4), pp. 27–37.

Dumez, H.; Jeunemaitre, A. (2010b): When Economics Fails to be Performative. A Case Study. In *Débordements. Hommage à Michel Callon* (12). Available online at http://hal.archives-ouvertes.fr/hal-00555201.

Dunn, E. C. (2005): Standards and Person-Making in East Central Europe. In A. Ong, S. J. Collier (Eds.): Global Assemblages. Technology, Politics, and Ethics as Anthropological Problems. Malden: Blackwell Publishers, pp. 174–193.

Dunn, E. C. (2007): Of Pufferfish and Ethnography: Plumbing New Depths in Economic Geography. In : Politics and Practice in Economic Geography. London: SAGE, pp. 82–92.

Elyachar, J. (2005): Markets of Dispossession. NGOs, Economic Development, and the State in Cairo. Durham: Duke University Press (Politics, history, and culture).

Escobar, A. (2012): Encountering Development. The Making and Unmaking of the Third World. New ed. Princeton, N.J., Woodstock: Princeton University Press.

Escobar, J. (Ed.) (2013): Sistematización de Enfoques, Estrategias y Resultados Orientados a Negocios Agrarios Propuestos e Implementados por Instituciones Promotoras del Desarrollo Rural. Lima.

Essel, V. (2014): Cashew Association Pleads for Government Intervention as Côte d'Ivoire Bans Cashew Imports. 04.02.2014. Edited by Graphic Online. Ghana. Available online at http://www.ghanaweb.com/GhanaHomePage/NewsArchive/artikel.php?ID=299731, checked on 6/15/2015.

European Commission (12.2013a): Commission Tables Proposals on Animal Cloning and Novel Food. MEMO/13/1170 18/12/2013. Available online at http://europa.eu/rapid/press-release_MEMO-13-1170_en.htm.

European Commission (12.2013b): Regulation of the European Parliament and of the Council on Novel Foods. COM(2013) 894.

Fanali, C.; Dugo, L.; Cacciola, F.; Beccaria, M.; Grasso, S.; Dachà, M. et al. (2011): Chemical Characterization of Sacha Inchi (Plukenetia volubilis L.) Oil. In *Journal of agricultural and food chemistry* 59 (24), pp. 13043–13049. DOI: 10.1021/jf203184y.

Feed the Future (2015): Ghana. Approach, Results, Opportunities, Activities. With assistance of USAID. Available online at http://www.feedthefuture.gov/country/ghana, updated on 4/3/2015, checked on 4/3/2015.

Ferguson, J. (1990): The Anti-Politics Machine. Development, Depoliticization, and Bureaucratic Power in Lesotho. Cambridge: Cambridge University Press.

Ferguson, J.; Gupta, A. (2002): Spatializing States: Toward an Ethnography of Neoliberal Governmentality. In *American Ethnologist* 29 (4), pp. 981–1002. DOI: 10.1525/ae.2002.29.4.981.

Fernandes, P. (2014): Cashew Prices Soar to All-Time High. The Times of India. Available online at http://timesofindia.indiatimes.com/city/goa/Cashew-prices-soar-to-all-time-high/articleshow/32256099.cms, updated on 9/1/2015, checked on 9/1/2015.

Fernandez, V. R. (2014): Global Value Chains in Global Political Networks: Tool for Development or Neoliberal Device? In *Review of Radical Political Economics. DOI:* 10.1177/0486613414532769.

Ferraro, F.; Pfeffer, J.; Sutton, R. I. (2009): How and Why Theories Matter: A Comment on Felin and Foss (2009). In *Organization Science* 20 (3), pp. 669–675. DOI: 10.1287/orsc.1090.0432.

Ferraro, F.; Pfeffer, J.; Sutton R. I. (2005): Economics Language and Assumptions: How Theories Can Become Self-Fulfilling. Research Paper Series Paper No. 1849. In *Academy of Management Review* (30 (1):8-24.).

Fine, B. (2003): Callonistics: A Disentanglement. In *Economy and Society* 32 (3), pp. 478–484. DOI: 10.1080/03085140303128.

Fine, B. (2005): From Actor-Network Theory to Political Economy. In *Capitalism Nature Socialism* 16 (4), pp. 91–108. DOI: 10.1080/10455750500376057.

Flick, U.; Kardorff, E.; Keupp, H. (1995): Handbuch Qualitative Sozialforschung. Grundlagen, Konzepte, Methoden und Anwendungen. Second edition. Weinheim: Beltz.

Fligstein, N.; Dauter, L. (2007): The Sociology of Markets. In *Annu. Rev. Sociol.* 33 (1), pp. 105–128. DOI: 10.1146/annurev.soc.33.040406.131736.

Foss, N. J.; Klein, P. G. (2010): Critiques of Transaction Cost Economics: An Overview. In P. Klein, M. Sykuta (Eds.): The Elgar Companion to Transaction Cost Economics: Edward Elgar Publishing.

Fosu, A. (2013): Achieving Development Success. Strategies and Lessons from the Developing World. Country Role Models for Development Success: The Ghana Case: Oxford University Press, checked on 5/25/2014.

Fotuhi, M.; Mohassel, P.; Yaffe, K. (2009): Fish Consumption, Long-Chain Omega-3 Fatty Acids and Risk of Cognitive Decline or Alzheimer Disease: A Complex Association. In *Nature clinical practice. Neurology* 5 (3), pp. 140–152. DOI: 10.1038/ncpneuro1044.

Foucault, Michel (1991): The Birth of the Prison. London: Penguin.

Fourcade, M. (2007): Theories of Markets and Theories of Society. In *American Behavioral Scientist* 50 (8), pp. 1015–1034. DOI: 10.1177/0002764207299351.

Fourcade, M.; Healy, K. (2007): Moral Views of Market Society. In *Annu. Rev. Sociol.* 33 (1), pp. 285–311. DOI: 10.1146/annurev.soc.33.040406.131642.

Friedland, W. (1984): Commodity Systems Analysis: An Approach to the Sociology of Agriculture. In *Research in Rural Sociology and Development* 1, pp. 221–235.

Fynn, M. (2011): Joint Sector Review. Analytical Summary Report on VCD in the Agriculture Sector in Ghana. Edited by GIZ-MOAP. GIZ. Accra.

Garcia-Parpet, M.-F. (2007): The Social Construction of a Perfect Market: The Strawberry Auction at Fontaines-en-Sologne. In D. MacKenzie, F. Muniesa, L. Siu (Eds.): Do Economists Make Markets? On the Performativity of Economics. Princeton: Princeton University Press, pp. 20–53.

Garfinkel, H. (1967): Studies in Ethnomethodology. New Jersey: Prentice Hall.

Garmendia, F.; Pando, R.; Ronceros, G. (2011): Effect of Sacha Inchi Oil (Plukenetia Volubilis l) on the Lipid Profile of Patients with Hyperlipoproteinemia. In *Rev Peru Med Exp Salud Publica* 28 (4), pp. 628–632.

Geertz, C. (1973): The Interpretation of Cultures. Selected essays. New York: Basic Books. Available online at http://worldcatlibraries.org/wcpa/oclc/737285.

Gereffi, G. (1999): A Commodity Chains Framework for Analyzing Global Industries.

Gereffi, G. (2014): Global Value Chains in a Post-Washington Consensus World. In *Review of International Political Economy* 21 (1), pp. 9–37. DOI: 10.1080/09692290.2012.756414.

Gereffi, G.; Humphrey, J.; Sturgeon, T. (2005): The Governance of Global Value Chains. In *Review of International Political Economy* 12 (1), pp. 78–104. DOI: 10.1080/09692290500049805.

Gereffi, G.; Korzeniewicz, M. (Eds.) (1994): Commodity Chains and Global Capitalism. Political Economy of the World-System Conference. Westport, Conn.: Greenwood Press (Studies in the political economy of the world system, no. 149).

Gereffi, G.; Korzeniewicz, M.; Korzeniewicz, R. (1994): Introduction: Global Commodity Chains. In G. Gereffi, M. Korzeniewicz (Eds.): Commodity Chains and Global Capitalism. Westport, Conn.: Greenwood Press (Studies in the political economy of the world system, no. 149), pp. 1–14.

IDS Bulletin. Globalisation, Value Chains and Development (2001). 32 volumes. Edited by Gereffi, G. Humphrey, J., R. Kaplinsky, H. Schmitz: Institute of Development Studies (3).

Gerstberger, I. (2011): Innovationen durch Lebensmittel aus anderen Kulturkreisen. In *ZLR*, pp. 425–442.

GFU (n.d.): Underutilized Crops in Peru: Some Conceptual and Political Consideration. With assistance of S. Pastor, B. Fuentealba, M. Ruiz, Crops for the Future. Global Facilitation Unit for Underutilized Species (GFU); GRPI; Pro Uso Diversitas; SPDA. Rome, Italy. Available online at http://www.cropsforthefuture.org/publication/strategic-document/underutilized_species_policies_and_strategies_peru_lr.pdf, updated on n.d., checked on 2/19/2014.

Gibbon, P.; Bair, J.; Ponte, S. (2008): Governing Global Value Chains: An Introduction. In *Economy and Society* 37 (3), pp. 315–338. DOI: 10.1080/03085140802172656.

Gibbon, P.; Ponte, S. (2005): Trading Down. Africa, Value Chains, and the Global Economy. Philadelphia: Temple University Press.

Gibson-Graham, J.K (2008): Diverse Economies: Performative Practices for `Other Worlds'. In *Progress in Human Geography* 32 (5), pp. 613–632. DOI: 10.1177/0309132508090821.

Giere, R.; Moffatt, B. (2003): Distributed Cognition: Where the Cognitive and The Social Merge. In *Social Studies of Science* 33, pp. 301–310.

Gille, Z.; Riain, S. O. (2002): Global Ethnography. In *Annu. Rev. Sociol.* 28 (1), pp. 271–295. DOI: 10.1146/annurev.soc.28.110601.140945.

Giovannucci, D. (2008): How New Agrifood Standards are Affecting Trade. MPRA Paper No. 17203. International Trade Centre World Export Development Forum. Available online at at http://mpra.ub.uni-muenchen.de/17203/, updated on 6/18/2015.

Giovannucci, D.; Ponte, S. (2005): Standards as a New Form of Social Contract? Sustainability Initiatives in the Coffee Industry. In *Food Policy* 30 (3), pp. 284–301. DOI: 10.1016/j.foodpol.2005.05.007.

GIZ (2009): Guía Metodológica de Facilitación en Cadenas de Valor. With assistance of PDRS-GIZ, inwent. Lima, Peru: GIZ.

GIZ (Ed.) (2013): La Cadena de Valor del Sacha Inchi en la Región San Martín. Análisis y Lineamientos Estratégicos Para su Desarrollo. Lima.

GIZ (2015a): Peru. Deutsche Gesellschaft für Internationale Zusammenarbeit (GIZ) GmbH 2015. Available online at http://www.giz.de/de/weltweit/400.html, updated on 7/1/2014, checked on 3/15/2015.

GIZ (2015b): Peru: Wirtschaft & Entwicklung. Das Länder-Informations-Portal der GIZ. With assistance of Länderinformationsportal. Edited by G. Basurco. Gesellschaft für Internationale Zusammenarbeit (GIZ). Available online at http://liportal.giz.de/peru/wirtschaft-entwicklung/, checked on 3/15/2015.

Glass, M. R.; Rose-Redwood, R. (2014): Performativity, Politics, and the Production of Social Space. New York: Routledge, Taylor & Francis (Routledge studies in human geography, 51).

GlobalGAP (2015): What We Do. Available online at http://www.globalgap.org/uk_en/what-we-do/index.html, updated on 7/10/2015, checked on 7/13/2015.

Gluckman, M. (2002): "The Bridge": Analysis of a Social Situation in Zululand. In J. Vincent (Ed.): The Anthropology of Politics. A Reader in Ethnography, Theory, and Critique. Malden, Mass.: Blackwell Publishers (Blackwell anthologies in social and cultural anthropology, 3), pp. 53–58.

Gobierno regional de San Martín (2008): Plan Concertado de Desarrollo Departamental 2008-2015, checked on 5/13/2015.

Goffman, E. (1961): Encounters: Two studies in the Sociology of Interaction. Indianapolis: Bobbs-Merrill. Available online at http://worldcatlibraries.org/wcpa/oclc/710786.

Goldman, M. (2007): How "Water for All!" Policy Became Hegemonic: The Power of the World Bank and its Transnational Policy Networks. In *Geoforum* 38 (5), pp. 786–800. DOI: 10.1016/j.geoforum.2005.10.008.

Goldschmidt, N.; Becker, P.; Lenger, A. (2014): Das Zusammenspiel und die Erfassung individueller und institutioneller Bedingungen wirtschaftlicher Entwicklung. In Thomas Apolte (Ed.): Transfer von Institutionen. 1. Aufl. Berlin: Duncker & Humblot (Schriften des Vereins für Socialpolitik, 340).

Gorriti, A. (2010): Toxicidad Oral a 60 días del Aceite de Sacha Inchi y Linaza y Determinación de la Dosis Letal 50 en Roedores. In *Revista Peruana de Medicina Experimental y Salud Pública* (27 (3)), pp. 352–360.

Gorriti, A. (2013): Actualización de la Monografía Sacha Inchi. Plukenetia Volúbilis L. Proyecto de Perúbiodiverso. With assistance of Diana Flores. Lima, Peru.

Gorriti, A.; Arroyo, J.; Quispe, F.; Cisneros, B.; Condorhuamán, M.; Almora, Y.; Chumpitaz, V. (2010): Oral Toxicity at 60-days of Sacha Inchi Oil (Plukenetia Volubilis L.) and Linseed (Linum Usitatissimum L.), and Determination of Lethal Dose 50 in Rodents. In *Revista Peruana de Medicina Experimental y Salud Pública* 27 (3), pp. 352–360.

Government of Ghana (2013): FASDEP II- Food and Agriculture Sector Development Policy. Published on 17.12.2013. Accra. Available online at https://opencontentghana.wordpress.com/2013/12/17/fasdep-ii-food-and-agriculture-sector-development-policy/, checked on 3/20/2015.

Granovetter, M. (1985): Economic Action and Social Structure: The Problem of Embeddedness. In *American Journal of Sociology* 91 (3), pp. 481–510. DOI: 10.1086/228311.

Grewal, D. S. (2008): Network Power. The Social Dynamics of Globalization. New Haven: Yale University Press.

Gupta, A.; Ferguson, J. (1997): Discipline and Practice: 'The Field' as Site, Method, and Location in Anthropology. In A. Gupta, J. Ferguson (Eds.): Anthropological locations. Boundaries and Grounds of a Field Science. Berkeley: University of California Press, pp. 1–46.

Gutiérrez, L.; Rosada, L.; Jiménez, A. (2011): Chemical Composition of Sacha Inchi (Plukenetia volubilis L.) Seeds and Characteristics of Their Lipid Fraction. In *Grasas y Aceites* 62 (1), pp. 76–83. DOI: 10.3989/gya044510.

Guzmán, A. T. (2013): Sistematización de la Mesa Técnica de Sacha Inchik en la Región San Martín. Periodo 2006 - 2012. Documento interno - Versión 2.0.

Haggblade, S.; Gamser, M. (1991): A Field Manual for Subsector Practitioners. Tools for Microenterprise Programs: Nonfinancial Assistance Section. GEMINI Technical Notes.

Hall, S. (2008): Geographies of Business Education: MBA Programmes, Reflexive Business Schools and the Cultural Circuit of Capital. In *Trans Inst Br Geog* 33 (1), pp. 27–41. DOI: 10.1111/j.1475-5661.2007.00288.x.

Hamilton, G.; Gereffi, G. (2009): Global Commodity Chains, Market Makers, and the Rise of Demand- Responsive Economies. In J. Bair (Ed.): Frontiers of Commodity Chain Research. Stanford: Stanford University Press, pp. 136–161.

Hanssen, H.-P.; Schmitz-Hübsch, M. (2011): Sacha Inchi (Plukenetia volubilis L.) Nut Oil and Its Therapeutic and Nutritional Uses. In V. Preedy, R. Watson, V. Patel (Eds.): Nuts and Seeds in Health and Disease Prevention: Elsevier, pp. 991–994.

Hardie, I.; MacKenzie, D. (2007): Assembling an Economic Actor: The Agencement of a Hedge Fund. In *The Sociological Review* 55 (1), pp. 57–80. DOI: 10.1111/j.1467-954X.2007.00682.x.

Harsch, E. (2008): Closing Ghana's National Poverty Gap. North-South Disparities Challenge Attainment of Millennium Development Goals. Edited by Africa Renewal Online. UN. Available online at http://www.un.org/africarenewal/magazine/october-2008/closing-ghana%E2%80%99s-national-poverty-gap, checked on 5/22/2015.

Henderson, J.; Dicken, P.; Hess, M.; Coe, N.; Yeung, H. (2002): Global Production Networks and the Analysis of Economic Development. In *Review of International Political Economy* 9 (3), pp. 436–464. DOI: 10.1080/09692290210150842.

Henriksen, L. F. (2013): Economic Models as Devices of Policy Change: Policy Paradigms, Paradigm Shift, and Performativity. In *Regulation & Governance* 7 (4), pp. 481–495. DOI: 10.1111/rego.12031.

Henson, S.; Reardon, T. (2005): Private Agri-Food Standards: Implications for Food Policy and the Agri-Food System. In *Food Policy* 30 (3), pp. 241–253. DOI: 10.1016/j.foodpol.2005.05.002.

Herbert, S. (2000): For Ethnography. In *Progress in Human Geography* 24 (4), pp. 550–568. DOI: 10.1191/030913200100189102.

Herr, M. L.; Muzira, T. J. (2009): Value Chain Development for Decent Work. A Guide for Development Practitioners, Government and Private Sector Initiatives. Geneva: ILO (International Labour Office). Available online at http://www.worldcat.org/oclc/769190103.

Higgins, V.; Larner, W. (2010): Calculating the Social. Basingstoke: Palgrave Macmillan.

Higgins, V.; Lawrence, G. (2005): Agricultural Governance. Globalization and the New Politics of Regulation. New York: Routledge (Routledge advances in sociology, 17).

Holm, P. (2007): Which Way is Up On Callon? In D. MacKenzie, F. Muniesa, L. Siu (Eds.): Do Economists Make Markets? On the Performativity of Economics. Princeton: Princeton University Press, pp. 225–243.

Holmes, D. R.; Marcus, G. E. (2008): Collaboration Today and the Re-Imagination of the Classic Scene of Fieldwork Encounter. In *Collaborative Anthropologies* 1 (1), pp. 81–101. DOI: 10.1353/cla.0.0003.

Hughes, A.; Reimer, S. (2004): Geographies of Commodity Chains. New York: Routledge (Routledge studies in human geography, 10).

Humphrey, J.; Navas-Alemán, L. (2010): Value Chains, Donor Interventions and Poverty Reduction: A Review of Donor Practice. Brighton, UK (IDS Research Report, 63).

ICRA (2009): Greentech Retire Son Brevet sur la Graine de Sacha Inchi. Première Grande Victoire Contre la Biopiraterie en France. With assistance of Fondation Danielle Mitterrand. Edited by France-Libertés, checked on 5/7/2015.

IICA (2000): CADIAC: Actor-Led Change for Efficient AgriFood Systems. Handbook of the Participatory Actor-Based CADIAC Approach. CGPRT No. 39. With assistance of Robin Bourgeois, Danilo Herrera: UN. Available online at http://ageconsearch.umn.edu/handle/32727, checked on 2/11/2015.

IICA (2006a): Gestión de Agronegocios En Empresas Asociativas Rurales. Módulo 1: Sistema Agroproductivo, Cadenas y Competitividad. Curso de capacitación. IICA-PRODAR, FAO. Lima.

IICA (2006b): Medium Term Plan 2006 - 2010. Promoting Rural Prosperity In The Americas. San José, Costa Rica.

IICA (2011): Strategic Plan 2010 - 2020. Summary. San José, Costa Rica: IICA.

Indecopi (2011): Normalización de Productos Agrícolas en el Perú. Comisión de Normalización y de Fiscalización de Barreras Comerciales no Arancelarias. With assistance of Rosario Uría Toro. Indecopi. Lima, checked on 5/6/2015.

INIA (2006): Cultivo de Sacha Inchi. Dirección de Investigación Agraria. Estación experimental agraria “EL PORVENIR”. With assistance of Emma MANCO Céspedes. Tarapoto, San Martín (El Porvenir).

ITC (2014): GRAS Assessment Dossier Prepared for Peruvian Sacha Inchi. 5.05.2014. International Trade Centre (ITC). Available online at http://www.intracen.org/news/GRAS-assessment-dossier-prepared-for-Peruvian-Sacha-Inchi/, checked on 5/13/2015.

Jackson, P. (2002): Commercial Cultures: Transcending The Cultural and The Economic. In *Progress in Human Geography* 26 (1), pp. 3–18. DOI: 10.1191/0309132502ph254xx.

Jackson, P.; Ward, N.; Russell, P. (2006): Mobilising The Commodity Chain Concept in the Politics of Food and Farming. In *Journal of Rural Studies* 22 (2), pp. 129–141. DOI: 10.1016/j.jrurstud.2005.08.008.

James, A.; Martin, R.; Sunley, P. (2008): The Rise of Cultural Economic Geography. Introductory Chapter. In R. Martin, P. Sunley (Eds.): Economic Geography. London, New York: Routledge (Critical concepts in the social sciences). Available online at www.geog.qmul.ac.uk/docs/staff/4516.pdf, checked on 8/25/2014.

Jones, A.; Murphy, J. T. (2011): Theorizing Practice in Economic Geography: Foundations, Challenges, and Possibilities. In *Progress in Human Geography* 35 (3), pp. 366–392. DOI: 10.1177/0309132510375585.

Jöns, H. (2011): Centre of Calculation. In : The SAGE Handbook of Geographical Knowledge. 1 Oliver's Yard, 55 City Road, London EC1Y 1SP United Kingdom: SAGE Publications Ltd, pp. 158–170.

Juarez Nima, E. (2007): Estudio sobre Sistematización de Avances de Investigación y Propuesta de un Modelo Productivo Competitivo Para la Producción de Sacha Inchi en la Región San Martín. Informe de Consultoria. Moyobamba, Perú.

Kaplinsky, R. (2005): Globalization, Poverty and Inequality. Between a Rock and a Hard Place. Cambridge, UK, Malden, MA: Polity.

Kellermann, M. (2011): Thoughts on a National Quality Policy. Discussion Paper 4/2011. Braunschweig, checked on 6/18/2015.

Kera, D.; Tuters, M. (2011): Actor-Network Theory. Online version. In D. Mulvaney (Ed.): Green technology. An A-to-Z guide. Los Angeles: Sage Publications (The Sage reference series on green society: toward a sustainable future, 10), pp. 2–6.

Knorr-Cetina, K. (1981a): Introduction. In K. Knorr-Cetina, A. V. Cicourel (Eds.): Advances in Social Theory and Methodology. Toward an Integration of Micro- and Macro-Sociologies. Boston: Routledge & Kegan Paul, pp. 1–45.

Knorr-Cetina, K. (1981b): The Manufacture of Knowledge: An Essay on the Constructivist and Contextual Nature of Science. Oxford New York: Pergamon Press.

Knorr-Cetina, K. (1992): The Couch, the Cathedral, and the Laboratory. On the Relationship between Experiment and Laboratory in Science. In A. Pickering (Ed.): Science as Practice and Culture: University of Chicago Press, pp. 113–138.

Krigbaum, J. (n.d.): First Steps in the Construction of a Market of Oil of Sacha Inchi in Japan. With assistance of Jim Krigbaum. Edited by 2020 Development Consulting. Available online at 2020dc.com/press/Sachi_report_PRA.pdf, checked on 5/13/2015.

Krivankova, B. (2007): Sacha Inchi: A Promising Oilseed Crop from Peruvian Amazon. 9.-11.10.2007. Tropentag. Czech University of Life Sciences Prague. Witzenhausen, 2007.

Krivankova, B.; Cepkova, P. H.; Ocelak, M.; Juton, G.; Bechyne, M.; Lojka, B. (2012): Preliminary Study of Diversity of Plukenetia volubilis Based on the Morphological and Genetic Characteristics. In *Agricultura tropica et subtropica* 45 (3). DOI: 10.2478/v10295-012-0023-6.

Künkel, J. (2015): Urban Policy Mobilities Versus Policy Transfer. Potenziale für die Analyse der Neuordnung. In *sub\urban. zeitschrift für kritische stadtforschung* 3 (1), pp. 7–24.

Larner, W. (2002): Globalization, Governmentality and Expertise: Creating a Call Centre Labour Force. In *Review of International Political Economy* 9 (4), pp. 650–674. DOI: 10.1080/09692290220000021844.

Larner, W. (2003): Neoliberalism? In *Environment and Planning D: Society and Space* 21 (5), pp. 509–512. DOI: 10.1068/d2105ed.

Larner, W.; Laurie, N. (2010): Travelling Technocrats, Embodied Knowledges: Globalising Privatisation in Telecoms and Water. In *Geoforum* 41 (2), pp. 218–226. DOI: 10.1016/j.geoforum.2009.11.005.

Latham, A. (2002): Retheorizing the Scale of Globalization: Topologies, Actor-Networks, and Cosmopolitanism. In A. Herod, M. W. Wright (Eds.): Geographies of Power. Oxford, UK: Blackwell Publishers Ltd, pp. 115–144.

Latour, B. (1983): Give Me a Laboratory and I Will Raise the World. In K. Knorr-Cetina, M. J. Mulkay (Eds.): Science Observed. Perspectives on the Social Study of Science. London, Beverly Hills: Sage Publications, pp. 142–170.

Latour, B. (1986a): The Powers of Association. In J. Law (Ed.): Power, Action, and Belief. A New Sociology of Knowledge? London, Boston: Routledge & Kegan Paul, pp. 264–280.

Latour, B. (1986b): Visualisation and Cognition: Drawing Things Together. In *Knowledge and Society: Studies in the Sociology of Culture and Present* 6, pp. 1–40.

Latour, B. (1987): Science in Action. How to Follow Scientists and Engineers Through Society. Cambridge, Mass: Harvard University Press.

Latour, B. (1988): The Pasteurization of France. Cambridge, Mass.: Harvard University Press.

Latour, B. (1996a): Aramis or the Love of Technology. Cambridge, Mass: Harvard University Press.

Latour, B. (1996b): On Actor-Network Theory. A Few Clarifications Plus More Than a Few Complications. In *Soziale Welt* 47, pp. 369–381, checked on 6/4/2015.

Latour, B. (1999): Pandora's Hope. Essays on the Reality of Science Studies. Cambridge, Mass.: Harvard University Press.

Latour, B. (2004a): Scientific Objects and Legal Objectivity. In A. Pottage, M. Mundy (Eds.): Law, Anthropology, and the Constitution of the Social: Making Persons and Things: Cambridge University Press, pp. 73–113. Available online at http://www.bruno-latour.fr/node/213, checked on 1/17/2015.

Latour, B. (2004b): Why has Critique Run Out of Steam. From Matters of Fact to Matters of Concern. In *Critical Inquiry* (Vol. 30. No. 2.), pp. 225 - 248. Available online at www.unc.edu/clct/LatourCritique.pdf.

Latour, B. (2005a): From Realpolitik to Dingpolitik: How to Make Things Public. In B. Latour, P. Weibel (Eds.): Making Things Public. Atmospheres of Democracy. Cambridge, Mass., [Karlsruhe, Germany]: MIT Press; ZKM/Center for Art and Media in Karlsruhe, pp. 14–43.

Latour, B. (2005b): Reassembling the Social. An Introduction to Actor-Network-Theory. Oxford, New York: Oxford University Press (Clarendon lectures in management studies).

Latour, B. (2008): What is the Style of Matters of Concern? Two Lectures in Empirical Philosophy. Assen: Van Gorcum (Spinoza lectures).

Latour, B.; Callon, M. (1981): Unscrewing the Big Leviathan; or How Actors Macrostructure Reality, and How Sociologists Help Them To Do So? In K. Knorr-Cetina, A. V. Cicourel (Eds.): Advances in Social Theory and Methodology. Toward an Integration of Micro- and Macro-Sociologies. Boston: Routledge & Kegan Paul, pp. 277–303.

Latour, B.; Woolgar, S. (1986): Laboratory Life. The Construction of Scientific Facts. 2nd ed. Princeton: Princeton University Press.

Lave, J. (1988): Cognition in Practice. Mind, Mathematics, and Culture in Everyday Life. Cambridge, New York: Cambridge University Press.

Law, J. (1987): Technology and Heterogeneous Engineering: the Case of the Portuguese Expansion. In W. E. Bijker, T. P. Hughes, T. J. Pinch (Eds.): The Social Construction of Technological Systems. New Directions in the Sociology and History of Technology. Cambridge, Mass.: MIT Press, pp. 111–113.

Law, J. (1992): Notes on the Theory of the Actor-Network: Ordering, Strategy, and Heterogeneity. In *Systems Practice* 5 (4), pp. 379–393. DOI: 10.1007/BF01059830.

Law, J. (1994): Organizing Modernity. Oxford, UK, Cambridge, Mass., USA: Blackwell.

Law, J. (1997): Traduction/Trahison - Notes on ANT. Available online at http://www.comp. lancs.ac.uk/sociology/stslaw2.html, updated on 8/21/2014.

Law, J. (1999): After ANT: Complexity, Naming and Topology. In *The Sociological Review* 47 (S1), pp. 1–14. DOI: 10.1111/j.1467-954X.1999.tb03479.x.

Law, J. (2004): After Methodology. London: Routledge (International library of sociology).

Law, J. (2007): Actor Network Theory and Material Semiotics. Working Paper Version of 25th April 2007. Available online at http://www. heterogeneities. net/publications/Law2007ANTandMaterialSemiotics.pdf.

Law, J.; Hassard, J. (Eds.) (1999): Actor Network Theory and After. Oxford [England], Malden, MA: Blackwell/Sociological Review (The Sociological review monographs).

Law, J.; Singleton, V. (2013): ANT and Politics: Working In and On the World. In *Qual Sociol* 36 (4), pp. 485–502. DOI: 10.1007/s11133-013-9263-7.

Lawson, M. (2010): Foreign Aid: International Donor Coordination of Development Assistance. CRS Report for Congress, prepared for Members and Committees of Congress, checked on 3/18/2015.

Lee, J. (2010): Global Commodity Chains and Global Value Chains. In R. Denemark (Ed.): The international Studies Encyclopedia. Malden, MA: Wiley-Blackwell.

Lee, J.; Gereffi, G.; Beauvais, J. (2012): Global Value Chains and Agrifood Standards: Challenges and Possibilities for Smallholders in Developing Countries. In *Proc. Natl. Acad. Sci. U.S.A.* 109 (31), pp. 12326–12331. DOI: 10.1073/pnas.0913714108.

Ley, D. (1993): Postmodernism, or the Cultural Logic of Advanced Intellectual Capital. In *Tijdschrift voor economische en sociale geografie* 84 (3), pp. 171–174. DOI: 10.1111/j.1467-9663.1993.tb00648.x.

Li, T. (2007): The Will To Improve. Governmentality, Development, and the Practice of Politics. Durham: Duke University Press.

Lin, J. Y. (2012): New structural economics. A framework for rethinking development and policy. Washington, D.C.: World Bank.

Lins Ribeiro, G. (2013): Global Flows of Development Models. In *Anthropological Forum* 23 (2), pp. 121–141. DOI: 10.1080/00664677.2013.767183.

Loconto, A.; Busch, L. (2010): Standards, Techno-Economic Networks, and Playing Fields: Performing the Global Market Economy. In *Review of International Political Economy* 17 (3), pp. 507–536. DOI: 10.1080/09692290903319870.

MacKenzie, D.; Muniesa, F.; Siu, L. (Eds.) (2007): Do Economists Make Markets? On the Performativity of Economics. Princeton: Princeton University Press.

MacKenzie, Donald (2005): Opening the Black Boxes of Global Finance. In *Review of International Political Economy* 12 (4), pp. 555–576. DOI: 10.1080/09692290500240222.

MacKenzie, Donald A. (2006): An Engine, Not a Camera. How Financial Models Shape Markets. 1st MIT Press pbk. ed. Cambridge, MA, London: MIT Press (Inside technology).

MacKenzie, Donald A. (2009): Ten Precepts for Social Studies of Finance. In Donald A. MacKenzie (Ed.): Material Markets. How Economic Agents Are Constructed. Oxford, New York: Oxford University Press (Clarendon lectures in management studies), pp. 8–36.

Maertens, M. (2006): Trade, Food Standards and Poverty: The Case of High-Value Vegetable Exports from Senegal. Poster paper prepared for presentation at the International Association of Agricultural Economists Conference, Gold Coast, Australia, August 12-18, 2006.

Mallavarapu, S.; Prasad, A. (2006): Facts, Fetishes, and the Parliament of Things: Is There any Space for Critique? In *Social Epistemology* 20 (2), pp. 185–199. DOI: 10.1080/02691720600784782.

Marcus, G. E. (1995): Ethnography in/of the World System: The Emergence of Multi-Sited Ethnography. In *Annu. Rev. Anthropol.* 24 (1), pp. 95–117. DOI: 10.1146/annurev.an.24.100195.000523.

Massey, D. (2005): For Space. London: SAGE.

Massey, D. B. (1994): Space, Place, and Gender. Minneapolis: University of Minnesota Press.

McCann, E. (2013): Policy Boosterism, Policy Mobilities, and the Extrospective City. In *Urban Geography* 34 (1), pp. 5–29. DOI: 10.1080/02723638.2013.778627.

McCann, E.; Roy, A.; Ward, K. (2013): Assembling/Worlding Cities. In *Urban Geography* 34 (5), pp. 581–589. DOI: 10.1080/02723638.2013.793905.

McCann, E.; Ward, K. (2010): Relationality/Territoriality: Toward a Conceptualization of Cities in the World. In *Geoforum* 41 (2), pp. 175–184. DOI: 10.1016/j.geoforum.2009.06.006.

McCann, E.; Ward, K. (2011): Mobile Urbanism. Cities and Policymaking in the Global Age. Minneapolis: University of Minnesota Press.

McCann, E.; Ward, K. (2013): A Multi-Disciplinary Approach to Policy Transfer Research: Geographies, Assemblages, Mobilities and Mutations. In *Policy Studies* 34 (1), pp. 2–18. DOI: 10.1080/01442872.2012.748563.

McDowell, L. (1992): Doing Gender: Feminism, Feminists and Research Methods in Human Geography. In *Transactions of the Institute of British Geographers* 17 (4), pp. 399–416. DOI: 10.2307/622707.

McFarlane, C. (2011): Assemblage and Critical Urbanism. In *City* 15 (2), pp. 204–224. DOI: 10.1080/13604813.2011.568715.

Mennicken, A.; Miller, P. (2012): Accounting, Territorialization and Power. In *Foucault Studies* No. 13 (2012), pp. 4–24.

Mesa Técnica de Sacha Inchi (2013): El Sacha Inchik en la Región San Martín. Dirección de Competitividad Agraria (DRASAM), 02.2013.

Mesa Técnica de Sacha Inchi Región San Martín (2012): Experiencia de la Mesa Técnica de Sacha Inchi en la Región San Martín. With assistance of Shanantina SAC.

MiDA (2015): Millennium Development Authority: Reducing poverty through economic growth. Available online at http://mida.gov.gh/site/?page_id=31, checked on 4/2/2015.

Milberg, W. (2004): The changing structure of trade linked to global production systems: What are the policy implications? In *International Labour Review* 143 (1-2), pp. 45–90. DOI: 10.1111/j.1564-913X.2004.tb00546.x.

Miller, D. (2002): Turning Callon the Right Way Up. In *Economy and Society* 31 (2), pp. 218–233. DOI: 10.1080/03085140220123135.

Miller, D. (2005): Reply to Michel Callon. In *Economic Sociology: European Electronic Newsletter* 6 (3), pp. 3–14.

Miller, P.; O'Leary, T. (2007): Mediating Instruments and Making Markets: Capital Budgeting, Science and the Economy. In *Accounting, Organizations and Society* 32 (7-8), pp. 701–734. DOI: 10.1016/j.aos.2007.02.003.

Miller, P.; Rose, N. S. (2008): Governing the Present. Administering Economic, Social and Personal Life. Cambridge: Polity.

Ministerio de Agricultura del Perú (2012): Plan Estratégico Sectoral Multianual 2012-2016. Ministerio de Agricultura del Perú. Lima, Peru.

Ministerio de Agricultura del Perú (2013): Informe Técnico N° 44-2013-MINAG-DGCA-DPC-ERGO. With assistance of José Muro, Augusto Martinez. Ministerio de Agricultura; Dirección General de Competitividad Agraria. Lima, Peru.

Ministerio de Comercio Exterior y Turismo del Perú (2004): Plan Estratégico Nacional Exportador 2003-2013. Plan Operativo Exportador del Sector Agropecuario-Agroindustrial. Lima.

Ministry of Food and Agriculture (2007): Food and Agriculture Sector Development Policy (FASDEP II). Edited by Ministry of Food and Agriculture. MoFA. Accra, Ghana.

Ministry of Food and Agriculture Ghana (2010): Medium Term Agriculture Sector Investment Plan (Metasip). 2011 - 2015. Edited by Ministry of Food and Agriculture.

Ministry of Food and Agriculture Ghana (2013): Value Chains and Gains. Ghana: The Gateway to Africa. 17.09.2013. Accra, Ghana, 2013, checked on 3/27/2015.

Ministry of Food and Agriculture Ghana (2015): Development Partners Working Together For a Better Future. Agricultural Sector Working Group. Available online at http://mofa.gov.gh/site/?page_id=3575, checked on 4/2/2015.

Mirowski, P.; Nik-Khah, E. (2007): Markets Made Flesh: Performativity, and a Problem in Science Studies Augmented With Consideration of the FCC Auctions. In D. MacKenzie, F. Muniesa, L. Siu (Eds.): Do Economists Make Markets? On the Performativity of Economics. Princeton: Princeton University Press, pp. 190–224.

Mitchell, J.; Coles, C. (2011): Markets and Rural Poverty. Upgrading in Value Chains. London, Washington, DC: Earthscan.

Mitchell, T. (2002): Rule of Experts. Egypt, Techno-Politics, Modernity. Berkeley: University of California Press.

Mitchell, T. (2005): The Work of Economics: how a Discipline Makes its World. In *Arch. Europ. Sociol.* 46 (2), pp. 297–320, checked on 8/26/2014.

Mitchell, T. (2007): The Properties of Markets. In D. MacKenzie, F. Muniesa, L. Siu (Eds.): Do Economists Make Markets? On the Performativity of Economics. Princeton: Princeton University Press, pp. 245–279.

Mol, A. (1999): Ontological Politics. A Word and Some Questions. In J. Law, J. Hassard (Eds.): Actor Network Theory and After. Oxford [England], Malden, MA: Blackwell/Sociological Review (The Sociological review monographs), pp. 123–162.

Mol, A. (2002): The Body Multiple. Ontology in Medical Practice. Durham: Duke University Press (Science and cultural theory).

Mol, A.; Law, J. (1995): Régions, Réseaux et Fluides. L'Anémie et la Topologie Sociale. In *Réseaux* 13 (72), pp. 195–218. DOI: 10.3406/reso.1995.2720.

Morozov, E. (2012): So We're All In Agreement. Evgeny Morozov reviews "Standards: Recipes for Reality" by Lawrence Busch. In *The Wall Street Journal*, 1/18/2012. Available online at http://www.wsj.com/articles/SB100014240529702040120045770732538 71935524, checked on 5/8/2015.

Mosse, D. (2005): Cultivating Development. An Ethnography of Aid Policy and Practice. London, Ann Arbor, MI: Pluto Press (Anthropology, culture, and society).

Mosse, D. (2011): Adventures in Aidland. The Anthropology of Professionals in International Development. New York: Berghahn Books.

Mosse, D. (2013): The Anthropology of International Development. In *Annu. Rev. Anthropol.* 42 (1), pp. 227–246. DOI: 10.1146/annurev-anthro-092412-155553.

Muellerleile, C. (2013): Turning Financial Markets Inside Out: Polanyi, Performativity and Disembeddedness. In *Environ. Plann. A* 45 (7), pp. 1625–1642. DOI: 10.1068/a45610.

Mukhopadhyay, B. (2014): Taking Callon to Calcutta: Did Economist-Administrators Make Market in the Colony? In *Economy and Society* 43 (2), pp. 183–210. DOI: 10.1080/03085147.2013.827860.

Müller, M. (2012): Opening the Black Box of the Organization: Socio-Material Practices of Geopolitical Ordering. In *Political Geography* 31 (6), pp. 379–388. DOI: 10.1016/j.polgeo.2012.06.001.

Müller, M. (2015a): Assemblages and Actor-Networks: Rethinking Socio-Material Power, Politics and Space. In *Geography Compass* 9 (1), pp. 27–41. DOI: 10.1111/gec3.12192.

Müller, M. (2015b): Geography of Organization. Working Paper. In J. Wright (Ed.): International Encyclopedia of the Social and Behavioral Sciences. Amsterdam: Elsevier, checked on 9/15/2014.

Muñoz, R. (2006): Una Alternativa Preincaica. Ambiente & Ciencia

. Edited by El Litoral. Santa Fe, Argentina. Available online at http://www.ellitoral.com/index.php/diarios/2006/10/18/medioambiente/MED-02.html, checked on 2/26/2014.

Murdoch, J. (1997): Towards a geography of heterogeneous associations. In *Progress in Human Geography* 21 (3), pp. 321–337. DOI: 10.1191/030913297668007261.

Murphy, C.; Yates, J. (2009): The International Organization for Standardization (ISO). Global governance through voluntary consensus. London, New York: Routledge (Routledge global institutions).

Nadvi, K. (2008): Global Standards, Global Governance and the Organization of Global Value Chains. In *Journal of Economic Geography* 8 (3), pp. 323–343. DOI: 10.1093/jeg/lbn003.

Nang'ole, E.; Mithöfer, D.; Franzel, S. (2011): Review of Guidelines and Manuals for Value Chain Analysis for Agricultural and Forest Products. Edited by World Forestry Centre. ICRAF. Nairobi, Kenya (Occasional Paper, 17), checked on 5/26/2014.

Neilson, J.; Pritchard, B.; Yeung, H. (2014): Global Value Chains and Global Production Networks in the Changing International Political Economy: An Introduction. In *Review of International Political Economy* 21 (1), pp. 1–8. DOI: 10.1080/09692290.2013.873369.

Neilson, Jeffrey (2014): Value Chains, Neoliberalism and Development Practice: The Indonesian Experience. In *Review of International Political Economy* 21 (1), pp. 38–69. DOI: 10.1080/09692290.2013.809782.

Newiger-Addy, G. (2008): Abstimmung mit hohem Aufwand. In *welt-sichten* 12, 2008. Available online at http://www.welt-sichten.org/artikel/4249/abstimmung-mit-hohem-aufwand, checked on 3/18/2015.

NRGP (2009): Proceedings of Value Chain Practitioners Forum. 26-27.11.2009. With assistance of MOFA/IFAD/AfDB. Northern Rural Growth Program.

OECD (2011): Global Value Chains: Preliminary Evidence and Policy Issues. DSTI/IND(2011)3. Paris: OECD. Available online at http://www.oecd.org/dataoecd/18/43/47945400.pdf, checked on 3/10/2015.

OECD (2012): Managing Aid for Trade and Development Results. Ghana Case Study. Policy Dialogue on aid for trade. With assistance of Bernardin Senadza, Amarquaye Laryea, checked on 9/27/2014.

Ong, A. (1999): Flexible citizenship : the cultural logics of transnationality. Durham: Duke University Press. Available online at http://worldcatlibraries.org/wcpa/oclc/39538933.

Ong, A.; Collier, S. J. (Eds.) (2005a): Global Assemblages. Technology, Politics, and Ethics as Anthropological Problems. Malden: Blackwell Publishers.

Ong, A.; Collier, S. J. (2005b): Global Assemblages, Anthropological Problems. In A. Ong, S. J. Collier (Eds.): Global Assemblages. Technology, Politics, and Ethics as Anthropological Problems. Malden: Blackwell Publishers, pp. 3–21.

Ouma, S. (2010): Global Standards, Local Realities: Private Agrifood Governance and the Restructuring of the Kenyan Horticulture Industry. In *Economic Geography* 86 (2), pp. 197–222. DOI: 10.1111/j.1944-8287.2009.01065.x.

Ouma, S. (2012): Frontier Regions of Marketization. Agribusiness, Farmers, and the Precarious Making of Global Market Connections in Ghana. Inauguraldissertation. Goethe-Universität Frankfurt am Main, Frankfurt am Main. Institut für Humangeographie.

Ouma, S.; Boeckler, M.; Lindner, P. (2013): Extending the Margins of Marketization. In *Geoforum* 48, pp. 225–235. DOI: 10.1016/j.geoforum.2012.01.011.

Ouma, S.; Lindner, P. (2010): Von Märkten und Reisenden: Geographische Entwicklungsforschung oder Wirtschaftsgeographien des Globalen Südens? 62 (10), pp. 12–17.

Owusuansah, A. (2008): Study on Quantitative Assessment of Small and Medium Scale Value Chains. Report.

Paglen, T. (2009): Experimental Geography: From Cultural Production to the Production of Space. In N. Thompson (Ed.): Experimental Geography. With assistance of Independent Curators International. Brooklyn: Melville House, pp. 26–33.

PDRS (2013): Competitividad Rural: Una Estrategia de Lucha Contra la Pobreza y Uso Sostenible de la Biodiversidad. Lima, Peru.

Peck, J. (2011): Geographies of Policy: From Transfer-Diffusion to Mobility-Mutation. In *Progress in Human Geography* 35 (6), pp. 773–797. DOI: 10.1177/0309132510394010.

Peck, J.; Theodore, N. (2010): Mobilizing Policy: Models, Methods, and Mutations. Themed Issue: Mobilizing Policy. In *Geoforum* 41 (2), pp. 169–174. DOI: 10.1016/j.geoforum.2010.01.002.

Peck, J.; Theodore, N. (2012): Follow the Policy: A Distended Case Approach. In *Environ. Plann. A* 44 (1), pp. 21–30. DOI: 10.1068/a44179.

Peck, J.; Theodore, N. (2015): Fast Policy. Experimental Statecraft at the Thresholds of Neoliberalism: University of Minnesota Press.

Peters, M. (2001): Education, Enterprise Culture and the Entrepreneurial Self: A Foucauldian Perspective. In *Journal of Educational Enquiry* 2 (2), checked on 7/8/2015.

Phillips, J. (2006): Agencement/Assemblage. In *Theory, Culture & Society* 23 (2-3), pp. 108–109. DOI: 10.1177/026327640602300219.

Pickering, A. (Ed.) (1992): Science as Practice and Culture: University of Chicago Press.

Pickering, A. (1995): The Mangle of Practice. Time, Agency, and Science. Chicago: University of Chicago Press.

Pickering, A. (2010): Material Culture and the Dance of Agency. In D. Hicks, M. C. Beaudry (Eds.): The Oxford Handbook of Material Culture Studies. Oxford: Oxford University Press.

Pickering, A.; Guzik, K. (2008): The Mangle in Practice. Science, Society, and Becoming. Durham: Duke University Press (Science and cultural theory).

Porter, M. (1985): Competitive Advantage. Creating and Sustaining Superior Performance. New York, London: Free Press; Collier Macmillan.

Powell, S.; Chavarro, P. (2008): Toward a Vibrant Peruvian Middle Class: Effects of the Peru-United States Free Trade Agreement on Labor Rights, Biodiversity, and Indigenous Populations. In *Florida Journal of International Law* 20 (Special Edition 20), pp. 93–146. Available online at http://works.bepress.com/stephen_powell/3.

Preda, A. (2009): Framing Finance. The Boundaries of Markets and Modern Capitalism. Chicago: University of Chicago Press.

Rabeharisoa, V.; Callon, M. (2002): The Involvement of Patients Associations in Research. In *Int Social Science J* 54 (171), pp. 57–63. DOI: 10.1111/1468-2451.00359.

Rabinow, P.; Rose, N. (2003): Foucault Today. In P. Rabinow, N. S. Rose (Eds.): The Essential Foucault. Selections from Essential Works of Foucault, 1954-1984. New York: New Press, pp. vii–xxxv.

Raikes, P.; Friis Jensen, M.; Ponte, S. (2000): Global Commodity Chain Analysis and the French filière Approach: Comparison and Critique. In *Economy and Society* 29 (3), pp. 390–417. DOI: 10.1080/03085140050084589.

Rankin, K. N. (2003): Anthropologies and Geographies of Globalization. In *Progress in Human Geography* 27 (6), pp. 708–734. DOI: 10.1191/0309132503ph457oa.

Republic of Ghana (2009): Ecowas Agricultural Policy (ECOWAP) - Comprehensive African Agriculture Development Programme (CAADP). Support the Successful implementation of the Ghana FASDEP II. Edited by Republic of Ghana. Accra, Ghana.

ReSAKSS (2013): Trends in Public Agricultural Expenditures in Africa. Issue Note. With assistance of Samuel Benin, Bingxin Yu. Edited by Regional Strategic Analysis and Knowledge Support System (ReSAKSS). Washington (22). Available online at http://www.resakss.org/sites/default/files/pdfs/IB22%20-%20ATOR%202012.pdf.

Roberts, J. M. (2012): Poststructuralism against Poststructuralism: Actor-Network Theory, Organizations and Economic Markets. In *European Journal of Social Theory* 15 (1), pp. 35–53. DOI: 10.1177/1368431011423573.

Roberts, S. M. (2014): What Do We Want our Words and Our Concepts to Do? In *Dialogues in Human Geography* 4 (3), pp. 331–334. DOI: 10.1177/2043820614544605.

Rose, N. (1992): Governing the Enterprising Self. In Paul Heelas (Ed.): The Values of the Enterprise Culture : The Moral Debate. London, New York: Routledge, pp. 141–164.

Rose, N.; Miller, P. (1992): Political Power beyond the State: Problematics of Government. In *The British Journal of Sociology* 43 (2), pp. 173–205. DOI: 10.2307/591464.

Rose, R. (1991): What is Lesson-Drawing? In *J. Pub. Pol.* 11 (01), p. 3. DOI: 10.1017/S0143814X00004918.

Roy, A. (2012): Ethnographic Circulations: Space – Time Relations in the Worlds of Poverty Management. In *Environ. Plann. A* 44 (1), pp. 31–41. DOI: 10.1068/a44180.

Rushkoff, D. (2005): Commodified vs. Commoditized. 4.09.2005. Available online at http://www.rushkoff.com/blog/2005/9/4/commodified-vs-commoditized.html, checked on 5/13/2015.

Santos, A. C.; Rodrigues, J. (2009): Economics as Social Engineering? Questioning the Performativity Thesis. In *Cambridge Journal of Economics* 33 (5), pp. 985–1000. DOI: 10.1093/cje/ben058.

Sathe, S. K.; Kshirsagar, H. H.; Sharma, G. M. (2012): Solubilization, Tractionation, and Electrophoretic Characterization of Inca Peanut (Plukenetia Volubilis L.) Proteins. In *Plant foods for human nutrition (Dordrecht, Netherlands)* 67 (3), pp. 247–255. DOI: 10.1007/s11130-012-0301-5.

Sato, S. (2013): Comitć Técnico de Sacha Inchi y sus Derivados como Eje Articulador Intersectorial. Logros, Proyectos y Perspectivas. 13.05.2013. Lima. Available online at http://www.siicex.gob.pe/siicex/resources/calidad/431471990rad304B4.pdf, checked on 9/3/2015.

Schatzki, T.; Knorr-Cetina, K.; Savigny, E. (2001): The Practice Turn in Contemporary Theory. London, New York: Routledge.

Schipmann, C. (2006): Value Chains for a Better Integration of Smallholders to Trade - The Case of Chilli in Ghana. Master Thesis. Berlin.

SDC (2007): Donor interventions in Value Chain Development. Value Chains and Cluster Development – Improved Access to Local, Regional and Global markets. Available online at https://www.eda.admin.ch/deza/en/home/themes-sdc/private-sector-development/creating-incentives/value-chains-cluster.html, checked on 2/3/2015.

SDC (2013): Wertschöpfungsketten und Cluster-Entwicklung - Verbesserter Zugang zu lokalen, regionalen und globalen Märkten. Direktion für Entwicklung und Zusammenarbeit. Title page. Edited by Federal Department of Foreign Affairs (FDFA). SDC, checked on 6/25/2013.

Serres, M. (1974): La Traduction, Hermes III. Paris: Edition de Minuit.

Serres, M.; Latour, B. (1995): Conversations on Science, Culture, and time. Ann Arbor: University of Michigan Press (Studies in literature and science).

Sheppard, E. (2013): Rethinking Capitalism from a Geographical Perspective. In *Annals of the Japan Association of Economic Geographers* 59, pp. 394–418, checked on 9/15/2014.

Sheppard, E.; Leitner, H. (2010): Quo Vadis Neoliberalism? The Remaking of Global Capitalist Governance after the Washington Consensus. In *Geoforum* 41 (2), pp. 185–194. DOI: 10.1016/j.geoforum.2009.09.009.

Simopoulos, A. P. (2002): Omega-3 Fatty Acids in Wild Plants, Nuts and Seeds. In *Asia Pac J Clin Nutr* 11 (s6), pp. S163-S173. DOI: 10.1046/j.1440-6047.11.s.6.5.x.

SIPPO (Ed.) (2012): Market Brief for Sacha Inchi. An Introduction to the European Market for Peruvian Exporters. In cooperation with GFU: SDC.

SNV (2004): Metodología de Análisis de Cadenas Productivas con Equidad para la Promoción del Desarrollo Local. With assistance of Magda Salazar González, Heyden, Damien van der. [Lima, Peru]: SNV.

SNV (2015a): Peru | SNV World. Available online at http://www.snvworld.org/en/countries/peru, updated on 3/15/2015, checked on 3/15/2015.

SNV (2015b): SNV Ghana. Ghana Home Grown School Feeding Programme (GSFP). Available online at http://www.snvworld.org/en/procurement-for-hgsf/our-work/ghana#overlay=en/node/7693/, updated on 4/2/2015, checked on 4/3/2015.

Solarz, M. W. (2012): North–South, Commemorating the First Brandt Report: Searching for the Contemporary Spatial Picture of the Global Rift. In *Third World Quarterly* 33 (3), pp. 559–569. DOI: 10.1080/01436597.2012.657493.

Soto, H. (2003): The Mystery of Capital. Why Capitalism Triumphs in the West and Fails Everywhere Else. New York: Basic Books.

Springer-Heinze, A. (2004): Info-Cadena. Instruments to Foster Value Chains. First Draft. Eschborn: Gesellschaft für Technische Zusammenarbeit.

Springer-Heinze, A. (2007): ValueLinks Manual: The Methodology for Value Chain Promotion. Eschborn: Gesellschaft für Internationale Zusammenarbeit. Available online at www2.gtz.de/wbf/4tDx9kw63gma/ValueLinks_Manual.pdf, checked on 1/20/2014.

Stamm, A. (2004): Value Chains for Development. Policy Challenges for Trade Policy and the Promotion of Economic. Concept Study. Eschborn.

Stamm, A.; Drachenfels, C. (2011): Value Chain Development. Approaches and activities by seven UN agencies and opportunities for interagency cooperation. Geneva: ILO. Available online at http%3A//www.worldcat.org/oclc/794059692, checked on 2/19/2015.

Star, S. L. (1991): Power, Technologies and the Phenomenology of Conventions: Of Being Allergic to Onions. In J. Law (Ed.): A Sociology of Monsters. Essays on Power, Technology, and Domination. London,, New York: Routledge, pp. 26–56.

Staritz, C. (2012): Value Chains for Development? Potentials and Limitations of Global Value Chain Approaches in Donor Interventions. Available online at http://www.oefse.at/Downloads/publikationen/WP31_value_chains.pdf.

Stengers, I. (2011): Another Science is Possible! A Plea for Slow Science. 13.12.2011. Inauguratial lecture Chair Willy Calewaert 2011-2012. Faculté de Philosophie et Lettres, ULB. Brussels, 2011, checked on 6/7/2015.

Stiglitz, J. (2014): Economic Stagnation By Design. 6.02.2014. Social Europe Forum. Available online at http://www.socialeurope.eu/2014/02/economic-stagnation/, updated on 4/4/2015, checked on 4/5/2015.

Stone, D. (1999): Learning Lessons and Transferring Policy across Time, Space and Disciplines. In *Politics* 19 (1), pp. 51–59. DOI: 10.1111/1467-9256.00086.

Sturgeon, T. (2009): From Commodity Chains to Value Chains: Interdisciplinary Theory Building in an Age of Globalization. In J. Bair (Ed.): Frontiers of Commodity Chain Research. Stanford: Stanford University Press, pp. 110–135.

Temenos, C.; McCann, E. (2013): Geographies of Policy Mobilities. In *Geography Compass* 7 (5), pp. 344–357. DOI: 10.1111/gec3.12063.

Thomas, N. (1991): Entangled objects. Exchange, material culture, and colonialism in the Pacific. Cambridge, Mass.: Harvard University Press.

Tsing, A. (2005): Friction. An ethnography of global connection. Princeton, N.J: Princeton University Press.

Tsing, A. (2009): Beyond economic and ecological standardisation. In *The Australian Journal of Anthropology* 20 (3), pp. 347–368. DOI: 10.1111/j.1757-6547.2009.00041.x.

UN Economic Commission for Africa (2013): Economic Report on Africa 2013. Making the Most of Africa's Commodities : Industrializing for Growth, Jobs and Economic Transformation. With assistance of African Union. New York / Addis Ababa: United Nations Publication. Available online at http%3A//www.worldcat.org/oclc/856168486, checked on 5/22/2015.

UNCTAD (Ed.) (2006): Global Value Chains for Building National Productive Capacities. TD/B/COM.3/79.

UNCTAD (2007): BioTrade Initiative. BioTrade Principles and Criteria. UNCTAD. New York (UNCTA). Available online at http//www.unctad.org/biotrade, updated on http://www.biotrade.org/ResourcesPublications/UNCTAD_BT_PC_en.pdf.

UNCTAD (2013): Global Value Chains and Development - Investment and Value Added Trade in the Global Economy. http://unctad.org/en/PublicationsLibrary/diae2013d1_en.pdf.

UNCTAD (2014): Trade and Development Report 2014. Global Governance and Policy Space for Development. New York and Geneva: UNCTAD.

UNCTAD (2015): BioTrade Initiative. Available online at http://unctad.org/en/Pages/DITC/Trade-and-Environment/BioTrade.aspx, checked on 3/17/2015.

UNIDO (2011): Pro-Poor Value Chain Development: 25 Guiding Questions for Designing and Implementing Agroindustry Projects. United Nations Industrial Development Organization (UNIDO). Vienna, Austria.

UNODC (2011): El Modelo de Desarrollo Alternativo de la Región San Martín. Un Estudio de Caso de Desarrollo Económico Local. With assistance of Fernando Villarán De La Puente (Jefe de equipo). Lima. Available online at https://www.unodc.org/documents/alternative-development/San_Martin.pdf, checked on 2/26/2014.

Urry, J. (2007): Mobilities. Cambridge, UK, Malden, MA: Polity.

US Center for Food Safety and Applied Nutrition (2014): GRAS Notice Inventory - Agency Response Letter GRAS Notice No. GRN 000506. 10.09.2014. Edited by US Food and Drug Administration. Center for Food Safety and Applied Nutrition. Available online at http://www.fda.gov/Food/IngredientsPackagingLabeling/GRAS/NoticeInventory/ucm425865.htm, checked on 5/13/2015.

USAID (2015): Mobile Solutions Matter for Land. USAID Land Tenure and Property Rights Portal. Available online at http://usaidlandtenure.net/video/mobile-solutions-matter-for-land?utm_source=Mobile%20Solutions%20Spotlight&utm_medium=Top%20Spotlight&utm_campaign=Spotlights, updated on 4/3/2015, checked on 4/3/2015.

USAID-Peru (2012): Peru Country Development Cooperation Strategy 2012-2016. Lima, Peru. Available online at usaid.gov/sites/default/files/documents/1862/PeruCDCS, checked on 3/15/2015.

USDA: Organic Products Update 2008. Foreign Agricultural Service: Global Agriculture Information Network. GAIN Report Nr. PE8014. Lima. Available online at http://www.fas.usda.gov/gainfiles/200805/146294603.pdf.

Valles, C. (1993): Sacha Inchi Bautizado como "Maní del Inca". Tarapoto, San Martín: Oportunidades comerciales, pp. 4–12.

van Helvoirt, B. (2014): Product Factsheet: Sacha inchi oil in the EU and EFTA. With assistance of Netherlands Ministry of Foreign Affairs. Centre for the Promotion of Imports from developing countries (CBI). Available online at http://www.cbi.eu/market-information/natural-ingredients-cosmetics/sacha-inchi, checked on 7/20/2015.

Vera, L. (2014): Sacha Inchi: Ready to take off. 6.06.2014. Edited by Organic and Wellness News: The international newspaper for Organic Trade. Available online at http://organicwellnessnews.com/en/sacha-inchi-ready-to-take-off/, updated on 5/13/2015, checked on 5/13/2015.

Wagner, H.-J.; Oevermann, U. (2001): Objektive Hermeneutik und Bildung des Subjekts. Mit einem Text von Ulrich Oevermann: Die Philosophie von Charles Sanders Peirce als Philosophie der Krise. First edition. Weilerswist: Velbrück Wissenschaft.

Wallerstein, I.; Hopkins, T. K. (1977): Patterns of Development of the Modern World-System. In *Review* 1 (2), pp. 11–145.

Wallerstein, I.; Hopkins, T. K. (1986): Commodity Chains in the World Economy Prior to 1800. In *Review* 10 (1), pp. 157–170.

Ward, K. (2006): 'Policies in Motion', Urban Management and State Restructuring: The Trans-Local Expansion of Business Improvement Districts. In *Int J Urban Reg Res* 30 (1), pp. 54–75. DOI: 10.1111/j.1468-2427.2006.00643.x.

Weinberger, K.; Lumpkin, T. A. (2007): Diversification into Horticulture and Poverty Reduction: A Research Agenda. In *World Development* 35 (8), pp. 1464–1480. DOI: 10.1016/j.worlddev.2007.05.002.

Weisser, F. (2014): Practices, Politics, Performativities: Documents in the International Negotiations on Climate Change. In *Political Geography* 40, pp. 46–55. DOI: 10.1016/j.polgeo.2014.02.007.

Weisser, F.; Bollig, M.; Doevenspeck, M.; Müller-Mahn, D. (2014): Translating the 'adaptation to climate change' paradigm: the politics of a travelling idea in Africa. In *The Geographical Journal* 180 (2), pp. 111–119. DOI: 10.1111/geoj.12037.

Werner, M.; Bair, J.; Fernández, V. (2014): Linking up to development? Global Value Chains and the making of a Post-Washington Consensus. In *Development and Change* 45 (6), pp. 1219–1247, checked on 9/28/2014.

Whatmore, S. (2002): Hybrid Geographies. Natures, Cultures, Spaces. London, Thousand Oaks, Calif: Sage Publications.

Whitfield, L. (2011): Political Challenges to Developing Non-Traditional Exports in Ghana: The Case of Horticulture Exports. DIIS Working Paper 2011:29. Edited by Danish Institute for International Studies, DIIS. Copenhagen, checked on 3/18/2015.

Whittle, A.; Spicer, A. (2008): Is Actor Network Theory Critique? In *Organization Studies* 29 (4), pp. 611–629. DOI: 10.1177/0170840607082223.

WHO (2015): Post-Washington Consensus. Programmes: Trade, foreign policy, diplomacy and health. World Health Organization. Available online at http://www.who.int/trade/glossary/story074/en/, updated on 2/10/2015, checked on 2/10/2015.

Wight, C. (2006): Agents, Structures and International Relations. Politics as Ontology. Cambridge, UK, New York: Cambridge University Press (Cambridge studies in international relations, 101).

Woodward, K.; Dixon, D.P; Jones III, J.P; o (2009): Poststructuralism/Poststructuralist Geographies. In K. Woodward, D.P Dixon, J.P Jones III (Eds.): International Encyclopedia of Human Geography: Elsevier, pp. 396–407.

World Bank (2015a): Ghana | Data. Available online at http://data.worldbank.org/country/ghana, updated on 3/17/2015, checked on 3/18/2015.

World Bank (2015b): Peru | Data. World Bank. Available online at http://data.worldbank.org/country/peru, updated on 3/13/2015, checked on 3/15/2015.

World Bank Blog (2015): Agriculture as Enterprise: An Evolution of Thought and Perspective to Increase Outcomes for India's Farmers. 28.03.2015. With assistance of Parmel Kumar Gupta. Available online at http://blogs.worldbank.org/dmblog/agriculture-enterprise-evolution-thought-and-perspective-increase-outcomes-indias-farmers, checked on 6/17/2015.

Yarrow, T. (2011): Development Beyond Politics. Aid, Activism and NGOs in Ghana. New York: Palgrave Macmillan.

Zaloom, C. (2003): Ambiguous Numbers: Trading Technologies and Interpretation in Financial Markets. In *American Ethnologist* 30 (2), pp. 258–272. DOI: 10.1525/ae.2003.30.2.258.

Zaloom, C. (2006): Out of the Pits. Traders and Technology from Chicago to London. Chicago: University of Chicago Press.

Zegarra, C. (2008): Caracterización Química de Nueve Ecotipos de Plukenetia volubilis L. de los Departamentos Loreto y San Martín. In *Folia Amazonica* (1-2), pp. 39–45. Available online at http://www.iiap.org.pe/cdpublicaciones2011/documentos/pdf/piba/pu/4.pdf, checked on 1/20/2014.

MIX
Papier aus verantwortungsvollen Quellen
Paper from responsible sources
FSC® C105338

If you have any concerns about our products,
you can contact us on
ProductSafety@springernature.com

In case Publisher is established outside the EU,
the EU authorized representative is:
Springer Nature Customer Service Center GmbH
Europaplatz 3, 69115 Heidelberg, Germany

Printed by Libri Plureos GmbH
in Hamburg, Germany